OU†SPOKEN

FATHER
ROD BOWER

OU✝SPOKEN

EBURY
PRESS

An Ebury Press book
Published by Penguin Random House Australia Pty Ltd
Level 3, 100 Pacific Highway, North Sydney NSW 2060
penguin.com.au

First published by Ebury Press in 2018

Addresses for the Penguin Random House group of companies can be found at
global.penguinrandomhouse.com/offices.

Every effort has been made to identify individual photographers and copyright holders
where appropriate, but in some instances this has not been possible. The publishers
would be pleased to hear from any copyright holders who have not been acknowledged.

 A catalogue record for this
book is available from the
National Library of Australia

ISBN 978 0 14378 840 9

Cover image by Photo Pty Ltd
Cover design by Alex Ross © Penguin Random House Pty Ltd
Typeset in 12/17.5 pt Adobe Garamond Pro by Midland Typesetters, Australia
Printed in Australia by Griffin Press, an accredited ISO AS/NZS 14001:2004
Environmental Management System printer

For Kerry
Thank you for accompanying me on the journey
to a place where we now finish each other's sentences,
and share each other's dreams,
a place from which we can truly tell our story.

AUTHOR'S NOTE

WHEN THE INVITATION first came, the prospect of writing a book was exciting and the project seemed easily achievable. I settled each night in front of the open fire in the winter of 2017 while Kerry was visiting our daughter Kate, son-in-law Brad and grandson Liam in the United States. The words flowed easily, if painfully, as I began to tell my story. However, my life also became increasingly busy during this period with little time to think or write; the task began to seem daunting and eventually verging on the impossible. I became paralysed.

Then Kerry stepped in. Initially she had been reticent. We do so much together she desired that this be my own project, but seeing my discomfort she offered her very considerable skills. Bit by bit, the rest of the story emerged. On reflection it was obvious that this was the only way it could be. This collaboration made such sense because it is how we live the rest of our life together. Ultimately for the book to be written in any other way would have lacked integrity.

I would not be here, let alone have written a book, without Kerry. Her love, support and deepest partnership enables every aspect of who I am and who we are together. It has not only been Kerry's capacity for detail and her editing skills that have brought this book to fruition, but her unique ability to enter my heart and, by so doing, emerge with words I did not know were mine. While it is my name on the cover, *Outspoken* is our collaboration.

CONTENTS

PROLOGUE

The Question

On a beautiful autumn day in 2017, I was on my early-morning walk when an elderly parishioner broke my peace. The approach wasn't for a friendly chat, however. Fixing me with a glare, he said, 'Why aren't you like all the other priests we've had here before?'

I had no ready answer.

I knew him to be a local and respected businessman, a member of several service clubs. He was and is, I believe, a good man in the way our society assesses goodness. When I first came to Gosford I had been told that although he didn't regularly attend church, I was expected to visit him once a year and he would give me a cheque. Our conversations in his beautiful waterfront home involved me sitting politely in silence while he told me in various ways that the problems with this country were caused by dole bludgers, foreigners and socialists; he generally understood all three terms to be synonymous. I dutifully went two years in a row and then I could stand it no more. I didn't return the third year.

On this autumn morning we had a brief exchange – I gathered he was irate about something he had read about me in the tabloid press concerning my relationship with the Muslim community. Despite my protestations, he refused to believe he was basing his argument on misinformation. However, his question was a penetrating one. Why was I so different to my predecessors?

I will admit that my response to him on that morning was less than professional. He had fired the occasional barb at me as we passed on our walks for several weeks. Usually, I brushed them off with a good-humoured response, but on this particular occasion I caught his anger and fired it back at him.

When I clumsily suggested that I did what I did because I was following the example Jesus had set, he emphatically told me not to 'bring Him into it'.

His anger connected with anger deep within me, something that was difficult to control and at best could only be channelled.

Since then, I have pondered his question many times. Why am I different?

PART 1
JUST MY STORY

CHILDHOOD THROUGH TO MANHOOD

1

A Country Kid

I HAVE NEVER been anyone's first choice. I was certainly not the first choice for the young girl who found herself pregnant with me. Nor was I the first choice for the childless couple who could not fulfil their desire to procreate, so adopted me. My wife did not plan for her first marriage to break down, nor did her children expect to be separated from their father or for their mother to then marry me so that they had to form a new life with a stepfather.

I have spent my entire life seeking to be the best at being second choice. This has given me a particular empathy for others for whom life has not offered a first-class ticket.

I was conceived in March 1962 in the womb of a 16-year-old Newcastle girl from a working-class family. My father was an apprentice butcher. This situation was neither planned nor manageable for these two young people. Although my birth father did offer to do what he thought was the 'right' thing under the circumstances, my birth mother felt she had no choices other than to carry me to term and then to relinquish me at birth. She had been given no education about reproduction, and when pregnancy occurred she was powerless and was simply swept along by the cultural demands of the day. This however carried me from the potential of non-being into the potentiality of being. I will be forever grateful for the gift of life, the unplanned, unchosen and accidental nature of which seemed to set the pattern for how this gift would be lived out.

My parents – the couple who raised me – were married in 1954. Thanks to my father having had a bout of the mumps in his early adulthood, they were not able to conceive children. Dad came from a Novocastrian business family who were involved in the meat industry and Mum from a Hunter Valley grazing family, so theirs was a marriage of some synergy.

Without the responsibility of children, in hedonistic 1950s postwar Newcastle their social lives were a whirlwind of friends and acquaintances. In this context, my father's issues with alcohol began to emerge. When Mum's father died in 1959, it seemed like the perfect opportunity to remove themselves from the Newcastle party scene. They relocated to the more sedate and relatively safe environs of the NSW Hunter Valley and took over the running of my maternal grandfather's grazing property. This was Warakeela.

It was the place to which I was brought in early January 1963 and where I was to spend the first 14 years of my life. My first official outing was to my baptism at St Andrew's Anglican Church, Mayfield on 23 February, eight years to the day after my parents were married in that church. I would not return to that building until Christmas Day 1984, a day that would change the direction of my life forever.

My early childhood was for the most part idyllic. In place of the toys that most young boys long for, I had the real things: a real dog, real horse, real trucks and tractors, real farm animals. Like most of us, my recollections of this time rely on manufactured memories created from photos I have seen or stories I have been told.

One story, which again echoes in the space between being and non-being, comes from when I was about five years old. Because the tractor had a flat battery, it had been parked facing downhill above the house. I often used to wander out to the shed and climb onto the tractor and pretend I was driving – harmless enough in the safe confines of the machinery shed. On this occasion, I managed to release the brake and began to career down the hill screaming with joy and exhilaration at the ride, oblivious to the impending doom I faced. Providentially, my father was at the kitchen window and removed the door from its hinges on his way through to catch me just in time. This was not to be my last brush with death in the context of encounters with farm machinery.

My sister, Anne, arrived – also via adoption – in 1964. I have no recollection of the impact her arrival had on me, and although I grew to be somewhat protective of her we always seemed to inhabit different universes. She and I never enjoyed the depth of relationship between siblings that I observed in other families.

In January 1967 I began my formal education at a one-teacher country school. Eccleston Public School had 14 students, four of whom made up the kindergarten intake. My sense of a lack of identity, a foreboding consciousness of not quite fitting in, seems to date from this time. It inhabited my being and drove me hard for the next 30 years. The shadow of this remains with me today.

Schoolwork was not difficult for me, which had the unfortunate consequence of allowing me to be habitually lazy. This became my mode throughout my formal education. I was never particularly happy at school, partially because of my chronic introversion and identity struggle.

What compounded this struggle was the fact that my father was a city boy at heart. Unlike the other dads, who came from generations of farmers steeped in agrarian knowledge, his was a world I neither knew nor understood. He sat uneasily on a horse, wore a fedora instead of an Akubra and lace-up shoes instead of elastic-sided boots. All this was significant to a boy trying so very hard to fit in, to form an identity that relied on being like – and looking like – everyone else. My dad, of course, had no such need; he was his own man, and it is only in recent years that I have come to grasp the tremendous courage that it must have taken for him to abandon the life he knew in the city for this foreign existence in the bush.

During my middle primary-school years, I became aware of my father's drinking, as much as my mother tried to protect us. This began to impact my view of the world.

Children of alcoholics begin very early in life to take the view that a lie is always better than the truth. Creating the fantasy of a normal family life becomes habitual. Ultimately it is destructive, especially when one moves beyond the age where living in a fantasy world is either acceptable or productive.

While I can remember only isolated events, several have been written indelibly into my consciousness. Mondays were particularly difficult, because this was when the local cattle sales were held and they normally involved Dad going to the pub at lunchtime and not arriving home until late afternoon. He was, in sobriety, a gentle and decent man but with the addition of alcohol he could become aggressive. I recall on one particular occasion when I was a young boy, trying to position myself so that I could protect my mother and sister in the kitchen while Dad waved a rifle in our direction. From then on my job after school on Mondays was to remove the firing mechanisms from the rifles and hide the ammunition.

Then there was the morning he drove past our school while everyone was in the playground at recess. The night before he had not come home, which meant that he had been on a bender. Although nobody else knew this, I still felt the need to make up a story of where he may have been and why he was driving past the school at that time of day. As I look back on this now, I recognise the emerging need to fantasise and to create a world that was hospitable – one in which I had unshakably stable parents and an unassailable identity.

Fortunately, these occasions, while regular, were not the daily norm. Rather, I remember a loving and engaged father. As a small child, I used to wait and watch for Dad to ride in on his horse from the paddocks. I can still recall my joy and exhilaration as I ran to the far gate, to be pulled up in front of him in the saddle and to share those precious moments on the ride home. It is when I think back to times such as this that I am reminded how much I loved him. It was not until I began to raise children who were not – at least biologically – my own that I realised the extent of his love for me.

Those years and experiences implanted in me an understanding that the human condition is not a binary equation of good or evil but living in the flow of breaking and healing, of abiding in the tensions of eros and thanatos, in the balance between life and death. This is where my father lived; it is where I live; indeed, it is where we all live.

If primary school was not entirely comfortable for me, high school was a nightmare. After attending a tiny village primary school until the age of 12, it was a shock to be sent to a large regional high school where most of the other students in my year had already been together for seven years and had formed strong bonds and relationships. I found this horribly difficult. I struggled to form friendships, which only served to drive me deeper into my own private fantasy world. So, I found myself in a vicious cycle, full of self-fulfilling prophecies, friendships becoming impossible to form or to maintain.

Every day of my school life I longed for the final bell so I could retreat into the solitude and security of my fantasy world. There, with horse, dog and rifle, I could be ruler of my own domain and be whoever I wanted to be – anyone but myself, that is.

Yet there was one last daily hurdle. Between the final bell and the relative sanctuary of Warakeela lay a journey fraught with danger. There was yet another social order on the bus. It was also a place where strong bonds had been formed prior to my arrival and, given my understanding of the world – which I saw perpetually through the eyes of an outsider – I had no mechanisms through which to find a niche in the existing system. Inevitably there were the bullies in the back seat. I seemed to be a magnet to them; they sensed my vulnerability and knew how to exploit it for the singular purpose of supporting their own fragile egos. It was four hours per day of enforced fear and anxiety.

I can understand why young people who are bullied are at increased risk of suicide. While, looking back, I cannot remember ever seriously contemplating taking this path, the thought did provide a fleeting escape from the daily terrors of the school bus.

2

Religious Education

WHILE NEITHER OF my parents was particularly religious, Mum – who had been raised as an Anglican – thought it was important for my sister and me to receive basic religious instruction. During our primary-school years, this entailed two sessions of special religious education per week. The Anglican priest conducted one, and the Congregational minister took the other. Each week in term they would arrive at the single-room schoolhouse to ply their trade. The only two Catholic students would be ushered out – their instruction was managed by nuns at a different time.

The priest was an Oxford-educated Englishman with a hyphenated surname; I have no memory of anything he said apart from the suggestion made, during my confirmation lessons, that if I masturbated it could have a deleterious effect on my eyesight. This only served to add anxiety to the guilt and embarrassment I already felt about my emerging sexual consciousness.

He was an entirely different kettle of fish to Mr Herman of the Congregational Church. Mr Herman used to pick up my sister and me each Thursday evening and take us to a local home for 'Christian Endeavour', which was a program of religious instruction for all ages, and which Mum thought would be good for us. Mr Herman was a humble, jolly man from the reformed Protestant tradition. He was a fantastic storyteller, although there is only one lesson he delivered that I remember specifically from all those years ago. It was the story of Joseph interpreting the Pharaoh's dreams, which included Potiphar, the captain of Pharaoh's guard. We were told that the means of remembering his name was to think of the joining together of the words 'pot' and 'heifer'.

For me, the real attraction of attending Christian Endeavour was that, after we sang some songs – accompanied by Mr Herman on the accordion – then had a Bible-study session and some prayer time, we were allowed to play pool.

Even though the details of the songs or lessons have not stayed with me, I am to this day conscious of the decent, uncomplicated, humble Christian character of the minister. My admiration for him remains undiminished even after 40 years.

There was an unusual ecumenical arrangement in Eccleston. At some time in the past, the Congregational Church had not been able to appoint a minister and had asked the local Anglican priest to help care for the Congregationalists in the area. This arrangement continued in perpetuity, ironically excluding Mr Herman; he attended to two congregations in other local villages. Services were taken by the priest on alternate weeks – one week there was Holy Communion according to the Anglican rite in St Paul's, the Anglican building; on the alternate week, morning prayer, still from the Anglican prayer book, took place in the Congregational building.

For several years, my Sunday mornings were spent in Sunday School, which the Congregationalists ran. As a boy I formed the impression that Congregationalists were not only bereft of clergy, they were also deeply lacking in saints. They did, however, possess two wonderful Sunday School teachers who, through their sensitive, joyful and caring approach to Bible stories, laid a foundation for my faith that has always enabled me to be free from moralistic judgmentalism and fundamentalist interpretation. It was a religious upbringing that I was mostly very fortunate to receive.

The Congregationalists had brought with them, from the Welsh mining villages, a simple poverty of spirit – humility and openness – embedded in the Protestant work ethic and sober morality. They – for the most part, although many were now wealthy landowners – maintained a simple working-class demeanour. Mr Herman was the embodiment of this tradition.

The Anglicans in the local area tended to be slightly more 'born to rule' types who had been away to boarding school. The Rector, the Reverend Desmond Stuart-Fox, Archdeacon Emeritis, did nothing to detract from that perception. He was English; further, he was an Oxford graduate, with the accompanying air of authority that comes naturally to such men. He was an old-fashioned Anglo-Catholic, with a deep love of ritual and worship, and a skilled practitioner of the mystical arts.

It was in this rather polarised ecclesiastical environment that I received my early spiritual formation. Somehow or other, I was able to take the best from both worlds and mold them into a working Christian spirituality. From Mr Herman and the Congregationalists I discovered a love of scripture and the importance of simplicity, while from Father Stuart-Fox I received an appreciation for mystery.

As I look back now, I see the polarities of head and heart yearning for each other like two estranged lovers, desiring to come together in the life of one confused little boy.

At the age of 12, having endured the aforementioned confirmation lessons, I was duly presented before the Anglican Bishop. It was an important milestone. I can remember receiving a new set of clothes, feeling nervous and just a little bit special. The abiding legacy of this rite of passage was twofold. Firstly, it coincided with the first time as an adolescent that I did not wear hair oil. The Bishop had requested that we refrain from applying the greasy substance so as to not contaminate his hands as he laid them upon our heads. Secondly, and more importantly to me, was that I was now able to partake in the mystery of Holy Communion. This is where having a well-developed sense of fantasy was spiritually productive: I readily believed in and experienced the Divine presence in this sacramental act of the consecration and reception of bread and wine.

The Bishop who laid his hands on my head that day was the same Bishop who, 18 years later, would – through the identical actions – ordain me to the priesthood. Still without hair oil.

Once I'd been confirmed, I no longer attended Sunday School but remained in St Paul's with the adults to receive communion. As if it were yesterday, I can remember the feeling of awe and wonder I experienced in that tiny country church, and the sense that I was participating in something mysteriously sacred and beyond my knowing. I still feel the same today.

On the alternate weeks I also remained in the Congregational building to hear the sermon. The Rector was a good preacher, easily able to hold the attention of an adolescent boy. Looking back now I think that it was not so much what he said as the way he was able to say it that held me in so much awe.

DOWNLOAD 2 FREE AUDIOBOOKS WITH A 30-DAY TRIAL

1. Visit www.audible.com.au/2_free
2. Sign up with an Amazon account
3. Pick your free audiobooks from more than 200,000 titles
4. Download and listen using our free apps

3

Dad's Time Ends

AT HOME, AN important Sunday-morning ritual took place in the farm butchery before church. Dad – having learned his trade as a butcher in his family's business – was the local go-to guy for processing the home kill. Most weekends, starting at four o'clock in the morning, he and I would be found in the butchery dressing a carcass for one of the local farmers. From a very young age I had risen early to help him. Initially, I worked on the less complicated cuts, things like mince and sausages, but as time went on I was shown some of the finer arts of the trade.

This was sacred father–son time, the passing of knowledge and skills from one generation to the next. There was the still silence of early mornings, the crisp darkness broken by a single lightbulb in the shed, which had been set up to look like and function as a 1950s butcher shop. I wonder now if it was Dad's attempt to regain something of the life he had left behind. Was it that through sight, sound, smell and feel, he could for a few short hours on a Saturday and Sunday morning enter into a world where he was the expert? I picture him in that shed, always looking comfortable and confident. Was he warmed by the knowledge that he knew everything there was to know about what he was doing? The fact that everyone else had to rely on his skill and expertise? Those are the times I felt closest to him. Perhaps it's because that was when he was most at home in himself. On those mornings in that place, I too felt – unusually for me – as though I belonged. I treasure these moments as among the best of my childhood memories.

This all came to an abrupt end on a Tuesday in September, three months before my 14th birthday. It was mustering day. The usual pattern for mustering was that a number of locals would gather to help us drive all the steers from a bush paddock to a fattening paddock about 10 kilometres away. There they would grow to bullocks, at which stage they were shipped off for sale.

I had begged to stay home from school so that I could be part of the muster. Permission was denied, however, and consequently I was in a very dark mood. That morning I dragged my feet, resentful that I wasn't going to join the men for the muster yet still hoping that my parents might change their minds. They didn't, and soon I was in danger of missing the dreaded school bus. When I finally started to run for the bus, consumed by adolescent anger, I refused to say goodbye to Mum and Dad.

My anger continued throughout the day, festering in my soul in a way that a teenager can manage masterfully. When I saw my only friend at the time, I vented thoroughly. I said that I hated my father and expressed ill will towards him for treating me as a child and denying me the right to ride with the men. Even as the dark words spilled out, I held out hope that there would still be some work to do when I arrived home at five o'clock.

When the school bus pulled up at Warakeela and I saw men standing around talking as their horses grazed quietly around them, my mood lifted significantly. I could see cattle in the yards, which meant that the drive to the fattening paddock had yet to take place. It was obvious what I needed to do: run straight to the house, change clothes and catch my horse before they had a chance to leave without me. All these thoughts flashed through my mind in a matter of seconds and I failed to notice the expression on the men's faces. But suddenly one of them grabbed my arm and said, 'Before you go inside, we have something to tell you.'

Turning towards him, I registered a face that was kind but creased with worry. A tall man, he got down on one knee to look me in the face as he spoke to me. 'Your dad has collapsed and your mum has taken him to hospital,' he said.

I had so many questions: how, when, where, why? There were no answers. Something in me sensed that it was too late.

For some time, Dad had suffered from arteriosclerosis brought on by a mixture of bad genes, alcohol, cigarettes and a diet heavy in fatty red meat. He had endured a number of painful bypass procedures, but each time the outcome had fallen short of expectation. Later, I was to learn that Dad's last words were, 'Where are my cigarettes?'

Anticipating the imminent arrival of my sister and me from school, one of the local women had driven over to look after us. Well, I was having none of it. I was going on the drive. Questioning glances were exchanged among the men, but shrugs of agreement followed. I quickly changed out of my uniform before they could change their collective mind.

My father's horse was still saddled and hitched to the fence. The big bay mare was easy to handle, and to save more time I unhitched her, swung into the saddle and we were ready to go.

As I look back now, that simple and pragmatic action was so much more than just mounting a horse. By taking my father's horse and saddle I was doing something more deeply profound than saving time: I was assuming the mantle. At 13, in my fantasy construct, I was now the man of the house. This was only partially subconscious; there was a deliberateness in this act. I knew what I was doing, at least I thought I did. I was becoming a man.

What I did not know was that I was also abandoning my adolescence; that painful, awkward, lonely, excluded, bullied, confused adolescence. Why wouldn't I want to abandon it? The trouble is, with its abandonment went any hope I had of developing into a normal well-balanced human capable of healthy relationships.

An ominous darkness descended that evening as we drove the mob along the gravel road. A storm brewed and then hit with what seemed to me unusual speed and severity. Lightning flashed and thunder roared; both cattle and horses were spooked and difficult to control. It was a portent of the life I had now chosen, a window into the existence I was, for the next 20 years, to inhabit.

I have no sense of how long it took to drive the mob that night but eventually we arrived at the paddock we called Belgrave. I was to learn later that this was where Dad had taken his final breath, and the very place where my maternal grandfather had died at the age of 49 from a heart attack, just 17 years earlier. He also had died mustering cattle. My father was nine hours away from turning 46.

I left the horse with one of the men who lived nearby. Thoroughly drenched, frightened, exhausted and confused, I was driven home. Mum met me at the door and confirmed what my soul already knew, with the simple but life-changing words: 'Your father is dead.'

I only had two questions: one spoken; the other held in the secret places of my soul. I asked, 'What happens now?'

I wondered, Did I kill him?

4

The Bereaved

MUM'S DEFAULT MODE in times of crisis was to pack up and head to her mother's. This had been the pattern established when Dad's drinking had begun to make her feel unsafe and she felt the need to protect Anne and me. It seemed the only logical course of action in the shock and confusion of this stormy night.

We left sometime after nine and arrived in Newcastle just before 11 pm. Nana was woken by our pounding on the door, and the shocking news was broken.

A day later, we returned to Warakeela to collect the horse and dog from the neighbours. The priest arrived to arrange the funeral. On the drive back to my grandmother's place in Newcastle, there was no emotion, no conversation in the car, just silence and shock.

The next days passed with family and friends visiting, laden with casseroles and corned meat for the hundreds of sandwiches that would be consumed. Again, and again, I would be told by well-meaning relatives, who were struggling to know what to say, that I was now 'the man of the house'. As if I needed any encouragement to adopt that particular state of mind. If I had happened to have any doubts in this regard, they would certainly have been dissolved by these constant affirmations.

The funeral director was a stout man who didn't tuck his tie through the loop. I had never seen this before. Had he not finished getting dressed? I was tempted to point out his sartorial forgetfulness but thought better of it. But then I found myself rather more interested in his large Ford limousine. My interest picked up even more when Mum arranged for us to be picked up for the funeral in that car.

Anne, my sister, at the age of 11 was thought to be too young to attend the funeral, so it was Mum and me and my two grandmothers who set off in the big Ford limousine for the crematorium. Dad's parents had separated some 20 years earlier, so my grandmother had moved to Sydney to live with her sister and start over. Divorce still carried some stigma and so people in her new world were encouraged to believe that she was a widow.

That day, there was an uneasy greeting between the two. For that brief moment, they were united in grief. Their sole remaining connection, their only son, was dead. Dad's mother was inconsolable, crying out to some unseen power to 'bring him back'. In reply there was nothing but silence.

The priest conducted the service with the best of Anglican dignity and detachment, referring to Dad as 'Robert'. I had only ever heard him called 'Bob'. Given that Dad was a very lapsed Presbyterian with no discernible interest in religion, what would he have thought of this ceremony, being called by an unfamiliar name?

With those thoughts going through my head, I wondered if he knew I had wished him ill on the day he died. I wondered if he could forgive me.

Immediately following the funeral, I dissolved for a moment in tears in the arms of a neighbour. But I quickly pulled myself together; after all, men of the house do not cry. It would be another 30 years before I wept for my father again.

According to conventional wisdom, Anne and I needed to be sent back to school as soon as possible. Sympathies were expressed, awkwardly, and everyone moved on. At no point did I consciously process my loss; I wouldn't have known where to start. Whatever Mum was feeling, she kept her thoughts to herself. Anne and I never found the words to talk about our grief. What did happen was that my already questionable behaviour at home began to deteriorate – and would continue to do so. I retreated into myself and was sullen and stubborn.

School days were ten hours long. I would leave at 7 am and return at 5 pm and then, especially in the summer, work until dark, feeding cattle, moving irrigation pipes, ploughing and planting oats and clover for winter feed.

Weekends were even longer days, with 4 am starts. After lunch I'd ride out to check cattle and fences, cut wood for the fires and tend to machinery and hundreds of other tasks that are required to maintain a working farm. It never occurred to me that this was in any way onerous. I enjoyed the work; it was fulfilling. It made me feel like a man.

Toby, my black Labrador-cross, was my constant companion, my best friend and confidant. He wasn't a particularly good cattle dog – he was far too easily distracted. Other dogs were focused, disciplined and responsive to a whistle, word or even a look. But Toby was faithful, gentle and always by my side.

By chance, I discovered that he was a much better cattle dog at night than he was during the day – perhaps because there were fewer distractions. A semi-trailer arrived one night to load cattle. This was not according to plan; the truck was expected the next morning. But because the cattle were in a holding paddock nearby, I caught my horse, and Toby and I ventured into the darkness together to drive the mob into the yards. Toby was magnificent: he kept the mob together and guided them skilfully to their destination. He had never worked so well before and he never did it so well again, but without him that night I could never have yarded the cattle.

5

Boy–Man

ONLY WEEKS AFTER the funeral, a neighbour asked me if I felt able to cut up a body of beef for him. This now seems an incredibly strange thing to ask any 13-year-old, let alone a bereaved one, but at the time it seemed perfectly logical. I was of course overly keen to step into my father's shoes in this area, so I took it on. This was the beginning of my weekend work for the next several years. Many Saturday and Sunday mornings from 4 am I would be found in the butchery working away for two cents per pound, with the ghost of my father looking over my shoulder. I could genuinely feel his presence there in the pre-dawn silence and darkness and I imagined him to be proud of me.

Several months into this new venture, one of the local 'Pitt Street farmers', as we called the city-dwellers who farmed on weekends, arrived on a Friday night with a body of beef to cut up. The process was to let it hang overnight to chill so that it would be manageable in the morning. I was by this time quite proficient at handling carcasses of between 150 and 250 kilograms. My heart sank when I set eyes on this one, however: it weighed over 450 kilograms. Between us we hung it up and I scratched my head; it was going to be a lot of work.

Although, realistically, I had neither the skill nor the physical strength to handle the job, the next morning I rose at 2 am, knowing I would need extra time. At 9 am I rang to say I wouldn't be finished until after lunch, and I finally finished at four o'clock in the afternoon. Pitt Street farmers were usually wealthy medical specialists or barristers who bought up failing farms as weekend hobbies. This particular gentleman was a Macquarie Street specialist. When I suggested to him that I might be paid a little more for this task, he flatly refused and drove off in his Range Rover. It was a valuable lesson. Negotiate early, negotiate clearly, negotiate hard. I would not make this mistake again.

Many life-defining and even life-threatening moments occurred for me in those first years after Dad died.

A storm approached one summer afternoon. We had noticed that there was a loose sheet of corrugated iron on the roof of one of the hay sheds. That was a risk that needed to be sorted out. If the hay got wet in the shed it could, before it dried out, create such heat that it would spontaneously combust. Mum decided that I would have to climb up onto the roof of the two-storey shed and repair it before the storm hit. I had thus far been quite comfortable with heights: I loved to climb trees and rockfaces; I had often climbed onto the roof of the house, simply because I could, and I liked the view from up there. But on this occasion, something was different and I felt afraid. I still cannot say what it was: perhaps it was the impending storm or perhaps it was to do with the enforced nature of the exercise.

In the shed we had an old Electricity Commission wooden extension ladder. It was so heavy that I struggled to lift it, let alone pull the rope through the pulley to extend it so it could reach the second storey. Eventually, having achieved this, I made my way to the top with a pocketful of nails, a hammer in one hand and clinging on for dear life with the other while Mum steadied the ladder from the bottom. I made it to the top, clambered onto the roof and secured the errant piece of tin.

It was when it came time to descend that the trouble really set in. I just couldn't seem to manage to put my foot over the edge and onto the ladder to climb down. The storm drew closer and the wind started to get stronger, which only served to intensify my anxiety.

There are few more dangerous places to be in an electrical storm that on top of an iron shed. I was in fact clinging to a giant lightning rod. My mother's words of encouragement slowly turned to anxious pleading and then to frustrated shouts of insistence. But I simply froze; I could not move.

Eventually, the fear of being struck by lightning or blown off the roof must have outweighed the fear of the descent and I made my way, inch by inch, over the edge and down the ladder.

To this day, I have no head for heights. I do not understand what happened on that roof, but it left a lasting legacy on my psyche.

Life carried on in a never-ending cycle of school and work through 1977 to the end of 1978. As I neared the end of Year 10, it was clear that I had neither the desire nor the aptitude to go on to Year 12, so it was decided that it would be best for us all to move to Newcastle to live with my grandmother. Staying on at Warakeela never seemed an option; it would be managed on weekends and with the assistance of casual labour. Anne, who had recently turned 14, was enrolled in a Newcastle high school for the following year, and as I was now legally able to work, a key aspect of the move was that I could properly learn my trade.

Through the nearly two years since Dad's death, Mum had shown extraordinary strength and stoicism. She was a young woman – only 43 when she was widowed – who had been forced by circumstance to run a farm and raise two teenage children on her own, and the stresses during this time were enormous. Having an angry, out-of-control son must have made this all so much harder. She had done well to keep me turning up to school and had contained me as best she could, but it was becoming an almost impossible task.

It is easy to idealise and canonise the dead while demonising the living, and that is pretty much what I had been doing. When my father went, somehow all his many faults died with him; all that was left was the fantasy I created about him in my mind. My mother, on the other hand, was alive and always there – in my face every day, trying to hold the family together in the midst of her grief, confusion and anxiety. Her brokenness was all I could see; her faults were all I could focus on. These were tumultuous times for our relationship, and it is only in hindsight that I can truly appreciate her sacrificial love and patience. Sadly, for both her and me, it was my father's absence – not her presence – that dominated my consciousness.

Leaving Warakeela was no small matter. The list of things we needed to do before we walked out the door was long. There was one task that I kept putting off and that weighed very heavily on me: I had to say goodbye to Toby, the black Labrador-cross, my faithful friend through all those traumatic years. We had worked and played together; he was my companion and confessor. We had developed a single-minded devotion to each other. But he could not come with us; he could not stay by himself; and he would not go to anyone else.

Mum's solution to this dilemma was pragmatic but harsh; her words still echo in my soul: 'Go and shoot the dog.'

Country life is always lived out in the most immediate way in that liminal space between life and death; this reality is simply accepted and understood. I had grown up shooting things; shooting anything was not really a problem for me. There was on this occasion, however, the added and complicating factor of betrayal. This was the kind of betrayal that eats away at the soul of the perpetrator.

Upon receiving the instruction, I went straight into problem-solving mode. Where would the deed be done? Possibilities raced through my mind. Then I remembered that I had previously shot a cow that was in poor condition then burned the carcass. That had been on a ridge, beside a fallen tree. The place was chosen; now I just had to get it over with.

I took my rifle and, for the last time, Toby and I rode out. It seems so surreal now. When we eventually arrived at the place of execution, I tied Toby to what was left of the charred fallen tree, patted him goodbye, told him that I was sorry and took a few paces back.

He looked at me with a fearful knowing. I took aim and pulled the trigger. I can't remember feeling anything, just numbness. But I think something died in me that day, something that has always struggled to be reborn. I cannot articulate what happened to me in that moment. I had killed my best, perhaps my only, friend. I felt soul-less, dead inside, a non-person. I have never held a gun since that day.

Suddenly it was December 1978; in ten days I would turn 16. For the last time, I walked through the school gates. I felt totally liberated. Mum was waiting for Anne and me out the front, and the three of us drove straight for Newcastle. I had no plan, and absolutely no idea where this new stage of life would lead me. A very different chapter was about to start.

6

Newcastle

WHEN WE REACHED Newcastle on that great day of liberation, I suggested that we stop at the Stag and Hunter hotel in Mayfield. I knew this pub well from sitting outside waiting for my father. He would often drink there with a friend of his by the name of Frank Dwyer. Frank owned a butcher shop and I had worked for him during the previous Christmas holidays.

When I walked into the bar, sure enough, there was Frank.

'Any chance of a job?' I asked on a sudden impulse.

'See you at 6 am on Monday,' came the answer.

And then he ordered me a beer. When I pointed out that I was still only 15, Frank's response was simply, 'If you're old enough to work, son, you're old enough to drink.'

Suddenly, I was a not-quite-16-year-old apprentice butcher. My first few weeks in the workforce were, with the benefit of hindsight, deeply traumatising. I had for the most part been able – in the relative security of my own imagination, living at Warakeela – to maintain the illusion that I was a man, a grown man, with real grown-man thoughts and feelings. That illusion was immediately shattered. My workmates saw through me very quickly.

I didn't understand their jokes or their innuendos, and I soon found myself completely out of my depth. Sometimes I was treated in a way that could now only be described as intimidation and bullying, although at the time it was minimalised as joking around. Such humiliating, degrading and at times anxiety-producing initiation rites were, apparently, what one had to endure to find one's way into the inner sanctum of manhood.

Despite those pressures, adapting to life in Newcastle was no trouble; in fact, I started to enjoy myself outside of work and home, which was a first. More than half my class had left school at the same time as me, and most of them had also moved to Newcastle, where they worked at BHP or other associated industries. There was nothing in Newcastle in those days that was not in some way associated with the Big Australian.

Weeknights usually involved a few drinks after work. Again, no-one seemed to question a 16-year-old being in a pub. Then it was a case of a quick run home for dinner before catching up with the boys from school. I did feel slightly more at home with them away from Dungog. It was as if the old dynamic had been broken and we all had to make a new start together. Some of the boys who had left school a couple of years ahead of us had their driver's licence, and most nights now consisted of driving around town and more drinking.

One of the former school friends I ran across in Newcastle was Wayne; he was a Torres Strait Islander who had been adopted by Mr Herman, the Congregational minister. Wayne was an extraordinary athlete and as tough as nails. He was unbeatable over 100 metres, which made him a champion 5/8 on the football field, and he was also so hard that no-one was game to get in his way and he could fight like a thrashing machine.

All through school I had competed against Wayne at running: he would always beat me in the 100 and 200 metres but he would tire in the 400 and I could take him in the straight. On the football field I simply stayed out of his way. He also moved to work in Newcastle and caught the bus at the stop outside the butcher shop where I worked.

One of the junior's jobs was to sweep the footpath in the morning, so I would often stop briefly to chat to Wayne. One morning a new butcher, who had only started the week before, said, 'So, you talk to blackfellas, do you?'

I understood from his tone that this was in some way unacceptable. I wanted desperately to fit in, to be accepted, so I never again went out to sweep until Wayne had got on the bus. Of the many things I have to be ashamed of in my life, this memory for me remains one of the most agonising. I felt so ashamed about my decision that day: not only had I denied and betrayed a friend, I had done so for a despicable reason. I had colluded with racism. My actions had made me feel so unbelievably dirty.

This is one of the deep and abiding reasons I am so passionately opposed to all forms and expressions of racism today. Not only because it is wrong and diminishes humanity, but because I have some insight into how the racist really feels, deep down in the most secret place. There is a part in the racist psyche that feels so afraid – so, so imprisoned – that it must hide in the shadows aching for redemption but is never able to step far enough into the light to find it.

This was a defining moment and gave me some – albeit at this time unsophisticated – insight into the dynamics of prejudice and racism. What I was faced with, as I perceived it, was a choice between being included or excluded. Wayne had no such choice; he could not choose the colour of his skin.

To this day I continue to make choices about where I stand and with whom I stand. I have the luxury to do so; many do not. That is perhaps why I am so passionate about standing up against the marginalisation and exclusion faced by the Muslim community in our society.

At the time of writing this book there is, in my own community, a debate about the establishment of a mosque in a local suburb. An article about objections appeared in the local paper, so I put up a sign supporting the mosque. That day I received a phone call from a long-standing parishioner objecting to my sign.

This was a person I knew well. He was, and is, a good and decent man committed to his faith and to the wider community; he is honourable and worthy of honour. Immediately, I went to see him and to hear him out. I tried to explain that if we continued to marginalise the Muslim community, we would simply increase the possibility of young Muslim men being radicalised. I explained that by supporting the mosque we would draw the Muslim community more fully into the life of the wider community, which could only serve to make it a safer and happier community for everyone.

He would have none of it.

He was convinced that all Muslims were bad. I asked him if he had ever met a Muslim. He said he had not. I asked him if he would like to meet a Muslim. He said he would not. I asked him if he had ever read anything positive about Muslims. He said he had not. I asked him if he would like to do so. He said he would not.

This otherwise good man, who had served the parish community faithfully for many decades, who had literally poured his life into the Church, was about to walk away from his life's work. I suggested that before he made such a drastic decision, it would make sense to seek some more balanced information, to perhaps read a little more widely. He said he felt no need to do so.

In the face of such blind, implacable prejudice, I was speechless. I was also powerless. A deep sense of hopelessness filled my being, and I simply wept in front of him. It was not solely because this man had been friend, supporter and mentor to me, there was something else.

This man was born in 1930, the same year as my father; he was exactly the age my father would have been had he lived. He was a father figure to me. Sitting there in his office, I wept not only for the diminished humanity resulting from his bigotry, not only that I was in danger of losing a friend, but also that I was losing my father all over again. Perhaps more accurately I was losing the fantasy of the good father. I was being confronted in the most powerful way with the reality of broken, fallible, confused humanity, unable to see beyond our own narrow cultural terms of reference and comforting shibboleths. This latter point perhaps was what most deserved my tears. But the deep and traumatic realisation was that if my father were still alive, if he had lived long enough to outlive the fantasy construction I had built for him, he probably would have held these same prejudiced views and we would be at odds on these issues.

7

Who Am I?

As THE JUNIOR apprentice, the work was heavy, hard and often demeaning. Wednesday was the worst; it was sausage day. The process really began after lunch on Tuesday, when I had to mix up by hand 20 batches, 23 kilograms apiece, of sausage meat. This was back-breaking labour, and just to make it more unpleasant, ice would be placed in the mixture to chill the meat. Effectively, I had to work for four hours up to my elbows in ice. My hands would turn red and ache with a numb, unrelenting pain that would permeate my whole body. When Wednesday dawned, I faced the relentless tedium of making 450 kilograms of sausages.

Fairly quickly it emerged that I was actually quite good with people, so during the busy days – Thursday, Friday and Saturday – the manager had me serve in the shop. Unfortunately, this never resulted in a release from the enslavement to the sausage machine.

On Saturdays – in those days – butcher shops closed at 11.30 am. Usually I was out of the door by noon. Mum would be waiting to pick me up for the one-and-a-half-hour drive to Warakeela, where

I would set about working for the afternoon. Numerous Sunday mornings were now spent cutting up meat for the locals, followed by more farm work and then back to Newcastle late in the afternoon ready to start work Monday morning.

During this time, at a party up the river, I met my first post-school girlfriend, the gorgeous Kate. Actually, we had spent time in primary school together but she had gone to a different high school. Local legend among our classmates is that we kissed behind the flagpole in kindergarten but I have no memory of this, so I date our first kiss to this party. However, I do remember as clearly as if it were yesterday the day I set eyes on Kate.

There were four of us starting school that day. Two of the girls I knew well – one lived just across the river and the other I knew from Sunday School. But Kate was a Catholic and lived further up the river; I have no memory of ever having met her prior.

The image seared in my five-year-old psyche is of this vision of loveliness in a white blouse and a red tartan skirt, and blonde hair blowing in the breeze. No doubt there is some appropriate music to go with this scene. I think I fell in love that day as only a five-year-old boy can. While I don't believe we did kiss behind the flagpole during our days together at that school, I used to wish we had. Eleven years on, our love finally blossomed.

Kate was still at school studying for the school certificate, so we began to correspond by letter. It seems so old-fashioned now. Every week I longed for her letter to come. That sweet agony of delayed gratification is a loss to our culture in so many ways.

When Kate eventually graduated and came to Newcastle to begin her nursing career, our relationship crashed and burned in less than a year. What I see as I look back now is that not only were we too young, but that it is impossible for someone like that young man – the person I was then – who wasn't sure who he was, to have an authentic relationship with anyone.

In the meantime, Mum's love life was doing far better than mine. She had met Trevor. Trevor was above all else a salesman. He had the unshakeable confidence required for his profession; he was worldly wise, intelligent and forceful. My perceived position as head of the house was under threat but I had neither the resources nor experience to defend myself. This sent me into an even deeper spiral of anger and self-destruction.

Trevor had been in the habit of working only long enough to make some money and then he would go fishing for months on end. Mum changed that. As soon as they were married they began developing a frozen-food company, and I was recruited to look after the meat side of the business. This was an uneasy relation-ship at the best of times and generated even more conflict between Mum and me.

For me, this was the era of working hard and playing even harder, so I had plenty of distraction. Some mornings I would turn up at the abattoirs at 4 am in a dinner suit, having come from an all-night party. I would grab a couple hours of sleep during the day and then I would party all night again.

During this period, I moved in with a mate, Alan, who had rented a large five-bedroom house. Three of the rooms were sublet. Mostly the housemates were girls, with some of whom we had fleeting relationships. It was a party house.

I became infatuated with . . . let's call her Nadia. She and I shared a love of horses, theatre and parties; we were inseparable for months. Then one day she came to me and told me it was over and that she had had a pregnancy termination. That left me devastated, speechless and I did not know what to do or think.

While I was certainly in no place to form a healthy relationship or to raise a child, I have come to recognise that I have always grieved for that child. I imagine him to be a boy; he would be 35 now, perhaps a father himself. This was the only child I was ever to father and his non-being will continue to be, until the day I die, a source of unending grief. Nadia and I met once more, several years later, on a beach in Newcastle. It was at the height of the AIDS epidemic and I noticed she had lesions on her body. I didn't ask around, but I have always wondered about her. Did she live through the terrible time or did she, far too young, join our son in death?

It was after this that I met Dianne and everything changed. She was considerably older than me, with a young son. Dianne was sophisticated and cultured, and I was enthralled. We quickly moved in together and I took up the father role with her son. I would have been barely 20 years old myself.

Dianne and I did love each other, deeply, but there was a lot against us, especially our own individual brokenness. I had been unseated as man of the house by Trevor, and my relationship with Dianne helped re-establish this position in my psyche.

It was a tumultuous relationship and not healthy for either of us but I have never wept as much as I did the day I left. We did manage to re-establish a friendship and I eventually became her son's godfather but I still cannot escape the feeling that I failed as a partner and as a father.

This period of emotional upheaval and failure left me burned out, so when the chance to return to Warakeela for some months presented itself, I grabbed it. Mum had decided to sell up and wanted me to make the farm presentable. The place had been neglected for several years and I set about mending fences and generally tidying up the place. For a while the isolation was a relief: there was just me; no relationships, not another human being to worry about, to please or to fail. In the evenings I sat on the verandah with a beer and listened to the sounds of darkness.

Eventually, the isolation got the better of me and I returned to Newcastle, where I proceeded to work in various aspects of the meat industry. During this time, I lived with Mum and Trevor. Even though this was not always easy, they were often away, so we managed to survive in the same space. Thankfully, it was a rather large house.

When Warakeela was sold, the effect on me was catastrophic – I experienced unbearable grief. I could rationally understand why the decision had been made but there was nothing rational about what I felt. As usual my grief was expressed as anger, and the upshot of this was a rift between my mother and me that took many years to heal. This is one of the many regrets I have about the choices I made at this time.

To the outside world, I had perfected the art of fitting in. Despite being retiring by nature, I was every inch the personable, efficient butcher.

By my early 20s, I was feeling as if I had made it. I was earning good money, enough to indulge my love of expensive cars, and my social life was extremely busy. I was a regular at Newcastle races, and the people I mixed with were others of the mercantile class: accountants, businesspeople, public servants. On Fridays we wound up at the local watering holes and had, for the most part, a very good time.

There were, however, occasions when the mixture of alcohol and testosterone became volatile. These occasions sometimes deteriorated into physical violence. While my strength and agility often helped me to prevail, there were occasions when my teeth were loosened and my eyes blackened.

DISCOVERING FRAGMENTS OF SELF

8

Epiphany

On Christmas Day, 1984, I woke up with a raging hangover. For reasons not altogether clear to me at the time, I decided, it being Christmas Day, I should go to church.

I found my way to St Andrew's Mayfield, where I had been baptised 21 years earlier. Up to then, my only experience of church had been St Paul's Eccleston, a tiny village church with a reed organ that was pumped by foot pedals, and a dozen or so parishioners. On this day St Andrew's, a large neo-Gothic building, was packed to overflowing. The large pipe organ rang out Christmas carols, the choir sang and the incense billowed.

Something stirred deep within me that day, something about the mystery that I had glimpsed in the tiny country church as a boy was now writ large. The colour, the movement and the transcendence took me to a place I never knew existed. I was captured. An otherworld had opened wide its arms and engulfed me.

This was my introduction to Anglo-Catholicism and I was completely blown away. I eagerly awaited the following Sunday so

I could return to mass, as I now knew to call it. The parish priest, Father George Parker, welcomed me enthusiastically, as did several leading laypeople. After that, I never missed a Sunday

And yet, as epiphanies go, it was low key. The wine-women-and-song lifestyle abated somewhat, but I did not completely abandon it – I just happened to turn up at church on Sunday as well. Consequently, my life was lived in the contradictory tensions of outward religious observance but inwardly hedonistic behaviour.

My pattern of spending most evenings with a few drinks after work and then heading home for dinner continued. On one such winter evening, I arrived home to the flashing light of police cars in the driveway; a tarpaulin covered something in the front of the garage. A police officer met me and said there had been an accident.

'Is my mother okay?' I asked.

'Yes,' he replied, to my relief, and then he told me that she was inside waiting for me. I rushed in only to hear her say, 'Trevor is dead.'

He had been taking a loaded gun out of the car and dropped it on the concrete. The gun discharged and the bullet lodged in his brain. He was dead before he hit the ground.

The police asked me to identify his body. Afterwards, I was flooded with emotion. Recently, I had begun to develop a sneaking admiration for Trevor and to appreciate his giftedness in many areas of life. Now, of course, it was all too late.

He was, I think, my mother's great love, and her level of devastation was overwhelming. By the age of 53, she had now lost two husbands, dead in front of her. I felt powerless to help or to comfort. During the following weeks and months I hung around more to offer some company, but I don't think it eased her suffering much.

Eventually, she began to live again but something had withered permanently within her this time.

Over time, my regular church attendance expanded and I took on various roles and responsibilities. I became a member of the Parish Council and part of the altar team. My social life began to revolve around the church, the clergy and parishioners who had become friends.

My close circle were all as immersed in the church as I was. Many of them were couples but I remained single. Before long some of them started saying things like, 'Rod, have you ever thought of the priesthood? You seem like a natural.' It hadn't occurred to me.

While the thought had some appeal in terms of my fantasy construct, even I could see that this couldn't work out. Priesthood would provide a ready-made identity for someone seeking one so desperately, but even I wasn't deluded enough to think that I could actually be a priest. But as I kept hearing the comments, this planted a seed.

The seed bore fruit; people persisted long enough for me to take it seriously. All the while, my parish priest, Father George Parker, was a mentor. Quietly and gently supportive, he seemed to understand my fantasy construct. While being careful not to collude with it, he tried to guide me towards a place that was a little more real.

It took a while, but I decided to present myself to the Assistant Bishop, Richard Appleby, to discuss the possibility of offering for the priesthood. Part of me assumed he would send me on my way after a polite conversation, but this did not happen. Next Appleby chatted to Father George. Once satisfied, he referred me to a panel of chaplains tasked with examining candidates. By this stage it was 1988.

By July the panel had decided that I should attend a selection weekend during which a group of examiners would seek to discern if I, along with other candidates, had a vocation to the priesthood.

About a dozen of us attended the September weekend, a motley crew from all walks of life. There were teachers, tradespeople, public servants, full-time mums – although at this stage, women could only be ordained as deacons and not priests. The program consisted of personal interviews with examining chaplains, psychiatrists and other professionals. We participated in role plays so we could be observed interacting with each other. The psychiatrist even supplied copious amounts of wine during dinner so again we could be observed as to how much we drank and how we behaved when we did. I probably drank more than I should have and talked far more that I should have, but why would that matter? They wouldn't pick me anyway, so I figured that I might as well enjoy myself.

In my wildest dreams I could not have imagined that I would be accepted, but to my surprise a week later a letter arrived in the mail inviting me to enter St John's College, Morpeth in the January of 1989.

9

Priest in Training

I HAD GROWN accustomed to an abundance of money, however in anticipation that I would be without income during my three years at college I sold my Ford Fairlane and bought a bottom of the range Daihatsu Charade. With the profits from this transaction, my work savings and a small inheritance from my recently deceased maternal grandmother, I arrived at college the day before my first term at St John's, Morpeth with a bank balance of $20,000 to see me through.

Only four of us had made it through selection, and the other three students were married and lived in the family accommodation, so I effectively had Robinson House, the singles residence, to myself. It was a long two-storey building that in its heyday would have housed up to 60 young men training for the priesthood. Now there was just me.

I had been told that as a single student I would be assigned a study and bedroom. Upon my arrival I discovered that these were one and the same room. Undeterred, and with my fantasy of the semi-monastic life of the seminary intact, I unpacked my clothes and my few books and hung up my cassock so it would be ready for chapel at 7 am the next day.

Although the married students used some of the rooms for study, on this first night I was there alone, as I would be on many nights for the next three years. The dining room was closed because term had not yet begun. I sat at my empty desk, looked at my nice new black cassock hanging behind the door. I looked at the crucifix on the wall, one of only three left in Robinson House from the 1940s. Apparently the wife of a former warden, in a fit of Protestant fervour and rampant iconoclasm, had stormed through the students' rooms one morning while they were at chapel and smashed every one she could find.

After sitting there for a while, alone, silent and increasingly hungry, I decided to take the ten-minute walk down to the town to find something to eat. Finding the Commercial Hotel, I entered and ordered a beer. One of the locals, noticing I was dressed in the black trousers and white shirt common to theology students, came over and asked me if I was from the college. Happy to have someone to talk to, I welcomed him and we had a beer together and then another and then another. Sometime after midnight, I staggered back to my room, still having not eaten.

Again, I was greeted by silence, emptiness. An unfamiliar foreboding gripped me. It was understood that if you were single you were to be celibate. The fantasy of the celibate priest, utterly committed to his vocation, a warrior for Christ, was again an appealing fantasy, one that been instilled in me by my mentors. But there on that first night in the silence and the aloneness, my emotions emancipated by alcohol, I recognised that it was indeed fantasy. Doubt blossomed: could I do this? A voice inside me screamed, 'No!'

The threat of my confirmation lessons came back with a vengeance, the disapproving crucifix looked down on me. I took the cruciform down from the hook and put it in the cupboard, I couldn't bear the guilt of failure even before I had started my first day. I wondered if this was how this particular crucifix had survived the iconoclastic maelstrom in the first place.

I awoke the next day at 6 am feeling unbearably hungover. I staggered up the hallway to the shower and – fumbling with every one of the mandatory 39 buttons – managed to get my cassock on. Putting on a brave face, I made my way along the narrow path to the chapel, where I took my place. Not an auspicious start. It accurately foreshadowed the mental state I would be in most mornings over the next three years as I passed through the doors to the chapel.

Breakfast followed chapel at 8 am. On this first morning, I was both starving and unable to eat. I braved a piece of toast and a coffee, which I managed to keep down just long enough to get to the bathroom. Orientation was scheduled for 9 am, after which introductory lectures would begin.

I was about to enter the strange new world of theology. Never in my life had I written an essay. Much of the time, neither the words being used nor the concepts being discussed meant anything. By lunchtime I had decided I would politely sit through the first day's program, then I would discreetly bow out and leave. After dinner, however, a few of us got together for drinks, the first of many such evenings, and I realised we were all in the same boat. Things, I figured, could only get better.

Theology was once known as the Queen of the Sciences and is the foundation of the world's great universities. To study pure theology is to develop the discipline of thinking universally. This discipline has nothing to do with the straw men set up and knocked down by secularists and militant atheists. It is something far more complex than anything that can be communicated in sound bites or in popular tabloid media. Once I learned the language I began to revel in the thought processes.

For some students, the disintegration of some of the 'Sunday School' theological constructs proved challenging and, in some cases, even damaging to their faith. Some clung to the safety of biblical literalism; others adopted 'churchianity' and became overly focused on the right practice in conducting church services. I was drawn to and felt liberated by the deconstruction, and those who became my closest friends during this time felt the same way.

There were only a dozen students in the college by this time, only really enough to form two cliques. Mine nicknamed the other clique the Circumcision Party, after a group who opposed the teaching of St Paul. I don't know what they called us. For the most part, except for the occasional heated exchange, we all got on reasonably well – especially considering the deep emotional turmoil that accompanies the process of priestly formation.

Partway through my first year, I discovered that it was not only my theology that was being deconstructed; my whole concept of self was starting to fall apart. These were the dying days of robust Christianity – a treat-'em-mean-and-keep-'em-keen philosophy that was probably always damaging. Whereas in former eras there had been dozens of single students, all in the same boat, able to support and commiserate with each other, here was I alone in Robinson House every night, my sense of identity – my very life – falling apart and no-one to talk to.

Although an Examining Chaplain had been appointed to each of us, someone we were supposed to talk to, these were generally senior clergy – the last people you would tell if everything was not okay. My Examining Chaplain was the then Archdeacon of Newcastle, the Venerable Jim Ely, a kind, wise and decent man I liked very much. But he was still an archdeacon, the third most senior cleric in the diocese. There were some things I did not feel safe to tell him. So, most nights after dinner, when I should have been studying but the loneliness overwhelmed me, I could be found wandering the college, a bottle of whiskey in hand, looking for someone to drink with. I often found willing partners in other students seeking to numb the pain of their process of metamorphosis.

It would be generous to refer to the food in college as inadequate. I was used to large meals and plenty of meat; I found neither in the college dining room. Most nights I would sit alone picking over the meagre offerings. Occasionally, a fellow student's in-laws, who owned a wheat and sheep property in Young, would send a side of lamb and I would be invited to feast. The experience of having more than two chops was for me a little taste of heaven. This would usually result in more drinking and a very seedy start to the next day.

At the end of 1989, when the Christmas break came, all the other students departed to their various homes and families. I felt going home to be a backward step, and hoped I might get the opportunity to spend the break overseas. During the year I had applied for a scholarship to spend these holidays in Calcutta working with the Australian priest then running the male version of Mother Teresa's Sisters of Charity. Unluckily for me, another student was awarded the funding for the purposes of studying church growth on the West Coast of the United States. Admittedly, unlike that candidate's extensive and neatly typed submission, mine had been written on the back of an envelope. I felt that my mode of presentation was totally in keeping with my goal of working with the poor. Sadly, that synergy in my presentation seemed to escape the notice of the judges.

With his customary generosity, Father George Parker offered me a room in the rectory at Mayfield and a paid job for the holidays. The work was not very onerous and basically consisted of helping at the daily masses and taking communion to some old folk who could no longer get to church. That all changed at 10.27 am on Thursday, 28 December 1989.

I was standing in the laundry of the rectory doing my washing when I heard what sounded like an air force jet approaching. Mayfield is only minutes from the Williamtown Air Force Base, so it wasn't out of the ordinary to hear jets. This one did seem unusually low, however. A huge explosion followed the roar, and the house seemed to lift off its foundations by about a metre.

Father George came rushing down the hallway accusing me of blowing up his washing machine. I suggested to him that it could be a little more than that – had a jet hit the church tower perhaps? We rushed outside to be greeted by a strange sight: the tower was still standing; not a jet was to be seen. Inside the church, the large stainless-steel cross that hung above the altar, a gift from local industry, was swinging like a pendulum.

We had lost all electricity and it took another ten minutes to locate some batteries and to tune in a transistor radio to the news. Then we heard that an earthquake had hit Newcastle. Within half an hour there were reports of devastation in the city and multiple casualties. We decided that we should make our way to the local hospital to see if we could be of any help.

The closest hospital was the Mater at Waratah. When we arrived, the building was being evacuated for fear that it would collapse and so we spent the day holding sheets over the patients to protect them from the heat and making sure they were hydrated until they could be evacuated to other hospitals. In the evening, we split the parish roll and tried to identify the most vulnerable of parishioners and visit them. Many of them we found sitting in their damaged homes in a state of shock.

Thirteen people were killed in the earthquake; we took the funerals of five of them. In the following days, many other people would die, mostly the elderly and mostly from the emotional shock and trauma of the earthquake. By 15 January we had conducted over 30 funerals. St Andrew's was one of the only churches in the city able to be used for weeks after, and we became the go-to place, not only for funerals but also for trauma counselling and community debriefing. It was for me a baptism of fire. There was no time to learn the finer points of funeral ministry, so I just had to make do with what little I knew and what I had learned watching Father George.

This was, I discovered, the Anglican Church at its best: doors flung wide open, a civic Church, broad enough in its theology and practice to provide a safe place for people from all walks of life to do whatever they needed in order to survive the trauma of a catastrophic event. I saw in those weeks the positive effect the Church could have in the community, and to this very day I continue to apply what I learned in those precious and devastating few weeks.

*

I returned to college in the February of 1990 freshly animated by the meaningful experience of ministry that I had encountered during the Christmas recess. By Easter that afterglow began to wear off. Once again, a dark cloud started to descend on my soul. The loneliness took its toll and I became acutely aware of the incredibly abusive nature of the environment in which I found myself. The power imbalances were quite destructive to the soul. Many of the students had held senior positions as lay people in the Church or in their professional life. Now, as candidates for ordination, we were no longer exactly lay people but neither were we clergy. In this space we were, ecclesiastically speaking, disenfranchised and highly vulnerable beings.

Some individuals took advantage of that powerlessness. The then Archdeacon of Maitland, the Venerable Peter Rushton, was not only malevolent but lived in close proximity to Morpeth College, a terrible circumstance because it made it hard to escape him. Ironically, his opposition to the ordination of women protected the female students from experiencing the immediacy of his power. Although he was aware of the trouble Peter Rushton kept causing, the Bishop continued to place students at St Mary's Maitland on Sundays. These were often men considered by the Bishop to need extra training in the liturgical area of ministry; that is, the way in which worship is ordered. Some people are just not particularly gifted in this area and it was often these who were sent to Rushton. What invariably then happened was that the student was subjected to the humiliation of having his character defamed to other priests around the Church. As a consequence, students who may have been depressed to begin with could become almost suicidal.

On one hand, I was in a slightly better position. As a protégé of Father George Parker, I was seen as the 'disciple' of the catholic wing of the Church. I also had a gift with liturgy, so I was less likely to be defamed by Rushton. On the other hand, I had no option but to sit by silently while he defamed some of my friends and fellow students, which was agony. I felt, and indeed was, powerless to defend them. This powerlessness was accompanied by the inevitable diminishing of the soul that goes along with being in a position that I felt trapped in. I hated being around Rushton but I knew if I was seen to leave the 'catholic club', then I would be defamed along with everyone else. The 'club' although not an official entity of any kind was understood to be made up of priests, mostly single, who had a very 'high' or catholic view of the Church and priesthood. They could be identified by their black suits and shirts, always clerically attired, and when in church, clothed in elaborate vestments. They were jokingly referred to as the 'gin and lace set'.

In my second year I was appointed to East Maitland for my Sunday placement. Father Rod Turner was my supervising priest. He was a wise, kind and decent man and when I went to him in second term and told him that I didn't want to go to church anymore and I wasn't even sure I believed in God, he simply said, 'Okay, come back if and when you're ready.' Wisely, he gave me nothing to kick against.

Many priests in his position would have seen this as a challenge to their authority, which in some ways it was, but Father Rod – being a truly humble man – didn't care about this; he just gave me the space I needed to explore the road ahead of me. By the beginning of third term I was ready to return. I turned up on the first Sunday, acting as if nothing had happened, and resumed my position in the sanctuary.

On one particular night during this dark time, when I had consumed far too much alcohol, I encountered one of my lecturers in the college quadrangle on my rather unsteady way back to my room. I have no memory of our encounter other than that our paths had crossed, but the next morning he called me in to his office and simply said, 'No matter what you do, I'm not going to throw you out, so stop trying.' But I didn't stop trying to sabotage my vocation.

10

Seeking My Birth Mother

THE FOLLOWING CHRISTMAS recess, four of us were packed off to Royal North Shore Hospital in North Sydney for three months of Clinical and Pastoral Education. This module was based on an action-and-reflection model of education and was designed to give us not only a taste of hospital chaplaincy but also further intensive ministry formation. It was undoubtedly one of the most important parts of not only my priestly formation but of the evolution of my humanity. I went through a phase – one that drove everyone around me completely mad – of responding to every statement with the probing question, 'How do you feel about that?' This enthusiastic embrace of the action-and-reflection approach morphed into an educational experience of a life-changing nature, one that would take some time to integrate fully into my being.

My assigned supervisor was known as 'The Toe Cutter'. She was, to say the least, a no-nonsense, straight-to-the-point woman. It was my first real encounter with the discipline of supervision and I did not like it one little bit.

I was appointed to two wards: surgical and spinal. Each of us also had to do one night a week on call. Every night I was on, somebody died and it was suggested my nickname should be 'The Angel of Death'.

The thing about the action-and-reflection model of learning is that life has an annoying way of presenting us with the things we need to learn; in my case it was dealing with my own loss and grief, something I had to face if I was ever to have an effective ministry as a priest. Thus began a journey that would take another 20 years and probably isn't over yet.

On one particular shift, I was called to Emergency about 1 am. A man aged 45 had died, and with him in the room were his wife and two children – a boy aged 13 and a girl of 11. In the midst of their shock and disbelief, other relatives were beginning to arrive and some were saying to the boy that he had to be strong because he was 'the man of the house' now.

After about the third time I heard this, I swung around to this well-meaning aunt and went for her. I told her that this was a totally inappropriate and potentially damaging thing to say. The room fell silent. What had I done? I didn't really know but I did know that I had made a terrible mistake. Needing to find a way out of the room with some dignity, I offered to say a prayer over the man. The offer was nervously accepted, and then I left.

Although I understood enough to know where my inappropriate behaviour had come from, I knew I still had to disclose this incident to my supervisor. I expected to be taken to task about my behaviour, and she didn't disappoint. The upshot to this and many other incidents during these three months was that my supervisor recommended that I go into psychotherapy and that while I was in this therapeutic relationship I might explore the issues of being an adopted person. While it did take me another two years to enter productively into therapy, I did begin to seriously consider searching for my birth mother.

In the middle of my final year, I began to explore the possibility of finding my mother. I first went to the records department of Royal Newcastle Hospital where I had entered the world in 1962. It was there that I ran into an old acquaintance. Leanne and I had hung around with the same group about six years earlier and had lost touch. We were, in the past, always friendly if not exactly friends, but there was a little spark in our conversation and we agreed to catch up for coffee after I finished college.

Later, a college friend explored other avenues by which I could engage further in the journey of finding my birth mother. The laws regarding these records had recently been changed, providing better access to both relinquished children and relinquishing parents. The Department of Family and Community Services had subsequently put out a helpful kit to guide people through the process. I had just enough information to apply for my original birth certificate, and after several anxious weeks of waiting, the longed-for documents arrived. My original name was Mark Andrew Burchell, and my mother's name was Anna.

There stood a jacaranda tree outside the college chapel that bloomed each year towards the end of October. The college mythology was that if you weren't ready for the exams by the time the jacaranda bloomed, it was too late. Just as the package arrived, the jacaranda tree outside the chapel began to break forth with its blossoming. So, I put away the envelope and the whiskey and hit the books to prepare for the exams.

But I have jumped ahead of my story.

*

The return to the loneliness of college for my final year came with its customary trauma and abuse of alcohol. I did not, nor was I able to, take my studies particularly seriously. These were the days when a theological qualification was awarded on the strength of one's ability to pass exams. All I needed to do was to read a book in late October and regurgitate the information in early November to gain 51 per cent in the exam and I would be ordained.

Under the modern system of progressive assessment, I probably would not have passed and would never have become a priest. It does trouble me that people like me – who learn in different ways and don't respond well to things like requirements for excessive footnoting – would not be ordained now. I am all for a good academic requirement for ordination, but it should not be the be all and end all. As it turned out, I managed far in excess of 51 per cent in all my subjects and discovered something of a flair for ethics, the theology of St John's Gospel and preaching, all of which I continue to be passionate about 25 years later.

By the time the exams began in the first week of November the flowers had begun to fall from the jacaranda, and we walked across a glorious carpet of purple for our encounter with destiny.

Several weeks prior to this, a long-awaited letter had arrived. This one was from the Bishop telling me that he intended, God willing, to ordain me as a deacon on the first day of February in the coming year, contingent of course on my passing all the exams. He also instructed me to contact Father David Simpson, the Rector of Cessnock, because he wished to appoint me to that parish after the ordination.

In the preceding weeks and months, my fellow students and I had engaged in much speculation over our appointments. This posting did fill me with trepidation. Father David had something of a reputation as a 'curate killer'. Curate is the rather old-fashioned term, now fallen into disuse, for the junior deacon or priest in a parish.

Determined to make the best of it, I contacted Father David and made an appointment to see him as soon as I had sat my final exam. He invited me for lunch. Despite his many failings he was above all else a most hospitable man. At the meeting he laid out clearly his expectations, which could be summed up as, 'Do as you are told.' He then sent me off to meet the curate I was to replace and to see the house I would live in.

Father Michael O'Brien was a good and decent man. He had once shown me a simple but very great kindness, so I trusted him when he told me in graphic detail what a living hell his previous two years had been.

I returned to the college for evening prayer in the certain knowledge that for the foreseeable future I would remain trapped in an environment of power abuse as someone who was utterly powerless. That night, I wept openly in the chapel. Yet again I felt helpless, abandoned and forsaken. At a time when I was beginning to get in touch with feelings relating to my birth, this sensation was particularly intense and devastating. The exams having finished, I once again took comfort in the whiskey bottle.

The college valedictory was held on St Hugh's day – 17 November – and after lunch I left the college for the last time as a layman. By now I had gone without any income for almost three years, except for the minuscule amount I had earned during the first Christmas holidays. Father George Parker once again offered me room and board and a small stipend to tide me over until February, which I gratefully accepted.

And so it was at my desk in Mayfield Rectory two days later, on 19 November, that I sat down to write a letter to my birth mother, not knowing where she was or even if she still lived.

The Department of Family and Community Services kit suggested that if I knew my mother's name and the area in which I was born, I should write to everyone in the phone book with that surname. This was not a common name, so I only had to send out half a dozen letters. The document, dated 19 November 1991, read as follows:

> *Dear Sir/Madam*
>
> *I am writing to you in the hope that you might be able to help me.*
>
> *I am trying to find Anna Burchell. We were very close in 1962 while she was in Newcastle, but unfortunately due to circumstances, we have lost contact over the years and now I would dearly love to contact her again.*
>
> *I would greatly appreciate any assistance you may be able to render me in finding her present address. If you know her whereabouts but feel for some reason you would not like to inform me of it, would you please pass this letter on to her so that she can contact me if she wishes.*
>
> *Yours sincerely,*
> *Rod (Mark Andrew) Bower*

A combination of emotional release after finishing college and the tension of writing that letter left me feeling extremely tired, so I had decided to take a week off and sleep in every morning.

Five days after posting my letter, I received a reply. Father George had collected the mail from the post office. The manner in which he opened the door of my room and tossed the letter on my bed suggested that he thought I should be up by this time.

I ripped open the envelope and scanned the contents. The brief and cautious letter indicated that, for the writer, the year 1962 did indeed hold particular significance. The letter went on to say that I was welcome to write back with more information as to why I desired to be in contact. It was signed Anna Burchell. My mother.

This was the first communication with her in almost 29 years.

For a very long time, I just sat there in bed feeling numb; I think I was in shock. Eventually, I managed to gather the energy to get up and talk to Father George about this correspondence. His response was cautiously noncommittal; it eventually emerged that this was his way of showing concern. Later in the day, I gathered the emotional resources to reply to the letter, giving further details. In another five days, a note returned with the suggestion of a time and place to meet.

In the midst of all this, I had made good on my promise to catch up with Leanne, and our friendship was moving into a deepening – if early – stage of relationship, albeit I was somewhat distracted.

The appointed time arrived for my mother and me to meet: 10 am, 7 December, outside David Jones in Newcastle. She had described what she would wear, and I was to carry a newspaper in my right hand so I could be identified.

That aspect of meeting went like clockwork. In fact, our meeting had a surreal quality to it; we walked up to each other, embraced, and just started chatting. It was, for a moment, as if the intervening 29 years had never existed. We decided to walk over to the foreshore and find a place to sit and talk.

It's strange the things you register in this acute state of aware-ness. As we walked up the mall, the infamous Professor of Classics at Newcastle University, Doctor Godfrey Tanner, greeted me with his customary salutation, 'Nice to see you, dear boy. And sober, too!'

I doubt my mother has retained any memory of this but I remember wondering what impression this might create. Once we sat down, she broke the news to me that my birth father had died 15 years earlier, a year after my adopted father had died. It is the only detail I recall from the several hours of conversation that day. We sat in the blazing December sun, oblivious to the fact that we were both getting burned, our skins reddening – Anna was as fair-skinned as me – and we each shared the first instalment of the story of our preceding 29 years.

The next anxiety-producing task was to break the news to my mum that I had found, well, my mum. I should, of course, have known better; she handled the news in her usual pragmatic and stoic manner and simply assured me that she would have been willing to help me and that she looked forward to meeting Anna.

The two of them met at Mayfield Rectory in the January. I can remember being more nervous than they seemed to be, running in and out of the room like a little boy, producing various pieces of ecclesiastical haberdashery that I had collected for my impending ordination and showing it all to them.

I need not have worried. Twenty-five years later, they remain in contact as an expression of the love they have for the son they share.

11

On Being Adopted

I CAN REMEMBER engaging in a 'pissing competition' with one of my school friends about whose family had been in the valley the longest. Having traced our ancestry back to the same forbear it was a stalemate at six generations, and then he delivered the winning blow.

He said, 'Yes, but that doesn't count because you're adopted.'

It was a decisive and unarguable victory, but the look on my face communicated, even to a twelve-year-old boy, that he had ventured into a place that was best left alone.

The feeling, I can still remember, was one of having been robbed. As if you've come home to the door wide open and that box, with all the special things, missing. The family photos are gone, the cards the kids made in primary school, the pressed flower that contained so much significance, all gone. To add insult to injury you know that the thief will find no value in the box, but without its deeply meaningful contents you feel set adrift, diminished in some way and less yourself than you were.

I am sure this boy has no memory now of his comment or the effect it clearly had on me, but I have never forgotten it or the profound insight it brought to me.

I was not who I thought I was, nor was I who I said I was. It dawned on me that nobody else believed me when I said who I was either. So, how do I live in a world where nobody knows who I am, especially not me?

Along with approximately 150,000 people between 1951 and 1975 I was adopted.[1] I belong to a very select group who experience a higher rate of identity, attachment and abandonment issues, psychological distress, mental illness and suicide.

It was a rainy cold winter's day when I was about eight that my father decided to bring out my adoption papers and explain to me the finer details of how I came to be in this family. I have no memory of what he actually said but I do remember us both feeling somewhat uncomfortable about the conversation. When he asked me if I had any questions, I said that I didn't and went on playing with my Meccano set.

I had a million questions, most of which my eight-year-old brain did not yet have the maturity to formulate or articulate. But it seemed to me that to show any undue interest in my family of origin would be to, in some way, betray my adopted family. For months after, when my parents were out, I would sneak to the cupboard where the papers were kept, take them out and stare at them for ages. The papers were the only connection I had not only to my birth mother, but to a yearning that I could not understand. It was my guilty secret.

My family always expressed their love and care for me, so I don't understand where this concept came from, but I always had an overdeveloped sense that I owed them for adopting me.

This later became a crippling and disabling component of my physiological framework.

Growing up in a small community surrounded by strong family and generational identities further compounded my lack of self-identity and more deeply entrenched my proclivity towards overcompensation with identity issues.

The more obsessed I became with my family identity the more the wider community seemed to resist this. There was a neighbour who would constantly refer to my grandfather, who had died before I was born, as my 'uncle'. There was an element of discomfort in him about referring to him as my grandfather, so he would opt for the common surrogate uncle concept that recognises relation-ships other than blood. While this did seem strange to me it always communicated the message that I did not really belong.

What I could not know then, or begin to understand, was that this feeling of not belonging would remain with me until my ordination as deacon in 1992. At last a square peg in a square hole. Here I would find my place and my people . . . well, at least I thought I had.

12

Ordained at Last and Off to Cessnock

THE DAY OF my ordination drew near and the candidates entered retreat at Bishopscourt, the official residence of the Bishop. Very few of the individuals who started at the Morpeth seminary with me that first day in January 1989 were emerging at the other end of the process as newly minted deacons. The Bishop's residence was a large art-deco house perched on the hill near the cathedral in Newcastle. We were to stay there for four days prior to the ordination; an archdeacon was on hand to give us prayerful and spiritual guidance in preparation for the upcoming ceremony. Meals were to be taken formally, in cassocks and in silence. The doors were locked at 9.30 pm sharp, so if we were to go for a walk after dinner we had to be in by then. I was, in fact, most interested in a constitutional after dinner as Leanne lived only a brisk 15-minute walk from Bishopscourt and I was keen to catch up.

There was so much going on for me at this time: I had a new girlfriend, I had met my birth mother, I had just left the college community and was about to not only enter a new community but to do so as a new person – not a layman but a clergyman.

I recall nothing of the retreat except the breathless walks to Leanne's and back each night and the meeting with the Bishop on the eve of the ordination. We were taken, one by one, into his rather imposing study, and sat in a chair considerably lower than his, as if he needed this device to make us feel intimidated. His charge to me was brief and to the point. 'I am sending you to Cessnock because no-one else will go. You will have a terrible time there, but I don't want you to tell me about it lest I should feel that I have to do something. If you need to talk to somebody, talk to Dean Lawrence.'

And that was it. What I had been told in no uncertain terms was that I was being abandoned to an abusive boss and that I was to collude with the system that was abusing me. The strangest thing about this is that it all seemed perfectly natural and normal; I even had a sense that I was entering into the fine and venerable tradition of the junior priest. One was expected to endure abuse and neglect: it was character-building, and the older clergy had all been through it and survived. One priest even suggested to me that if I kept my head down and my mouth shut I would one day have my own curate to abuse.

And so, it was in the midst of this reeling confusion that I got up early on 1 February 1992, showered, then dressed in a brand new black clergy shirt. I applied my 'dog collar' for the first time and donned my cassock. I sat in St Michael's Chapel waiting for the ordination to begin and wondered how I could have possibly got myself into all this.

As I knelt before Bishop Alfred Holland that day, I did so with all the anxiety, doubt and self-sabotage that I had managed to gather along the journey to this point. And as his arthritic hands descended towards my head, I was filled with the most awful dread, as if I were some terrible impostor about to be uncovered in front of a filled cathedral.

And then the Bishop voiced the words of ordination, I felt the pressure of his hands on my head, and immediately there was a knowing. Not only was I filled with the most sublime peace, I knew for the first time in my life that I was where I truly belonged. It was right. Doubt vanished. I was where I needed to be, doing what I was supposed to be doing.

I have doubted many things before and since but I have never doubted the truth of that moment.

I was no longer a layperson; now I was officially a clergyman.

The removalist's van had arrived in Cessnock the morning before I went into retreat, so I arrived that Saturday afternoon at a house with unopened boxes containing my meagre belongings. I was virtually penniless, but thankfully my pre-college savings had enabled me to keep my car. As much as I dreaded my curacy at Cessnock, I was eager to be earning an income again. The Rector phoned that evening to make sure I was clear on the service times the next day and to be assured I knew what I was doing. He also informed me that I was taking a funeral on Tuesday, which I needed to arrange on Sunday afternoon, and that he would graciously condescend to give me Monday afternoon off to unpack. But on Monday morning I would be busy because I had four scripture classes to teach; there were 16 in total for the week.

I had no training as a teacher, and yet I was expected to cope with half a full-time teacher's load along with my other duties.

As a deacon, I could not solemnise marriages, so I was useless on Saturdays and I was given the day off, at least between Morning Prayer at 7 am and Evening Prayer at 5 pm.

In the first year I took more than 100 funerals and taught over 600 scripture classes, undertook hospital and nursing-home visits, turned up at all parish functions and preached hundreds of sermons. It was exhausting and wounding to the spirit. The only thing that kept me going was the support of several good friends. One in particular was the Senior Curate, Father Michael Cooper. He was single also, and most evenings after prayers we would retire to one of the local pubs and drown our sorrows. Father Michael was affable and wonderful company and we became good friends. We remained so up until his death 20 years later.

Being in Cessnock also meant that we were in the midst of the Hunter Valley vineyards, and many of the renowned winemakers had an historic relationship with the parish. One of the less arduous tasks of the junior curate was to visit one such vineyard to collect the donation of communion wine. Little did I know that there was a ritual connected to this task: on the first visit, the unsuspecting priest would be invited to partake in an extended wine tasting, only to be picked up later in the evening and deposited home somewhat worse for wear. And it came to pass; and I was impressed.

My relationship with Leanne stumbled along for about six months but I was unable to make a deeper commitment and we gave up. Despite our promise to remain friends, we lost touch several months later. I had matured a lot since my break-up with Dianne, but I was still in no space to develop a relationship. It wasn't purely the lack of time; it was more that I was struggling with my identity as an ordained person and the fantasy at least of the celibate priesthood.

While I had already worked out that I was not called to celibacy, I was in some strange way not yet free of the fantasy of it. This was compounded by working with Father Michael and not inconsiderable pressure from Father George Parker, Rushton and some of the other unmarried priests. This expression of the priesthood was held up as in some ways superior to that of those who chose to marry. I found myself trapped between the ideal and the reality, a dilemma that would take me another seven years to resolve.

My newly single status seemed to send a signal to those we euphemistically referred to as the 'single men'. I received an invitation to dinner at the Deanery. This was cause for some excitement for me, because I knew Dean Graeme Lawrence to be a very powerful man who could be helpful to my career. By this stage I was also feeling that I needed to raise the issue of the difficult relationship with my Rector. Perhaps this dinner would be helpful on both these issues.

Present at the dinner were Lawrence and his male partner, along with a young male nurse. There was good food, lashings of wine and engaging conversation. After dinner we adjourned to the sitting room, where things became a little friendlier than I was comfortable with, so I made my excuses and left. After this awkward encounter, the Dean opposed my preferment at every level. This conflict would come to a dramatic and public climax 25 years later.

Women had been able to be ordained deacons since 1986, but it wasn't until my deacon's year that the Church passed legislation to allow for the ordination of women to the priesthood. Coming from the Anglo-Catholic wing of Anglicanism, I had entered college staunchly opposed to the ordination of women. The ideal priest, in my eyes, was just like me – male and single. Any other expression of priesthood was, to my way of thinking at that time, not only somewhat diminished but also diminished the ideal.

By the end of my first year in college, however, I had been brought kicking and screaming to a change of mind. There were a number of female students with me in training. At that stage, they were courageously preparing themselves for something that did not yet exist. Some of them should never have been accepted for ordination but it must also be said that neither should have some of the men.

There were, however, several women whose vocations were undeniable and it was in the end not only the quality of their characters, or their obvious gifts and competency, but the clarity of their calling that convinced me that I was wrong.

I am positive that had women been ordained in Christian churches 50 years earlier, we would never have been in need of a Royal Commission into child sexual abuse. The ordination of women ushered in a revitalised culture to the clergy and to the Church, one that was much less reliant on power and so much more genuinely focused on love. The boys' club began to dissolve and now, 25 years on, has completely disappeared – in the Diocese of Newcastle at least.

Nevertheless, there were still some challenges for me to overcome in this area. As my ordination to the priesthood approached and the legislation to ordain women was passed, it became evident that I would be ordained with the first cohort of women. There were 11 female deacons in the diocese by then and three male, of which I was one. There was naturally a heightened sense of interest in this ordination and quite a bit of press coverage. By early December, the participation of males in this process had been reduced to the phrase 'and three men'. The women had waited a long time for this and it was indeed special – I fully appreciated that – but I had to fight those old feelings that the ordination of women was taking something away from my particular priesthood.

The ordination took place on St Thomas's Day – 21 December – 1992. It was excruciatingly hot as all 14 of us lined up in front of Bishop Jeffrey Parker.

At the crucial moment, there was none of the deep peace in my heart that I had felt at my deaconing. While I supported the women wholeheartedly, I couldn't help feeling a little brushed aside in the euphoria as 2000 years of ecclesiastical male dominance was overturned.

My rector, Father David Simpson, remained a staunch opponent of the ordination of women, so he opted not to attend the ceremony on St Thomas's Day; instead, he preached at my first mass, the following evening. Tradition dictates that, unless there is a bishop present, it is the presider at the mass who takes the last place in the procession into the church. This was going to be my first time filling this position; it was a big moment. The church was full and there were a number of visiting clergy in the procession, all of them senior to me. I took my place at the end, resplendent in my new vestments, only to have Father David take up a position behind me. The message came through loud and clear: I may be a priest now but he was definitely still in charge.

Since 2 February, I had experienced plenty of such displays of passive-aggressive power from him but having become an 'also ran' the previous day, I had hoped to feel a little bit special for my very first mass. For a few minutes, again I felt robbed. Happily, I managed to rise above the pettiness and enjoy my first mass immensely, surrounded by friends, family and love. It was, in the end, a beautiful night in every way.

Getting to know my mother was my personal focus during my two years in Cessnock. Literally, we had to start from the beginning. I seemed to regress to young childhood, needing her to nurture me and her needing to nurture. By the time I left Cessnock, I was the rebellious teenager ready to leave home.

There is a fractured bond between a relinquishing mother and a relinquished child that can become enmeshed and entangled; this was certainly true for me. This vulnerability is so deep within the psyche and so subconscious that it can govern much of the emotional life without ever being recognised or dealt with. This entanglement can and does create unhealthy relationships and disable potentially healthy ones. For me, this journey has revealed its dangers at every turn and is an ongoing one.

Being brought to my knees trying to deal with Father David was what forced me to seek help in the form of therapy; it proved to be a gift. Initially, my motivation was simply to survive the trauma. I was at the same time discovering the mother and dealing with the abusive 'father', all the while trying to learn who I was as a person and as a priest. Although that first stint was relatively brief, the journey of psychotherapy was to be my path, off and on, for the next 20 years. Slowly but surely, I talked everything out and came to a place of self-acceptance that wasn't perfect but allowed me to breathe more easily than I ever had.

I finally took the Bishop's advice and contacted Dean Lawrence, suggesting that Father David be moved, rather than me, so that no other young priest would be subject to his mental and emotional abuse. This was a significant step for me, taking back my adult authority and ability to stand firm in myself and not to run away from a bully. In time, he was moved to a parish where he was unlikely to have a curate, but then in typical Church style he floated to the top and was made an Archdeacon.

Not long after the departure of Father David, I was contacted by the then Archdeacon and asked if I would like to spend two years in the parish of Dee Why on Sydney's Northern Beaches. I knew nothing about Dee Why but I said yes without thinking. My only regret was leaving some of the close relationships that I had formed in Cessnock. However, I could not have anticipated the personal and professional insights or deep sense of peace I would experience, nor the wonderful friendships I would form over the next two years.

THEN THERE WERE FOUR

13

Paris in the Spring

DEE WHY WAS a healing time for me. The Rector, Father Robert Wheeler, was a good and gentle man who allowed me space to heal, learn and develop. The people surrounding me were loving and generous; without them all it is unlikely that I would have survived long in the priesthood.

The curate's house was a former holiday shack built from fibro, and not far from North Curl Curl Beach. To me it was paradise. The workload was considerably lighter than in Cessnock and I soon found myself looking for things to do. I had time to read and think, and to take retreats. I discovered the Jesuits and the spiritual exercises of St Ignatius of Loyola; my proximity to Royal North Shore Hospital enabled me to undertake further study in Clinical and Pastoral Education, which in turn sent me back into therapy. All in all, it was a time of powerful growth and development for my ministry and for me.

The Right Reverend Roger Herft had become Bishop of Newcastle not long before I had moved to Sydney and I had promised him that I would return to the Diocese of Newcastle when my time in Dee Why had finished. We had stayed in touch and when I learned that he was leading a pilgrimage to England, France and Italy in mid-1995 I decided to join the group. Bishop Herft was to become a close friend during this time, but there was another relationship that came as a complete surprise to me.

In Paris in the spring of 1995 I fell in love.

By the time we reached the end of the pilgrimage in Rome, I was completely smitten with a fellow Australian pilgrim. However, while I was returning to Australia, my new girlfriend was going back to London. After we parted at the airport in Rome, I threw myself into the Bishop's arms and wept.

This love dominated my consciousness for the coming year. We wrote every week, and I returned to London in the northern summer of 1996, where we did the grand tour of Europe. I had in my mind to propose in the wedding church in Salzburg, but it was obvious that my girlfriend was not ready to return to Australia, so I decided to bide my time.

While in Geneva I received an exciting message from the Bishop that when I returned he would like me to consider the parish of Toukley on the Central Coast. That put an end to any thoughts I may have had of staying on in the UK. Another tearful and heartbreaking separation in an airport ensued.

I was inducted into the Parish of Toukley in the August. Shortly after, the Bishop went to London for a planning meeting to organise the forthcoming Anglican Communion Bishop's Conference at Lambeth. While there Bishop Roger visited my girlfriend and discovered that, unbeknown to me, my relationship was essentially over. As with many long-distance relationships, a deep emotional connection was difficult to maintain, and my girlfriend had moved on. The Bishop advised she should immediately communicate our relationship was over, or he would, and she did so accordingly.

Now freshly single and with a renewed commitment to the celibate life, I threw myself into the life of my parish. For the next three years I worked hard and enjoyed the fruits of my labour.

Toukley is a beachside suburb and it was a lovely place to live. My mornings began with a walk along the beach and often ended with dinner with parishioners. There was a large and hospitable team of volunteers and administrators. The parish was well served and it was flourishing.

I was as happy as I had ever been. My career was heading in the right direction, despite opposition from some of the power brokers. I wanted for nothing. I had few living expenses and my abundance of expendable income had allowed me to save enough to treat myself to a new, red BMW 318i. I had even come to terms with the single life: while perhaps not my preferred option, I was now at peace with it.

14

Meeting Kerry

It was late 1998 when Kerry and I started our friendship, which rapidly blossomed into love. We met through work where Kerry was employed as a funeral director. Her role was primarily to visit the family and organise the logistical aspects of the funeral service. One of these tasks was to liaise with the priest, minister or civil celebrant the family chose to preside over the service. Those new to the industry and learning their craft would often be allocated to funeral services where I was officiating so I could provide instruction on religious protocol in the funeral context.

One such trainee was Kerry Maxwell, and we developed a pleasant and cordial working relationship.

Kerry had started in the industry with a company that had been known, during the time I had worked at Dee Why in Sydney, for employing lesbians. While she no longer worked for this firm, I assumed that she was same-sex attracted. As it turns out, she assumed that I, being a single priest in my 30s, was gay; it dawned on us both at some point that our assumptions about one another were incorrect.

On one occasion I distinctly remember looking up as Kerry walked past the chapel and momentarily losing my place in the service. It was then that I realised that I did indeed find her very attractive. We had had several pastoral conversations and I became concerned that this be resolved before boundaries became blurred in me between personal and professional relationship.

I decided to come clean with her and tell her how I felt, expecting to look like an idiot but hoping that she would take pity on me and not tell anyone else that I had made such a fool of myself. I made a time to see her and to explain my feelings. I don't know who was more surprised: Kerry, that I had feelings for her, or me when she revealed that those feelings were reciprocated. We went out to dinner that night, 2 November 1998, and have been inseparable ever since.

Well, almost inseparable. Our relationship was tested only several months on when my London ex-girlfriend finally came home and made contact. I was thrown into a deep confusion; however, on revealing this conflict to Kerry she described her pain at having experienced this scenario before, and she clearly had no desire to repeat it. While affirming her love, Kerry expressed her greatest desire was for my happiness; her parting words that I should choose the person I could see myself spending the rest of my life with, and with that she was gone. I remember going immediately and sitting in the church and having an all too rare experience of absolute clarity. I had left my ex-girlfriend physically but not emotionally, and as I prayed it was as if a wall came down between her and me. I rang Kerry within the hour and said, 'It's sorted.'

From that moment I was truly free to give myself to Kerry, and I did.

In this situation, however, it wasn't just about Kerry: she had two children, 15-year-old Kate and 14-year-old John. My growing commitment to Kerry was also a growing commitment to them. As I fell more deeply in love with her, I also fell in love with them; they were engaging and funny and welcoming, and certainly more generous and open to me than I had ever been to my stepfather.

When Kerry and I started dating I quickly became aware that she was struggling financially. She had made a significant and uncompromising commitment to the kids' education, sending them to a Steiner school in Sydney, where they were both flourishing. She worked many weekends on call in her funeral director's role to supplement her income and would at times go without food herself just to pay the school fees. Consequently, a car was well outside her budget. When the bus ran late, trains were cancelled, or her and the kids were tired of carting heavy shopping bags home, she would tell them that one day she would buy a red 318i BMW.

Kerry has an amazing capacity for optimism, no matter how hard life gets, and this mantra became their standard joke and circuit breaker. The first time I turned up to meet Kate and John, I knew there was some kind of private joke going on between them all; however, I wasn't in on it and I was too polite and nervous to ask. Later I discovered that it was all about my vehicle: I had turned up in the exact same car, which had for so long symbolised a less stressful future for the family.

After I left that evening, the kids said to Kerry, 'You're going to marry Rod.' I am not sure how they arrived at that conclusion:

was it me or the car? Both? However, they all made a light-hearted pact not to tell me about the car or their bold assumption, lest they should frighten me away.

The kids were correct though: by the end of May 1999 I had decided to ask Kerry to marry me. Before I proposed, I put a lot of thought and prayer into the family that we would form together. On Wednesday, 2 June I took Kate and John out to lunch. I'm not quite sure why; I think I was confirming in my mind my love and commitment for them as my children. From that day to this and for all the days that I live, I will continue to love them as my own.

That night was our seven-month 'going out' anniversary, and I had invited Kerry to spend the evening with me in Sydney. After dinner, we saw a play at the State Theatre, and we followed that with drinks at the Ritz Carlton and then a walk down to the Opera House. I had been incredibly nervous during the evening. When we arrived in the city I drove the wrong way up a one-way street, spilt food down my tie and shirt during dinner, and was nearly thrown out of the play because my mobile rang in a very significant scene. I kept thinking, 'She must be on to me, I'm acting so weird.'

It was a beautiful winter's night. As we stood looking across Sydney Harbour, I found myself quoting some complex lines from the play that had been spoken by an Hasidic rabbi: 'If I am who I am because I am who I am, and if you are who you are because you are who you are . . .'

Not romantic words, but they encapsulated my inner desires to maintain my dawning and precious identity in the becoming of two as one.

'. . . and if I promise to be truly me and you promise to be truly you, then will you marry me?'

For a moment time stood still. Kerry was confused and didn't initially discern a marriage proposal in my words. I was a little scared. Had I misjudged her feelings? But when it dawned on her she said 'Yes!' without hesitation and threw herself into my arms.

The first issue at hand was a strange ecclesiastical tradition: I had to get the Bishop's permission to marry and we couldn't tell anyone until his permission was granted. The next day I phoned Bishop Roger Herft and told him I was seeking his consent to marry. His initial reaction was to check that it was not my ex-girlfriend from the Europe pilgrimage. After giving him those assurances, I made a time for Kerry and me to meet him in his office one week later.

As an obedient priest I followed the rules; we did not tell anyone, not even Kate and John, which went against Kerry's better judgment. They are highly perceptive and were sure they had picked up that a proposal was on. Each day they would question Kerry as to whether this was the case, which she continued to not-very-convincingly deny. A couple of days later, Kerry phoned me to say she refused to keep our impending marriage a secret from the kids any longer. And so, three days after my proposal we came clean.

They were extremely upset we'd kept them in the dark, and rightly so; this was a life-changing decision that impacted them as much as Kerry and me and we had withheld it from them. It was inconsiderate and hurtful and unjust, and I would never do it this way if I could have my time over again. Sadly, it was a decision informed by my priestly formation; my Bishop's authority was all-encompassing and not negotiable, even when it came to my marriage proposal.

Furthermore, it would be an understatement to say that, at the age of 41 with two children, Kerry was less than impressed about needing to ask permission to marry and that the rather quiet 90-minute drive to the Bishop's office in Newcastle seemed to take forever.

Bishop Herft was his usual charming and insightful self, and after a two-hour conversation he granted us permission to marry. As we were concluding our meeting, he found an available spot in his diary to officiate at our wedding: the date set for 11 September at 11 am. We called Kate and John with the message, 'Officially we are a go!'

On the drive home Kerry revealed that leading up to the meeting she had been paralysed by the fear that the Bishop would deny us the right to marry on the grounds that she was a divorcee. The thought of the cruel irony of meeting and falling deeply in love, then having to end our relationship had been almost more than she could bear. It was an emotional return journey. Following that week of anxiety, Kerry's tension dissolved into tears of joy as we eagerly planned our announcement to our families and friends.

15

Marriage

NEITHER KERRY NOR I wanted a big wedding but our visions of being married in a small, private ceremony were swept aside. The Bishop would have none of it; he would marry us in the cathedral. Apparently, I was a public figure and our wedding was to be a public event. Consequently, numerous shopping trips ensued. We had to get everyone kitted out for the big day; a suit for John and a taffeta dress for Kate. Due to the now grand scale of our wedding Kerry requested we pick out her wedding dress together, much to the chagrin of some staff and other brides-to-be in bridal shops.

More than 400 people attended our 'quiet, private' wedding. Although it wasn't what we would have chosen, it was a momentous day: exuberant, spontaneous and full of joy. There was some noise from a few of the conservative guests that a bride marrying a priest in the cathedral had worn a wedding gown which bared her shoulders, however no amount of disapproval could dampen the magic of our day.

We had not wanted a reception either, but that was also taken out of our hands when Dean Lawrence generously insisted on hosting family and close friends after the service in his residence on the cathedral grounds. Apart from our families, Kerry knew half a dozen guests, the kids even fewer. It was an overwhelming and unfamiliar context for them and Kerry's small immediate family. Nevertheless, they, like me, savoured every moment of it.

At last, we were officially four.

Our children in good hands with Kerry's parents, we headed off to Melbourne for a brief honeymoon, spending our wedding night in a sleeper carriage on the overnight train. It was captivating and romantic, and as the world sped by us we indulged in reliving every detail of the day numerous times over. It was here, while cocooned in our own private universe, that Kerry shared with me the details of a recurring dream she had been having.

The dream had begun a few weeks prior to our first date, and had returned to Kerry three or four times, each time advancing further, like a movie unfolding scene by scene.

Initially Kerry was swimming in deep, calm, crystal-clear water, an island visible in the not-too-far-off distance. With her heightened senses, she relished the intensely vibrant colours, and the peace and consolation the dream presented. There was no hurry, only a sense of everything unfolding in its right time as she leisurely swam toward the distant shore. At no stage were there any feelings of danger, and Kerry regularly stopped to tread water and allow the surroundings to further infuse her blissful state.

As the dream progressed, she began to swim past significant people in her life. They appeared in chronological order. Some swam, others were in boats or lying on blow-up devices. They happily acknowledged her and waved her on, and in each dream, every time she got closer to the shore, the sense of anticipation of something extraordinary awaiting her gained momentum.

At this point in the story, she paused and laughingly admitted that at the time she did wonder if she was going to die sometime soon, and this was a pre-death premonition.

The final dream saw Kerry arrive at the island. She stepped out of the water and onto the white sand. The landscape was bathed in glorious light, and she could feel the warmth from the sun on her skin. 'And there is a person standing on the sand in front of me . . . we embrace . . . and we kiss . . . and that person is you.'

I knew that, because I had seen the dream unfolding before Kerry said the words.

16

Rings

THE NIGHT BEFORE our wedding, I had knelt in the church and was suddenly overcome by the most terrible grief. Tears rolled down my cheeks as I stared at the ring on the second finger of my left hand. This ring had to come off and be replaced by another the next day, and it was breaking my heart. I was confused and conflicted.

The English word 'believe' is derived from the German 'lieben', which means 'to love'. This ring symbolised my fidelity to the Church, to the faith and to my vocation as a priest. The wearing of this ring also embodied some submerged belief that the celibate priesthood was in some way superior to its married equivalent.

Belief is really not giving assent to a set of doctrines but a falling in love. My emotional and theological conflict was that I now 'believed' in Kerry and the kids in a way that seemed indistinguishable from my belief in God. In some weird, irrational way, it felt a bit like adultery. As I removed the ring from my finger, I wept for what seemed like the loss of my life, without really knowing what kind of resurrection the next day would bring.

A couple of years after Kerry and I married, I lost my gold wedding ring in a shopping centre in Sydney. I sat in the car and wept the same tears I had cried on the night before our wedding.

Symbols are powerful. I bought a new wedding ring and eventually had it blessed by Bishop Roger Herft, who was by then the Archbishop of Perth. But it never seemed the same. Perhaps like many of the outward and visible signs of my faith, I no longer needed it to experience my depth of belief in Kerry.

A few days before our 18th wedding anniversary, while snorkelling off the coast of Western Australia, I also lost the replacement ring. This time there was no need for tears. When we returned home, I went to my desk drawer, removed my old priest's ring from where I had put it 18 years before and placed it on my wedding finger. I guess I had become comfortable with the reality that I could believe in both God and Kerry in similar ways and with equal measure, without conflict or confusion, and this one ring could be at once the unnecessary and yet potent symbol of both loves.

I don't think I really comprehended I had fallen in love with God until Kerry actually accessed the deeper parts of my heart. I had, of course, been in love many times before, deeply and truly, but never in this totally self-sacrificing way. It must, I realised, be how God also loves.

I continue to wear this ring to this day. Made of cheap metal alloy, I purchased it from a market stall for about 10 dollars while in college. Ironically, it has no financial worth, yet it serves as a priceless symbol of my abiding love and fidelity to my wife and my vocation.

17

The Fishbowl

THE FOUR OF US had spent a wonderful but brief 'courtship' consisting of family dinners, beach picnics and trips to the cinema, and from the time of the engagement we had all excitedly anticipated living together as a family in Toukley. But that was not where we started our new life. A week before the wedding I bid a tearful farewell to the Toukley community, even though I had loved my time there and been perfectly happy.

Nevertheless, when a priest marries there is a significant adjustment for all concerned and the Church tends to relocate the new couple so they can start afresh. Gosford – the second-largest parish in the diocese – had become vacant, and I not only felt that I was ready for something bigger, but it was so much better for our children, who were commuting to school in Sydney. When we returned from our honeymoon a week later, I took part in a ceremony in which Bishop Herft inducted me as Rector of the Parish of Gosford.

The four of us settled into the rectory and set about the process of learning to be a family together. For Kerry and the kids this constituted immense change. Our beautiful new home, 100 years old and in the Californian-bungalow style, sat just behind the main church and hall, adjacent the car park, with two hall buildings behind the house. All buildings were in use. The site is huge and open, with large expanses of lawn and no fences between the house, car park and church buildings.

For many years, Kerry and the kids had lived a quiet and private life. Now they had to adapt to life in a fishbowl, and the scrutiny was intense. The parishioners were incredibly excited to have two emerging adults living in the rectory and assumed Kate and John would bring with them a ready-made youth group. In that regard, they were to be disappointed.

For me, relishing challenge, those early days in the Parish were heady. Managing a large staff and the inevitable complexities that brings, as well as attempting to shift the psyche of the parish from the traditional mode, which was obviously on its way out, into something new and different, was something I could throw myself into, and I did. The parishioners had a lot of adjustment themselves, and it took a long time for the novelty of this new family to wear off. One of my tasks was to establish boundaries.

I made it abundantly clear to all concerned that decisions about whether or not Kate and John worshipped were entirely theirs, and theirs alone. They had spent their early years in a religious education setting that had not been a positive experience and consequently they had no desire to participate any further in organised religion. They chose not to, with my blessing.

This did not mean, however, that they were disengaged; intrigued by my vocation, they often questioned me on biblical and ethical precepts. I hoped that rather than dragging them into church, I could instead model for them a father attempting to walk the Christian talk as best I could.

Disappointingly, they did not live in the rectory without intrusion. Nosy parishioners would approach them anywhere at any time – even in the car park – and ask what they were up to. Thanks to the exposed position of the rectory, they would sometimes encounter drug-affected people, and occasionally things became dangerous. These incidences went from annoying to frightening, and on occasion downright humiliating.

One afternoon I answered the front door to a woman wanting to speak with me. This was not an unusual occurrence, so I invited her in. The rectory has a long hallway, with a door at each end, and no sooner had she entered the house she threw herself prostrate on the floor and, with arms and legs thrashing, started making loud noises like a clucking chicken. She interspersed these sounds with loud shouts, calling on God and the Holy Spirit to enter and cleanse the house. At this point Kerry came running from the kitchen alarmed and confused, just as John, who had recently started TAFE, walked in the back door with his new friend Ben, whom he had brought home for the first time.

Time stood still for an instant; everyone's gazes transfixed on the woman on the floor, who continued her behaviour unabated. Then John simply looked at both Kerry and me – it was a look of such painful humiliation – and turned and walked back outside without uttering a word. I felt helpless and gutted as I heard the car drive away, as I tried to manage the visitor who apparently had been given a 'message from God' to come and behave in our home in this way. While I had the capacity to manage her, it was a devastatingly embarrassing moment for John, who was having to come to terms with becoming a priest's son.

Kate, too, suffered humiliations. More than once people attending the rectory for meetings knocked and then walked into her bedroom unannounced as she sat on her bed in her pyjamas. Kate was mortified, but the parishioners didn't take a backward step, introducing themselves and trying to engage her in conversation before I could run interference and get them out. There were parishioners who told us that because the parish owned the house they had the right to come and go as they pleased. Both children took to locking themselves in their bedrooms at night.

There were always strangers somewhere on the block; mostly homeless men, often substance addicted, especially at night. The presence of these men made Kerry especially feel unsafe. While Kate was at university, she worked part time. Every Saturday morning, Kerry would surreptitiously watch her through the front windows, checking she made it down the long driveway to the road and the bus stop, because we could never be sure who was sleeping in the grounds, and how unsafe those people might be.

Having worked in the corporate world, Kerry also had a far broader understanding of professional boundaries than those in the Church at this time and would often ask me about OH&S issues that we were facing as a family. As a priest formed by a Church with its clergy living in on-site accommodation, I had difficulty seeing her and the children's grief. Kerry had worked hard to build a safe life for her and Kate and John, and here they all were now thrown into an unsafe one.

Then there was the incessant ringing of the phone and never-ending doorbell. I remember well one particular occasion when I left early to attend meetings in Newcastle, the kids were at school and Kerry was home alone. Enjoying the space and a leisurely coffee she then attempted to take a shower, but thanks to a steady stream of phone calls and people ringing the front doorbell, this was not to be. Over and over again she went through the ritual of undressing, only to have to put her clothes back on to answer the relentless intrusions.

Finally, three hours later, success. Into the shower, water on, and the doorbell rang again. Now Kerry was really furious. She stomped out of the shower and, dripping wet, wrapped herself in a bath sheet and her wet hair in a towel. She flung open the door and abruptly questioned the woman, a powerful and influential parishioner at the time, as to her needs. The parishioner was mortified, so much so she nearly walked backwards off the verandah in shock. Kerry suddenly saw the humour in the situation and had to work hard to keep a straight face.

When I arrived home that night, I did not find Kerry's story about the shower at all funny. Actually, I was very annoyed. Did she not understand that some sense of decorum was required by someone of her position? She began to cry. I regret to say that I had no understanding at that point that what Kerry had experienced was totally unacceptable, and that the problem wasn't with her, it was with me, and the Church, and the model it had given families to live their lives by.

Dinnertimes were every bit as trying. No matter how many times we rearranged our dinner timetable, the phone and doorbell always seemed to work in tandem and our family would eat dinner after dinner with my place at the table empty.

This was compounded by the fact that, as an ambitious young priest, I was out most nights of the week at meetings, literally leaving the family essentially undefended. When the children were with their father, Kerry would be alone in the rectory at night, and on several occasions, she found herself in threatening situations.

There were also times when she found herself left alone in restaurants to finish her dinner while I answered a hospital call.

All three quickly began to wonder what they had got themselves into. I was soon stuck, as most clergy are, between the needs of my family and the needs of the parish. This is a dynamic in which everyone loses, although this did not represent the only challenge we would face in those early years.

18

From Bad to Worse

BEYOND THE CONFLICTS arising from my workload and living arrangements, life began to present us with other difficulties. Kerry began experiencing recurring cardiac and other worrying symptoms, and over time her physical and mental health began to deteriorate. After a long search for answers she was finally diagnosed with Hashimoto's Disease, an auto-immune illness which attacks the thyroid gland. At this point Kerry was very unwell and consequently resigned from her day job, which perpetuated my experiencing, if somewhat irrationally, financial stress. Kerry's frustration in having to accept she was living with a chronic illness, and feelings of inadequacy in being able to contribute to the family's financial needs, burdened her greatly. My life experience of losing my father at a young age due to cardiac issues contributed to the fears I held around Kerry's health, and my overwhelm at carrying the family's financial responsibilities created anxiety for us both for some considerable time.

As if this wasn't hard enough Anna, my birth mother, was finding my marriage difficult to deal with, her response framed around feelings of me being stolen away from her again. For Kerry's part, her particular history made this dynamic difficult to bear. Subsequently, their relationship was strained. This was extremely gut-wrenching for me, and I had great trouble managing the tensions. I felt constantly torn between my birth mother and my wife; actually, there were times I chose my mother over my wife, something I never recommend any husband do. The enmeshing of a relinquished child and their birth mother is fraught with confusion and blurred boundaries. I had a long way to go before I 'left home' for good; it was a process that took many years, but when I finally did, more congenial relationships began to evolve.

Further conflict began to emerge from the fact that I had absolutely no idea what it was like to be a teenager. I had started work at 14; I had no experience of teenagers at play or their natural inclination to rebel or openly resist authority. It wasn't always easy for me to understand this difference at an emotional level and there were times that my expectations of John in particular were unfair and caused tensions between us all. I regret that I wasn't better equipped as a parent during these early years.

Kate tended to be more clandestine in her resistance but John at times could be blatantly oppositional. This often ended in a standoff. Kerry would understandably move to protect the kids from my anger at what I saw as their disobedience, which would cause further angst between us. Added to this was my overwhelming workload and absenteeism – it is a wonder we survived as a family at all . . . and then there were the 'diary fights' . . .

Kerry and I both vividly recall what we laughingly now refer to as the 'diary fights', a regular ritual that involved us both sitting down at the kitchen table with my diary to map out our family time for the coming month. No matter how hard we tried, we could rarely find spaces for us to spend quality time together, and it always ended in one of us, usually Kerry, leaving the room with the issue inflamed and unsolved. When we did spend time together there were so many unresolved matters that hadn't been attended to, it usually ended in tears.

It wasn't going well at home, and were it not for a wonderful, Christian counsellor named Daryll, we may not have made it. Kerry had spent five years in therapy with this insightful, humble man prior to us meeting, a man she credits with saving her life. Daryll agreed initially to help us emotionally prepare for marriage, however our life was so fraught with stress that we spent the first three years of our marriage seeing him regularly. The endurance of the family unit at all can be attributed to Kerry's love and patience, our mutual commitment to stay together, and Daryll.

19

Joy and Grace

EVEN IN THE midst of this turmoil there were many more moments of joy and grace. My relationship with Kate tended to be more the traditional father–daughter dynamic. We shared a number of interests, from philosophy to poetry, and engaged in lively conversations on many topics. I am not sure why, but I soon nicknamed her 'Possum'.

When it came to my relationship with John, I found myself asking, 'What interests can I nurture with my 15-year-old son?' Because I had lost my father when I was young I had no male role model to guide me through my own teenage years, nor due to my circumstances had I undergone my own adolescence, and I possessed little understanding of where to begin. And then I had a thought . . . For John's 16th birthday, I bought us both a set of golf clubs, and every Sunday afternoon we played nine holes together. On those Sunday-afternoon walks around the golf course, we slowly developed a bond that was beyond words. We understood that it was loving, deep, real and abiding, and it quietly endures to this day.

We weathered the barely tolerable conditions of living in the Gosford rectory for four years, long passing the blatantly obvious need to move into an off-site rectory. For much of this time my family had been overwhelmingly unhappy, and I worked incredibly hard to this end to salvage what was left of my marriage and my relationship with Kate and John. When we moved into our new home, we were free for the first time to live together as a family not bent out of shape by the relentless duress of living in the scary fishbowl. Life changed immediately and dramatically for the better; for Kerry and the kids, it was the first time they felt they had a 'normal' existence since the wedding.

From this new and private space, our children quite effortlessly transitioned into adulthood without drama; they were much better behaved than either Kerry or I had been at their age. Travelling the world, gaining degrees, establishing careers and falling in love – they did it all.

When John met Cassandra, it was very clear very quickly that this relationship was going somewhere. Cass is warm and gregarious and instantly became an integral and much-loved member of our family. Life flew by, and it seemed as though their wedding day arrived in no time at all.

I have two abiding memories of John's wedding day. First was the letter I wrote and gave him the week before the wedding.

Dear John

From time to time the question has crossed my mind about what advice I could give you as you entered married life. And here we are, a week away from your wedding. Well, I don't have much advice but there are a couple of things I would like to say to you.

Even after ten years I am still able to be shocked at the depth of love I have for you, as you know I am easily moved to tears because of this love, so I thought in order to avoid embarrassment to both of us, I might write you a letter.

I have had the privilege to watch you grow into an incredible and honourable man. I have the utmost respect for the love and commitment you have for Cassandra and I know you will make a wonderful husband and a fantastic father. I can see clearly that faithfulness is the greatest of the many great strengths in your character.

The commitment you have shown your relationship by buying your house and working full time while travelling to Newcastle in the evenings to undertake university studies demonstrates something of the depth of the man you have become.

I am so much looking forward to supporting you as you become a father and becoming a grandfather myself.

There isn't really much advice I can give you because I can see that the love you have for each other will see you through the ups and downs life will inevitably bring.

But for what it's worth; never do anything that you couldn't tell Cass about and you will have a peaceful life. Give all of yourself, as I can see you already do.

Words cannot express the admiration I have for you and I wish you and Cass every possible joy in your life together.

I know that I am not your father, but I want you to know how very proud I am to call you my son.

With all my love.

R

The other memory is of simply helping him do up his tie and put his cufflinks in. It was as if it was my last act as a parent toward a child, an expression of loving nurture. It was a moment of handing him over to himself to be the master of his own life.

I formed a clear image of John and Cass standing inside a circle drawn in the sand – their intimate circle, their own private universe. From now on he and Cass were the heads of their own household. While Kerry and I would continue to play a supportive role, we now stood outside the space that had become exclusively their own.

I am big on modelling . . . I believe we should always try to be the best example to others, because what we model they will often emulate. I consider this paramount as a parent. One of the great bones of contention in our early relationship was John's resistance to help maintain our rather extensive gardens. It was one of the proudest days of my life after he and Cass created a home of their own when John sent me a photo of himself watering their mani-cured lawn, with the simple caption, 'Modelling'.

We once held a wedding expo at the church, and Kate and John and their friends were models in the fashion parade. I played the priest as the brides walked up the aisle. There was a succession of brides but when Kate walked through the door in a wedding dress, I burst into tears. It was then that I knew that I could never conduct her wedding. I am still amazed that the kids and their friends partici-pated in this event, to be perfectly honest. I know that putting their embarrassment and discomfort aside, they did it for me.

Fairly soon after this, Kate started dating Brad, whom we had known for years because he was one of John's best friends. In many ways, Brad had long been a part of our family and we loved him already, his sense of humour and wicked wit always making him great company. While there were the initial bumpy adjustments as he moved from being John's best friend to Kate's boyfriend, we soon evolved into a loving family of six. Life was very good.

I wrote to Kate on the night before her wedding. She read the letter; we cried; there were no more words needed.

Well, Possum, here we are on the night before your wedding.

There is so much I want to say to you, but as we both know I will just end up in tears. So, to save us both embarrassment I thought I would write you a note.

I know I am not your father but I am so very proud to call you my daughter. Thank you for the unparalleled privilege of playing a fatherly role in your life. You have given me one of the greatest gifts of all.

I have watched you grow from the engaging 15-year-old I first met into an intelligent, professional, independent woman. I have cherished every day of that journey as we laughed and cried, discovered new wonders and explored ideas together.

You have challenged me and given me opportunities to discover deeper parts of myself. When you left home part of me went with you and now I have to completely hand you over to Brad. I cannot tell you how difficult that is. I guess I still want to see you as the little girl who needs my help and advice.

However, you are your mother's daughter, so I know that I can trust you to find your true path.

So, I release you into Brad's arms with faith, hope and love.

I love you. I always will.

R

Another handing over of a child to themselves, another intimate couple circle in the sand.

I was part of the busy morning behind the scenes on the big day. Kate got dressed at our house, and I was overwhelmed and so incredibly proud when she emerged from top-secret women's business in the bedroom as a stunning bride. But when it came to the public part of the ceremony, there was no room for two fathers to walk her down the aisle, so I chose to give up this privilege. I won't pretend it didn't hurt; this is sometimes the pain of the step-parent.

While I don't know what it is like to love a child who is biologically my own, while respecting of course that they have their own biological families, I cannot imagine a more abiding love than that which I have for Kate and John, and Brad and Cass . . . for they, too, have become my children.

Like most young, modern families, they have returned to live with us for the odd short stint at various times, bringing their children with them. Consequently, our hearts have broken when they have left. Yet ironically, if we as parents do our jobs well enough, we equip our children to grow up and leave home. This is the paradox of parenting. My admiration for these good and decent human beings, and now amazing parents, continues to ever deepen.

Kahlil Gibran, the 20th-century Lebanese poet and author, wrote so eloquently about raising children:

You may give them your love but not your thoughts,
For they have their own thoughts,
You may house their bodies but not their souls,
For their souls dwell in the house of tomorrow,
Which you cannot visit, not even in your dreams.

20

Gifts of Love

STEP-PARENTING IS A universe unto itself. My own experience of being a stepson was for the most part a messy mixture of positive and negative. I was at a difficult teenage stage when my mother remarried. I would not allow myself to enter into a relationship with my stepfather by whom I felt my position in the family was threatened. Regretfully, when I did allow this relationship to begin to grow, it was cut short with Trevor's tragic death.

At times I have not been able to stop myself offering unsolicited advice to my adult children. I should have resisted such temptation and feel blessed that all four have forgiven such intrusions. I am getting far better at shutting up . . . as is Kerry. Despite all of this – making lots of parenting errors and a few bad judgments along the way – we didn't do too badly.

And then there are our grandchildren. Not having raised infants, grandchildren brought me undiluted delight. Even changing dirty nappies allowed me to exercise my fatherliness in a way that I had never experienced. I found that I was a natural at settling grumpy babies and I took every opportunity to call in and play Pa.

To have our grandchildren live with us has been for me pure unadulterated joy. I lost a child to abortion, and Kerry and I had a number of miscarriages early in our marriage. My ever-present grief at not having children even prompted Kerry to ask early in our relationship if I wanted a divorce. Despite my dawning realisation that we would not have our own children, my response to Kerry was clear: I had not married her to be a baby incubator, but as my partner in life. There would be no divorce.

Consequently, to hold our grandchildren for the first time, and to feed them, and rock them to sleep on so many occasions has been for me a healing of the brokenness in my soul that I could neither have asked for nor imagined.

These three precious grandchildren have given me such joy and have taught me, albeit in my 50s, how to play and laugh and have fun, and derive the utmost pleasure from the simplest of things. I strive for a better world because Izzy, Liam and Lucas have given me my raison d'être. It is my intention, as best I am able, to continue to model for them that in standing up for issues of social justice, and in undertaking acts of service, we are best able to serve one another and ourselves. It is my most cherished hope that our children and grandchildren will be proud of the work Kerry and I do.

Moreover, I cannot imagine failing to leave them a world in which they can breathe clean air and drink pure water; I want them to live and grow in a safe, sustainable world. There is nothing more sobering than to hold in your arms a tiny, vulnerable, innocent new person. I recommend it as a way to give one perspective on what is important in life. I would joyfully give any of them my last breath.

THE VALLEY
OF TEARS

21

Unravelling at the Edges

IN 2001, THE already hectic pace of my professional life intensified. I was appointed as Archdeacon of the Central Coast, the youngest person ever to be promoted to that office in the diocese. Such an appointment meant that I was well and truly on the way up the ecclesiastical ladder. Even attaining the office of bishop, while not assured, would not be completely out of the question. I visualised a future in which I would fulfil a high calling.

With this promotion, I was effectively working two full-time jobs. Putting in 100 hours per week was nothing unusual. Often, I was away from home overnight, and when I was around I had to deal with the extraordinary range of tasks that is the lot of the parish priest. Presiding at church services, hospital visits, meetings, seminars, appointments and pastoral responsibilities all take a priest away from family.

Home was tough. Not going so badly at work. There was more than enough satisfaction in my day jobs and my wider diocesan roles. For instance, I was also a board member of the local grammar school. This involved regular meetings but particularly offering support to the Principal and senior staff members. As well, I sat on the Diocesan Council, which is like the board of directors of the diocese. For this I travelled to meetings in Newcastle and served as a conduit between the Bishop and my region of the Central Coast. There was also the Savings and Development Fund. Running a Diocese requires funds, and the funds need to be managed, regulations met and compliance standards adhered to. At the meetings, parishioners with business acumen sit alongside lawyers, bankers, property managers and senior clergy.

My career was definitely on its way. I was now at the centre of the decision-making body of the Diocese of Newcastle; well, at least I thought I was. Even in the midst of the heady upper echelons of ecclesiastical politics I began to notice that there were sentences that were not finished in my presence, decisions made when I was not in the room. I couldn't really put my finger on it but I began to see that there was more to ecclesiastical power than just being an Archdeacon.

I did, however, push those thoughts aside in favour of the trappings of power, the special seat in the cathedral, rather grand robes and being referred to deferentially as 'Archdeacon'.

Then one fateful evening I received a call from the Assistant Bishop: there was an emergency, he couldn't tell me what, and we were to meet with all the senior staff in Bishopscourt at 9 am the following day.

We gathered in the house on the hill at the prescribed time to hear that the Registrar, the person responsible for the financial affairs of the diocese, had stolen a large sum of money. I'm pretty sure I went into shock; perhaps we all did. This man had been my friend and colleague for 20 years, best man at our wedding; I really did not know how to respond.

A junior police officer had said to Bishop Herft the afternoon before, 'You lot will cover this up, you always do,' but the Bishop was particularly determined to be utterly transparent in the process. Everything was to be handed over to the police; justice had not only to be done, it had to be seen to be done.

I visited my friend several days later. He expressed his remorse and intention to plead guilty and to repay all the money.

I made a commitment to offer as much support as I could to him and his family during this difficult time.

A week later, there was a meeting of the Diocesan Council. The Bishop made a pronouncement that no-one on the council was to have anything to do with the former Registrar, and if we planned to do so we were to leave the meeting immediately.

This plunged me into deep conflict. I knew if I walked out of the meeting it would be the end of my career, but what was the point of being a priest if I couldn't, well, actually be a priest?

In terrible inner turmoil I slowly and quietly placed the business papers in my briefcase, stood and bowed to the Bishop as is customary in such a setting, and left the meeting.

The Bishop contacted me the next day and we agreed to meet. A few days later, over a cordial lunch, he reiterated that transparency was of the utmost importance and if I were to continue to offer pastoral care to the former Registrar, the Bishop would have no alternative other than to dismiss me as Archdeacon. I suggested that I could step down from Senior Staff until the case had been to court; this surely would not be more than a couple of months, because my friend had resolved to plead guilty. But the Bishop was resolute: I could not offer pastoral care to my friend and remain an Archdeacon. Transparency had to be absolute.

Ultimately, what his words meant to me was that I could not remain a priest, as I understood the office and staying true to my vows, and also remain an Archdeacon under the then regime of Bishop Roger Herft. I communicated this to the Bishop over dessert and he indicated that he would write to me and exercise an instrument of dismissal from my position as Archdeacon. I would remain a priest and Rector of Gosford.

Even though I knew it was coming, when the letter arrived from the Bishop stating that my licence as Archdeacon was revoked, effective immediately, I was paralysed with shock. I had worked extremely hard, cultivated all the right relationships, got on all the right boards and committees and chosen all the right appointments. Never for a moment had I entertained the possibility that I could lose my career prospects as a priest because of counselling someone in need and accompanying them on their journey to redemption.

While I knew I could never live with myself if I abandoned my dignity as a priest, I could not have anticipated how difficult it would be to live in the diminished state of a sacked Archdeacon.

On Saturday, 6 April 2002, the *Newcastle Herald* led with the headline 'Senior Anglican stripped of role'.

In his interview with the *Herald*, Bishop Herft suggested my position as Archdeacon created a 'conflict of interest' due to my relationship with the Registrar, and my sacking was for the 'common good'. The article however suggested murmurings within the church that some judged my dismissal as wrong. The Bishop had demanded my public silence on the issue, and consequently I was not permitted to speak to the press to defend my position. Although no such gag existed for him. When the press called I told them I was not in a position to comment. Once again, I found myself unquestioningly obedient. My wife and family were outraged at his handling of the matter, believing it fell far short of natural justice.

A leading layman phoned me later that day and said, 'Many of us understand and respect what you have done, but don't expect to get one vote at Synod,' and he was right. I became a pariah in the diocese. I would sit alone at clergy events, and I eventually stopped attending them. There were rumours, which still persist, that I had been an accomplice in the theft. Being on the boards of institutions that handled millions of dollars, I felt I had to resign my directorships.

In a matter of weeks, I went from being an up-and-coming to a has-been. The phone stopped ringing, invitations dried up, I was finished.

There was trouble at the parish level as well. With that demotion, my congregation numbers thinned and I encountered many an averted gaze.

Frankly, this reaction not only took the wind out of my sails in terms of energy, motivation and commitment, it dragged me down. Cumulative exhaustion from the many hundred-hour weeks I had been putting in contributed to my debilitation. Those around me suffered, for I tended to ruminate on what had happened. My unresolved identity issues resurfaced and I became depressed. The last thing a thriving congregation can cope with is a depressed priest, so the parish began to fail. The more people left, the more depressed I became, and the more depressed I became, the more people left. I knew that for my sake and the sake of the parish I had to take some time off, extract myself from this vicious cycle.

*

I was extremely blessed to have the support of my loving family. Kerry and the children put up with a lot from me during this period, and without their love I am convinced that I would have taken my own life. They were all I had left to live for.

When I returned to work I was also fortunate to be surrounded by a great team. I met with these colleagues every Tuesday morning for prayer and reflection; they sat and listened to my ramblings for over a year, without comment or judgment. When I had finally said all that I had to say, I was at peace and ready to move on. It was a startling transformation facilitated by the love, care, patience and forbearance of those closest to me, and I will be forever grateful to them.

I made a lot of changes. Initially, I took ten weeks off work, began a Masters in Christian Spirituality, and was enriched by my encounter with the sermons on the Beatitudes of Gregory of Nyssa (c. 335–394). Gregory was a thinker of big thoughts whose spiritual wisdom remains illuminating. It was useful to be reminded of the living tradition of the church, and to be taken out of my head. To be reminded that the truly blessed are the poor in spirit, the merciful and the peacemakers.

Reconstruction for me was both metaphorical and literal. Among the projects I threw myself into was restoration of the historic St Mary's chapel, the renovation of Christ Church and the building of a new rectory. The congregation started to return.

Wouldn't it be all hearts and roses if at this stage of the narrative, Kerry and I eased into our Darby and Joan life, sitting together doing the crossword puzzle; mass on Sundays and parish fêtes. No. Long unattended matters started to surface.

Throwing myself back into work and family life with such vigour, I didn't at first realise my mental health still wasn't okay. By now I was 48. My three fathers had all died before the age of 50, and there was a certain consciousness about that for me. Also, my grandfather had died at the age of 49, as had his father; it was as if there were something of a family curse.

The anxiety started while I was presiding at funerals, a mild tightness in the chest accompanied by a slight shaky feeling. I put this down to an irrational fear of my own mortality and undertook cognitive behavioural treatment and psychotherapy to address the feelings. But over the following year, the anxiety got worse and progressed to panic attacks, visual disturbances and heart attack-like symptoms, still often centred on funerals. It was not uncommon for me to be standing in front of 300 people in a funeral chapel and suddenly need to hold on to the lectern so that I would not fall, unable to focus my eyes on the page in front of me.

I tried medication but found that it reduced me to a quivering mess. This was burnout, but I could not afford to take more time off work. I was trapped, and again there were days where the only solution seemed to be suicide. I tend to look at my life as a series of defining moments. The thought of giving up work was to me like a spiritual death; not giving up work ultimately meant physical death. In a defining moment of sheer desperation, Kerry made an appointment for me at a local acupuncturist. After the first treatment I felt a little better, as if I might just be able to cope; after the second I was starting to manage; within six months of treatment I was not only functioning but flourishing.

Professionally my life would go on rather unremarkably for another few years until another hugely defining moment would launch me into a completely fresh chapter.

22

Losing Anne

As I LOOK at a photograph of my ordination as a deacon in February 1992, there is an obvious sadness in my sister Anne's eyes. On that day, I did not know that she had only 24 hours before been diagnosed with Myotonic Dystrophy.

Anne had difficulty giving birth to her daughter several years earlier. As it turns out, her birth mother had the same difficulty with Anne. Deterioration in her muscle strength had eventually led to this devastating diagnosis. It was a slow progression for Anne. Over the ensuing 25 years, she became less and less active, ended up in a wheelchair and was ultimately totally dependent on her husband for her care. She died of heart failure several months before her 50th birthday. I have long since stopped believing in the family curse, but it is a cause of great sadness that another family member did not make it to 50.

Anne and I just didn't seem to inhabit the same universe. It wasn't that we didn't love one another, because we did, but being adopted from a different set of parents, we just never deeply resonated.

Consequently, the depth of grief I experienced at her death surprised me. Kerry and I stayed with her during her last night and hours of consciousness. Kerry kept vigil while I dozed on and off. Before we left the following morning, in one of the most meaningful experiences of the sacrament I ever had, I administered the last rites through sobs.

I felt that I had not been a particularly good brother; I felt guilt at not being as supportive of Anne as I could have been. All the little mean things siblings do and say to each other came flooding back to me and I asked for her forgiveness and offered mine. I wish I could have done that 20 years earlier. It seems one of the strange contradictions of the human condition that when the separation of death is imminent, people are often able to feel closer than ever before.

My grief was not just the pain of the death of someone I loved, but also the pain of loving someone I often didn't understand. However, we shared the experience of growing up in a family together. Anne was the only other person in the world who really knew what that was like; with her death there was a part of me that felt totally alone and isolated, that no living person could ever know or understand.

23

The Royal Commission into Institutional Responses to Child Sexual Abuse

LIFE IS A messy place; it can be brutal, too often unjust, and sometimes beyond bearing. By default of our very humanness, we all endure our own dark nights of the soul, both individually and corporately. What was revealed in the Royal Commission into Institutional Responses to Child Sexual Abuse, Case Study 42: Anglican Diocese of Newcastle hearings held in Newcastle in 2017, following four years of intense and astonishing work by the Royal Commissioners and staff, was very dark indeed.

Sexual abuse is always about power, and that is never more devastatingly focused than when it is inflicted upon children. The evidence presented to the Royal Commission taught us that where we see abuse of power we should always look for sexual abuse of the most vulnerable.

Sexuality lies at the very foundation of our humanity; we are sexual beings, and for the most part we are broken beings. Our brokenness more often than not emerges and is expressed through our sexuality. This can be an expression of our desperate need for containment, which results in faithfulness to a partner or celibacy and abstinence, which are all honoured by our culture and are for the most part good for our society. Our brokenness can be and is also often expressed in less honourable and destructive ways, the extreme of which results in child sexual abuse.

We cannot avoid the issue of power in human society. I have often said that I do not want power, but I don't want anyone else to have it either. But that wish can never be a reality. In every relationship, in every organisation, in every community, in every society someone has power. And that is never truer than in the Church.

The structures of a faith community are such that the clergy speak from a position that is often literally six feet above contradiction. Canon law provides for the security of clergy often ensuring they cannot be outvoted or sacked. This at its best enables the clergy to speak truth to power and to express a prophetic voice; at its worst it can turn into abuses of power, with devastating consequences.

At its best the particular type of power expressed in a faith community is exercised with true humility, shared responsibility and sacrificial love; when it works it works well but that is rare because we are all wounded. So, it is a matter of ensuring a safe Church, which is best achieved by transparent processes, just accountability and professional supervision.

Prior to the Commission's hearings, Kerry and I had decided that as testimony to every courageous survivor, and in memory of those who did not survive, we would bear witness to each day's hearings. If we couldn't make it to court, we would watch or listen to proceedings via live broadcast. If I had appointments, Kerry would be my eyes and ears. It was an act of contrition on behalf of our faith community.

I am not conscious of when I became aware that adults sexually abuse children. As a child I, like most people, had the usual experiences of peer-to-peer exploration of each other's physicality, most of which I have no real negative memories of except perhaps for some residual guilt mostly imposed by nominal and moralistic Christianity. An adult never sexually abused me and this was never spoken about in the society in which I grew up, so I had no way of knowing it existed. I was never what could be called sexually naive but I was totally unaware of this particular aspect of human behaviour.

This issue was never raised while I was training for the priesthood. We were never warned to look out for such behaviours or what to do if we encountered them. I was shocked and devastated to learn that child sexual abuse was going on all around me, by priests I knew, and I had no idea that it was happening. Someone suggested that I would have been subtly 'sounded out'; perhaps a perpetrator would have said something that thinly veiled the sexualisation of a child and watched my reaction. If my reaction was negative, which it would have been, the conversation would have gone no further. I do not remember this conversation but I am assured it would have taken place. My dawning awareness that there was such an aberration as child sexual abuse, and that this was an issue in the Church, evolved slowly over years as perpetrators were charged and their offences reported in the media.

However, it was not until the revelations of the Royal Commission began that I became fully and devastatingly conscious of how deeply this evil had entwined itself so perniciously through the lives of so many innocent children.

Every courageous witness, every revelation, every cleric who responded with 'I don't recall' pierced my soul. I wept for the dignity and bravery of those who stood to give their testimonies, at times staring church employees down, at other times reduced to tears and succumbing to overwhelming emotions. I found myself crying most days for the evil that my Church had rained down on such innocents, whose whole lives had been lived in painful and torturous ways; their whole existence torn apart. For an unknown number of men and women, their journey was to end in premature death by their own hand.

This also awakened within me a dawning consciousness of the power abuses that existed within the Church with regard to my own life. I came to understand that where there is one kind of abuse, there are most certainly others. As further revelations about other clergy were reported in the media, I was less surprised as I had witnessed at first-hand their power abuses manifest in hideous bullying, although to be blatantly clear, this did not include sexual abuse.

And so it was to be that over the course of the Royal Commission's hearings I became aware that the priest who had married my parents and baptised me was an alleged perpetrator, as was Father George Parker, who mentored me and nurtured my vocation; as were many of his friends. The priestly robes I wore in Cessnock had been previously worn by one of the most vile and evil perpetrators in the diocese, Peter Rushton, and my friend and colleague, Father Michael Cooper, was an abuser.

The most devastating evidence for me revolved around Father George Parker, although his identity at the time was protected by a pseudonym. While driving back to the office and listening to the Royal Commission hearings I heard a crucial piece of evidence that revealed to me that the abuser the Commission was currently investigating was in fact Father George. Without doubt. I knew it was him.

I couldn't breathe. Pulling the car over to the side of the road I began to hyperventilate. I was numb. I thought I would vomit. I eventually called Kerry, by this time sobbing uncontrollably. All I could repeat over and over was, 'It's George.' She had been watching the proceedings live and had heard the evidence, not realising it was him.

The only other thing I could articulate to her was that in that moment I believed I could not continue with my vocation. No. Never putting my robes on again. My priesthood was done. It appeared insurmountable to consider ever again functioning in a place where so many of my peers and superiors were responsible for such despicable harm. Additionally there was the longstanding and entrenched culture of power abuses of us, the clergy. It was so ugly and devastating and evil.

I soon realised that my response had been precipitated by shock and grief, so rather than abandoning my vocation I sought some help to work through the issues and regain my equilibrium. However the way I perceive the priesthood and the church had changed forever. I now knew that I could never know what was truly in a colleague's heart, no matter how well I felt I knew them.

In 2001 it was revealed in the media that Father George, at that time working as a priest in Victoria, had been charged with historical child sexual abuse offences alleged to have occurred between 1971 and 1975 in the Newcastle Diocese. I simply did not believe that this could possibly be true. I had known Father George since 1984. He had been incredibly generous to me. He had mentored my vocation. I had lived in his rectory and worked closely with him. I searched my memory and agonised over the accusations, but I could not find one single thing that would indicate that there was a problem. I spoke to mutual friends and other clergy who had worked with him and we all came to a similar conclusion that, if anything, Father George 'appeared asexual'.

Father George had always stressed to me the importance of being truthful and I had always known him to be so. Immediately on hearing the reports I telephoned him and asked him straight out, 'Did you do this?' 'No!' he exclaimed indignantly. I believed him.

Perpetrators are incredibly good liars and manipulators; they use personal loyalties to cover their tracks and are adept in compartmentalisation and showing completely contradictory faces to different people in different situations. They are also very deliberate in choosing their victims, and often prey on those most vulnerable and less protected, thereby reducing the chances their victims will come forward, or be believed as credible.

This initial case against George Parker was 'No Billed' at a Newcastle Court hearing in that same year, and he was free to go. This does not mean the court found him not guilty, but that at the time there was insufficient evidence to continue the case. Parker had produced parish records which suggested he could not have been with the victim when certain offences allegedly occurred. I was relieved that the man I had come to love dearly as a mentor and priestly father figure was exonerated. Not so the man

George abused, who would now endure more than a decade and a half before he got the chance to be heard and vindicated.

I made it back to the office in time to watch this astonishingly courageous and dignified person give his evidence to the commission. He recounted details of the abuse he suffered, the effects on his life, and the 2001 hearing, including how on leaving court that day he observed what he described as Parker and two other men, one he identified as the then Dean Graeme Lawrence, laughing at him. My outrage and disgust at Parker, Lawrence and the other person was barely containable.

And then it happened: Counsel Assisting the Royal Commission into Institutional Responses to Child Sexual Abuse read out my name in court. My name had been given to the commission by Lawrence in suggesting it was not he, but I, who was one of the three who mocked the victim outside the court building. I was not where Lawrence said I was, and I had indisputable proof, but I was stunned.

The only consolation for me is that the survivor of Parker's abuse sought me out some months later and told me he knew that I was not there at court that day. I was able to ask for his forgiveness for not believing him back in 2001, and he graciously gave me that forgiveness. In spite of all the pain the Church, its priests and bishops had inflicted on this decent, gentle human being, he still had the grace to forgive. This is humanity in its fullness. This man understandably no longer holds 'the faith' but has clearly embraced something deeper and more real for him than Christianity is for most who claim its adherence.

The charges against George Parker were reinstated after the Royal Commission received the survivor's statements. There were allegations the records produced in achieving the 'No Bill' verdict in 2001 were doctored. Parker died several weeks later from cancer; he never lived to face either the man whose life he changed forever, or justice.

I was deeply disturbed and wounded by the disclosures that successive bishops and senior Church officials, often close friends, had mishandled reports and covered up crimes.

Roger Herft was Bishop of Newcastle from 1993 to 2005 and retired early from his position as Archbishop of Perth in 2017 following the Royal Commission Newcastle hearings. He admitted to having let down the people of the Hunter Valley while not admitting to anything in particular; however, in this single and very significant issue, he failed unconscionably. He did not exercise proper leadership when he should have, and this caused vulnerable people devastating consequences and pain. His failure to act appropriately put innocents at risk. This is diabolical. It should never, ever have happened.

Throughout the whole Royal Commission proceedings there is one bishop who emerged with impeccable integrity and credentials: The Right Reverend Greg Thompson, the now former Bishop of Newcastle. Bishop Greg, a survivor of abuse himself, put his own health at risk to ensure that the Diocese of Newcastle faced the past and engaged in a healthy future, but this was not without extreme personal cost. The old guard in the diocese circled the wagons against Thompson's agenda to expose the Church's history of child sexual abuse and the cover-ups that ensued.

Thompson was steadfast and resolute in his determination to see this through. He worked diligently with the Commission, spent endless hours pastorally caring for other survivors, ensured policies and processes were in place to determine that such crimes were never repeated and enabled proper redress to be paid to survivors and their families. At the end of the Commission's proceedings, Bishop Greg resigned so that he could recover from the ordeal that his prophetic ministry had led him though.

Prophets are not without honour, except . . . in their own house.
Matthew 13:57

As I write this I am reminded of a man who once came to see me. Kerry answered the knock on the door of the parish office to find an elderly man breathless and in tears, so distressed he found it difficult to articulate what he needed; he wanted to see a priest. Luckily, I was at my desk and heard the commotion. It would be no exaggeration to say that as he covered his face with his hands and wept openly, Kerry and I found it hard to contain our emotions.

Ushered into the sanctuary of my office, he acknowledged he had been convicted and sent to prison two decades previous for sex offences against a child. He explained that he had sought help in understanding why he did what he did and undertaken upon release to adhere to all conditions placed upon him. He described how vigilantes in the local community had hounded him out of his small rented flats three times over the past five years. He recounted how many times he had been followed, verbally abused in the street, and fiercely beaten. He told me of his inability to gain employment following his release from jail, and with nothing to fill his days, and no person to share his life, searched to find a reason to exist.

And so it was that he found solace in academic research, spending most of his days in the local library. Until today. Until today when the same local group who had harassed him for years, armed with a loud-speaker, entered the library. They approached him and identified him via megaphone, in this public space, as a paedophile. Following this 'outing' he somehow made his way up the road to the church, and here he sat in front of me; stooped and defeated . . . his pain, despair and humiliation tangible . . . his human brokenness as raw and open as a gaping wound. He knew there could be no more library visits; another dwelling place taken from his matchbox-sized universe.

This man's visit affected me profoundly, leaving me concerned that as a society we could be so self-destructive. This form of scapegoating can only serve to create conditions for reoffending. Those who behave in this manner do so under the banner of 'keeping our children safe', but they are doing precisely the opposite. An overwhelming number of studies have found that sex offenders who are surrounded by a caring and accountable community are far less likely to reoffend than those who are socially ostracised.

A community is safe for everyone or it is safe for no-one. Those of us who have not committed those crimes and have not participated in their concealment need to guard against self-righteousness and reflect upon the ways we have personally contributed to a culture and society in which these crimes could be committed and covered up.

I know that there will be those who would wish to twist my words here, so let me be absolutely and definitively clear. I stand firmly against all forms of abuse, but I find child sexual abuse to be an abomination; perpetrators must be sought out, tried, convicted and imprisoned for significant sentences. Generally speaking, however, they cannot be kept in prison forever and if we genuinely wish to protect children, then a safe and just community must surround the paedophile.

The Church is always in danger of creating a community that is so safe for one group that it becomes unsafe for others and that is not a Church. Proper training, processes and practices are what make an organisation safe for all. Transparency, accountability and supervision, especially for those in power, are what will ensure safety for the most vulnerable. Exclusion, marginalisation and ostracism only serve to place the vulnerable at greater risk. This is a difficult conversation to have and it may indeed still be too soon to have it. But for the Church and the wider society to have a healthy future, it is one that will have to be entered into sooner or later.

24

The Crossroads

Does not wisdom call,
and does not understanding raise her voice?
On the heights, beside the way,
at the crossroads she takes her stand;
beside the gates in front of the town,
at the entrance of the portals she cries out:
'To you, O people, I call,
And my cry is to all that live.'

Proverbs 8:1–4

I AM A white, Western, male, Christian heterosexual. I am therefore the absolute embodiment of the domination system in which we live. I live my life socially, economically and professionally at the centre, not on the margins. But because of my lived experience I live that life perpetually with the mind of an outsider.

I have come to a point in my journey where I am able to see this as a blessing rather than a curse. The reflections that follow are offered from the perspective of the crossroads where the centre and the edge are at their closest point.

A place where I have found the still small voice of wisdom whispers her timeless truths.

PART 2
JUST MATTERS

NEW LANGUAGE, ANCIENT WISDOM

25

Facebook and 'That' Post

IN 2010 I decided to establish a parish Facebook account, which grew out of a renewed focus on what was happening in the wider world. The timing was interesting. After a long and messy career journey I found myself back enjoying my work once again; not only with an altered identity in terms of what my role was and what the future held – and no longer held – for me, the way people interacted generally in society was undergoing a transformation as well. Social media was in its infancy.

However, my entrée into the social media world had a rather inauspicious beginning. The Bishop had decided he wanted to import a priest from England. Gosford was one of the few parishes that could afford an extra stipend, so he determined to appoint the priest to the parish. This particular priest was of a very conservative, evangelical persuasion and I did not feel he would resonate well with the team as it was. The Bishop, however, was not a man to change his mind once it was made up. My only chance was to change the mind of the priest. The Facebook page of the Anglican Parish of Gosford was born.

I asked the parish office manager to create a page that strongly reflected a commitment to LGBTI rights and marriage equality. This was, of course, entirely in keeping with my views. Next, I referred the prospective priest to the page as an efficient means of gathering information about his new posting. It wasn't long before he decided that Gosford was not the parish for him.

The page, having done its job, then sat undisturbed for some time until Kerry suggested it as a way of keeping people interested and informed about the activities of the parish. She started putting up posts – thoughts for the day – for which she would usually see a handful of likes.

Every once in a while, I would add a mild comment about current affairs. I was quite excited when something about LGBTI rights attracted 13 shares. That seemed like a success. Typically, one of our posts would get a dozen likes. But it was all very relaxed. Kerry and I were enthusiastic about it but it didn't require a lot of attention.

This was in 2013, when people were starting to feel a little more comfortable with social media and it was being adopted more broadly. A range of different conversations was beginning to take place, including commentary of a political nature. It didn't occur to me that we were seeing a technology-enabled ideas exchange. But then something happened that shook me to my core, and before I knew it, I wrote a much more deeply felt post. And that's when a massively defining moment occurred.

On 23 July 2013, I received a phone call from a woman whose brother was dying. She asked me if I would administer the last rites at his home. At the agreed time, I duly presented myself at the door in order to administer the sacrament. The man was unconscious, lying in a hospital-type bed in the living room of his well-appointed apartment.

His sister was there with another family member. After introducing myself, I invited them to tell me something of his story and prompted them with some questions. When I asked whether he lived alone, the answer was a slightly awkward, 'No.' I asked if he had a partner, and the answer was a slightly awkward, 'Yes,' accompanied by a glance towards the bedroom door. It was then that it dawned on me what was happening.

I said, 'Well, get him out here so that he can be part of this.'

The assumption was that the Church – and therefore, the family had figured, me as the Church's representative – was unable to accept a same-sex union as valid. I was deeply disturbed by this and incredibly troubled as I drove back to the church. The adrenaline was surging through me for a long time afterwards.

Kerry happened to be interstate visiting John, Cas and Izzy and, because I could be a bit slack about it, had given me strict instructions to continue changing the street sign and updating the Facebook page while she was away. In the office, I opened the software program I had acquired – a formatting system. You could key in a line and it would present the text to look like a roadside sign outside a church.

Still exercised about the exclusion I had just witnessed being visited on people even in the pressure-cooker of the end-of-life experience, I decided to make a public statement. I needed the community to know that I was personally supportive of LGBTI people. I needed my parish also to be welcoming of people from every colour of the rainbow spectrum of human sexuality expressed by consenting adults.

My post to the parish Facebook page read:

DEAR CHRISTIANS. SOME PPL ARE GAY. GET OVER IT. LOVE GOD

At that time, we had about 150 followers on our parish Facebook page. Almost straightaway, I noticed it starting to attract some attention – likes and shares – so I went down to the *actual* roadside sign – at the bottom of the driveway to the church – and put it up there, too.

Next, I rang Kerry to tell her I had possibly hit our street sign messages for six . . . play nice, be kind, buy someone a coffee . . . by doing something a little outrageous. Kerry, as an 'unchurched' person, had always lived beyond the conservative confines of the church – actually I would say she was downright challenging of them – and while her views and experiences were often helpful in allowing me to see outside of my 'club' mentality, these differences every so often caused considerable friction in our marriage. Not this time. She was over the moon. Although it wasn't long before Kerry's thoughts turned to what repercussions might befall me, her experiences meant she had little faith in the Church as an institution to act justly. We would soon come to know it was not the Church we most needed to fear.

By the end of that day the Facebook page had nearly 1000 likes. A week later that number had gone to 3000, and the numbers continued to grow steadily over the coming months. The post is estimated to have been viewed over 70 million times and shared many thousands of times. The sentiment behind the 'Some people are gay' post was deeply felt for my part and in turn it struck a nerve.

A sleeping giant had been aroused. I really hadn't done or said anything new, progressive or liberal, only acted in the spirit of what had always been part of the Christian expression but seems little known in secular Australia. The message was reported nationally and internationally in the UK and US press. Calls flooded in to the parish office – both of praise, including from the LGBTI community, and recrimination. Unsurprisingly, I received some very loud condemnation from conservative Christians.

It's just a blur when I look back on it now. While it was exciting to ignite something, when people engage with it on that scale, the momentum it generates is terrifying. How do you control a firestorm? You can't. It was difficult to predict what might happen from one moment to the next.

The media attention came on instantly and strongly. There were requests for appearances and comments from television, including the morning shows, and from radio and print journalism. I had no way of knowing if I would ever again get the opportunity to encourage people to engage with this issue, so I said yes to every offer that came my way. It was demanding and I tried hard not to become overwhelmed but to simply invite people to open their hearts and minds about giving a thought for those who are marginalised in our society. So, there I was, thrust onto the public stage. Ready or not.

Strangely, at that time, my thoughts turned to the plight of ordinary people who – often in life's tragic circumstances – get thrust into the media spotlight. How exhausting and overwhelming it would be to have to face that relentless attention.

By nature, I am not particularly extroverted, so it was a relief when it died down, by which time I felt as though I had ridden a tidal wave. Depleted and drained, I needed to reflect and make sense of it all. What I realised was that I had found a way to get people to engage with some big ideas. As a priest, that was what I constantly tried to achieve every time I delivered a sermon.

But now I had found a way to preach to more than the choir; it came in the form of a battered, traditional roadside sign displaying 56 characters.

A couple of weeks after the 'Some ppl are gay' post, I ventured out again . . .

DEAR KEVIN PNG IS NOT THE ANSWER

It drew 176 likes and 52 shares. It was extremely easy, I discovered, to find the words with which to connect with people on the social justice issues I most cared about. It seemed sensible to focus attention on asylum seekers, Indigenous rights, climate change and marriage equality. These were the things I wanted to open up conversations about because I believed they were issues that reflected the health of our corporate soul. They were sacramental in a sense, an outward and visible sign of an inward and spiritual grace.

I have continued on that path since then, looking for issues that reflect the state of the nation and analysing our responses in order to gain insight into our corporate spiritual health. It is what I was trained to do with individuals; I find the same rules apply for an entire nation.

There has been a lot of learning-by-doing. My conservative parishioner base was initially shocked and bemused. No-one had seen any of this coming, least of all Kerry or me. Far from minding the media attention, some of them seemed happy about it, possibly proud even. In some cases, people were positively energised by it. Surprisingly few parishioners were upset. I could count them on both hands.

Today the make-up of our congregation has changed; it is younger, more vibrant and certainly more engaged in the community. I have had to change, too. I don't get to do so much one-on-one ministry anymore; I now rely on others to help provide pastoral care, administration and general running of the parish. My focus is now outward from the parish rather than inwards toward the parish; this is also the parish's focus.

From that low-key beginning of the church's Facebook page, Kerry and I started putting a lot more time and thought into it. We developed a stratagem for moderating the page as well as a stratagem for our own self-care. We decided that we would stick to subjects that we knew about and, as worthy as they may be, stay away from those with which we are unfamiliar.

Sometime later, I became aware that this thing called Twitter existed. I signed up and started posting the signs there as well. Roadside signs are made for Twitter. They are a meme in themselves – a meme is essentially a picture with some text. Consequently, there is a natural synergy between the space constraints of Twitter and the size of a photograph of a roadside sign. At the time of writing we have 55,000 Facebook and 17,000 Twitter followers.

It's impossible to tell this story without also talking about the backlash. Not that I dwell on it as a rule. Conservative Christians were outraged that I would dare to support LGBTI people. This is exactly why the dying man's family had hidden his partner. In the minds of the conservatives, I was supporting an abomination, something that God had clearly condemned. Of course, this view was based on a misinterpretation of scripture, because the biblical writers had no understanding of what we now know as the spectrum of human sexuality. How could they? It is not possible for late bronze and iron-age people to have a modern scientific and physiological understanding of human sexuality.

THE AUSTRALIAN CHRISTIAN LOBBY DOES NOT SPEAK FOR US

Just as I had a steep learning curve in dealing with media attention, I had to adjust to dealing with searing criticism. This is where having cut my teeth on the floor of an abattoir came into its own. Colourful language and direct abuse don't tend to faze me.

As well as mail and messages and phone calls to my parish office, many calls went in to the diocesan office asking the Bishop to intervene. The supposition is that I would have been censured many times over. On the contrary, at no point did the Bishop pick up the phone and speak to me, let alone try to tell me how to behave.

The reality is that a bishop's job is a conservative one and there are many bishops who feel they have to toe the party line. However, there are a great number of those bishops who have a passion and concern for social justice and deeply care for those marginalised by society. These bishops are often delighted when they hear their priests speaking out in ways that they themselves do not feel able. I have not always had an easy relationship with the episcopate but I have been privileged to work under the authority of bishops who have a genuine care for the marginalised of every kind.

It wasn't the bishops who threatened to shut me down, but anonymous keyboard warriors. With my embrace of social media came a steady stream of what is now known as trolling – nasty, vitriolic, menacing comments online.

We had to work out how to deal with that phenomenon, and there were a few rookie errors. Initially we tried to engage but quickly discovered that there are a lot of skilled trolls out there. These people are essentially sociopaths. Their modus operandi is to control the conversation until they have attracted a number of new participants. They will inflame the situation and encourage others to become irrational and abusive – to do the dirty work for them.

We learnt how to deal with these arch manipulators the hard way – the best response is to ban them, not to engage. It wastes a lot of time and ultimately no good comes from it. There is an adage, 'Never feed the trolls.' There is a lot of wisdom in that.

I don't know how many people we have banned from our social media accounts, although I estimate it would be many, many thousands. The ban-and-delete policy has had its critics, especially among those who champion free speech above all else, although I must say that this is usually in the context of freedom to abuse. The view we have taken is that this is not anti free speech; people are free to say whatever they like on their own page, but we are under no obligation to listen. Our moderating rules have always been clear: abusive, violent, hateful, threatening, offensive, bigoted posts would not make it to page.

CIVILITY IS THE FOUNDATION OF PRODUCTIVE PUBLIC DISCOURSE

We are exercising our right to not hear. As the Mahatma said, 'I will not allow anyone to walk through my mind with dirty feet.'[1] I am also exercising my own freedom of speech and that is the freedom not to speak to certain people. We made a conscious choice very early that our target audience was the political centre, those who are called the 'persuadables'. We can only hope that at the end of the day those who believe that a diverse, just and harmonious society, along with those who have also been persuaded that such a society is of value, will, in this secular democracy, outnumber those who seek power through the manipulation of fear and creation of division. Although some days it feels like a losing battle . . .

26

Shutdown

In early November 2014, the media reported a small South Australian business, Fleurieu Milk Company, chose to end its $50,000-per-annum yoghurt supply deal with Emirates Airlines because of a large number of abusive responses from people who claimed Halal certification fees were being used to fund terrorism. The spokesperson leading this actual act of terrorism against Fleurieu, the anti-Halal group Halal Choice, was of course unable to substantiate her claims.

Appalled by this gross act of bullying, we put up this sign with accompanying commentary . . .

BOYCOTT THE BIGOTS AND BULLIES. BUY HALAL

This is not about Halal. This is about living in a civil society. We must stand up against bigotry and prejudice. A South Australian dairy company has been bullied out of a contract by the 'boycott halal' people. We call upon everyone who desires to live in a peaceful, harmonious multicultural society to speak out against this bullying by the Islamophobic lobby.

This post received over 240,000 views, 4200 likes and 3225 comments; sadly, 2153 of these were at best ignorant, and at worst hate-filled, racist, violent, threatening rants. Kerry and I tag-teamed moderating the page, banning the bullies and Islamophobic. Four days later, having had little sleep, saturated by the vitriol, and unnerved by personal threats made against my life, including being burned alive, beaten to death then urinated on, and stalked in the cross hairs of a rifle, we shut the page down.

TAKING A BREAK

In a further bid to escape we packed our bags and headed north to the beautiful village of Boomerang Beach. It was a blissful time away; swimming in the sea, walking along the beach, napping in the afternoon and going to dinner in the evenings, but we did not discuss that from which we had fled; it was too raw and we felt too vulnerable. As the sun was going down on our last night in Boomerang we sat on the verandah having a beer; the smell of summer and the sea pervading our senses, neither of us wanting to burst the bubble and begin the dreaded conversation. It began rationally, questioning whether we should continue with the social media project, the highs, the lows, but it soon escalated to tears as Kerry revealed her deep fears for my safety. After a couple of emotionally tough hours we decided it wasn't worth the risk, nothing was worth that great a risk.

By this stage I had received a number of substantial death threats which had been given to police for investigation; consequently I had been assigned my own detective. This was the last straw. We were done. We went to bed resolute that night that we wouldn't put the page back online. However, it was difficult to think about shutting it down, and on the drive home the next morning I turned to Kerry. It began with an apology, telling her

I thought we had somehow stumbled into something incredibly significant and there was no going back.

I understood the fear and anxiety – I lived with it too – but I couldn't ignore the call of the Gospels to continue to fight injustice. This work was life-giving and it seemed to be the right thing to do. Kerry didn't respond with words, just nodded, and we drove on in silence. Suddenly I was overcome by emotion, and I asked her to promise me that if the worst happened, she would carry on the work and make my death worthwhile.

We both cried, it was a gentle and generous moment of love and grace between us, and Kerry softly said, 'I never imagined we would be having this conversation. I don't want to admit it, but I agree.'

Facebook post, 23 November 2014:

We are back! We are even more determined to transform unjust social structures and to contribute to the evolution of a harmonious and peaceful multicultural society. We do hope you will join us. One of the most destructive forces to have been unleashed on Australian society in recent times is unbridled xenophobia. This is being given tacit approval by some leading politicians for the purpose of political gain. This trend must be arrested. This irrational fear of the stranger has found its recent expression in the recent 'boycott halal' movement and other likeminded groups. We call upon all good and decent Australians to stand up and help contain this divisive trend, to reach out across cultural, ethnic, and religious boundaries and to recognise and celebrate our shared humanity. It's great to be back.

The threats began with the 'Dear Christians' sign, and have not stopped. Sad to say, this is now our lived reality. We exist in a permanent and heightened state of anxiety; threatening, abusive people at the door, on the phone and via social media are commonplace. When I rode on the Mardi Gras float in 2014, I had received so many threats beforehand that as the float proceeded along its route, I looked for moving curtains in windows and red dots on my chest. As I left Kerry at the hotel to walk to the parade marshalling point, we had both been emotional. I told her how much I loved her and our kids and our grandchildren, and I was sure I would return . . . but if I didn't . . . I didn't finish the sentence. Public spaces are the most frightening of all.

We have back-to-base security and security cameras, and keep doors and windows locked and double-locked in our home. My staff's safety is always of deep concern for me; the office security door is always locked. If I don't come home when expected, or if I'm unavailable on my mobile for a certain time, Kerry will sometimes panic. Every once in a while, she will get in the car and drive into work looking for me. Most likely there will have been a wedding couple calling by to look at the church, or an emergency hospital call. As a consequence of Kerry's distress on such occasions, we communicate far more closely these days about my movements.

Since 2013, I have learned an immense amount about social media and what it brings out in people, including myself. At different stages, social media has become such a huge part of my life that it is unhealthy. Let's call it what it is: a performance. And to a huge extent it is about affirmation. You're putting something out there that people are responding to. That feeds something in the psyche; there is a certain energy that comes from the affirmation.

Most social media interaction occurs at night. When is enough enough? It requires discipline to turn off the devices, to switch off from it all. To return to relating to partner and family.

Such was the impact of 'that' post, life changed fairly rapidly for my family, and we all had to come to terms with the public profile. Our children, highly protective of their privacy, do not like to be identified publicly, as one can understand. Kerry and I, while chronic introverts and intensely private, have gradually become used to living a more public life, an incredibly privileged life we could never have imagined. Paradoxically a life overflowing with both blessings and menacing threats.

27

The Church Should Stay Out of Politics

IT'S NOT ONLY threats that bombard me, I am also often offered unsolicited advice, much of which I can't print here. But oh, if only I had a dollar for each time I have been shouted at down the phone or had rants posted on social media telling me I should 'stay out of politics', I would indeed be a very rich man. So why should I openly speak out against unjust and divisive systems within society? As a religious leader I believe I have an imperative, handed down to me by the founder of the firm, to focus my energy on creating a cohesive society.

As a Christian leader attempting to publicly challenge religious and political leaders on issues of social injustice, I am habitually criticised by those who vigorously maintain that Church and state should remain separate and consequently I have no authority to intervene with what they perceive as 'political commentary'. However, 'politics' is bigger than 'party politics', because politics refers to the way we human beings organise ourselves.

When the founder of the children's construction toy company Lego, Ole Kirk Kristiansen, named his business in 1932, he chose to combine two Danish words, 'leg' and 'godt', which means to play well. Kristiansen didn't realise until later that in Latin the word meant 'I study' or 'I put together', which is also the root meaning of the word 'religion'. 'Religeo' literally means to 'connect over and over again'. I like to apply Kristiansen's discovery of the Danish and Latin linguistic synergy of Lego to religious leadership; it is not only about getting people to 're-connect', but also to 'play well' together. I'm all for religious leadership, not just in faith organisations but also in the wider community.

This is, however, in a progressively secularising culture, becoming an increasingly difficult agenda to prosecute. The Reverend Dr Martin Luther King Jr had a dream, a dream packed with the biblical imagery that was well known by and resonated with his audience. Things are different now, so much more diverse, and so much more challenging when it comes to creating resonance.

The separation of Church and State is one of the most misunderstood concepts of our time. In historical terms, the Constitution of the United States was a reaction to, and insurance against, the dynamics of the established Church system in England, although it could be validly argued that religion has a de-facto position in the contemporary public life of America that was neither desired nor envisaged by the authors of the Constitution.

For Australia and New Zealand, the dynamic is markedly different; while we have no established Church and, unlike the United Kingdom, Anglican bishops have no ex-officio seats in our parliaments, our Head of State, presently Queen Elizabeth II, must be of the Anglican faith.

For us it is in reality a predominantly benign cocktail of secular democracy and soft theocracy; a system more easily supported by tradition and culture than political rationalism. In practical terms, separation of Church and State means balance and mutual accountability, it is part of the system of checks and balances that creates a healthy society. Although, for Australia I would favour the clearer separation that a republic would afford, and certainly no prayers in parliament, which would reflect the reality of religious diversity. This would serve more of a symbolic than practical purpose.

The State has a responsibility to ensure that religious organisations always act for the total wellbeing of their members and the community at large, as was powerfully demonstrated by the work of the Royal Commission into Institutional Responses to Child Sexual Abuse.

CHILD ABUSE. WE WILL NEVER BE SILENT AGAIN

Religious bodies, and other organisations that have a predominantly moral and ethical foundation, have a responsibility to call the State to remember its duty to govern with justice, equity and compassion. Recent examples include the Australian Government's treatment of asylum seekers and refugees, and the socially divisive rhetoric of vilifying ethnic and religious minorities for the purposes of political gain.

MR ABBOTT LEADERSHIP NEEDED TO STOP RACISM

Human rights are best served when there is a healthy interaction and mutual moral accountability between all parties. To some extent society depends on the religious to transform narratives from 'them' to 'us', to speak in prophetic voices, to live on the edge, be courageous and outrageous, to illuminate and celebrate the 'good other'. We are called to stand against oppressive politics of fear by challenging those who act divisively, and we rely on society to call us out when we are acting divisively. It is an interdependent relationship; when it works well it works very well, and when it doesn't work it has catastrophic consequences.

In this area of conversation there must be clarity of definition between politics and government. Politics, as I have said, is simply the way we organise ourselves, government for us is a particular form of representative democracy that is charged to make decisions for the greater good of all. Religion should always be involved in politics but never in government.

28

The New Marketplace

Whereas Jesus took his message to the marketplace and people gathered around to listen, and St Paul had the *areopagus*, a place of exchange of ideas and debate in ancient Athens, social media is the new arena for public conversations. Twitter, Facebook, Instagram and the like constitute the marketplace from which I operate as I engage in public conversations, in a movement I see as essential.

Although this is perhaps not yet the norm, neither should it be surprising. I am tapping into a tradition of adapting to technology. Early Christians took letters from Christian leaders such as Paul and reproduced them over and over again. Through the Dark Ages the monks kept the candle of knowledge burning by copying manuscripts. Mediaeval stained-glass windows were memes of the day. The Church was an early adopter of the printing press; the Bible is the first mass-produced book.

Social media has become the influencer of our time. That is not the same thing as determining people's opinions. It's not super strong in that sense. It cannot change people's minds or convince them of the rightness or wrongness of an argument. There is no doubt, however, that it influences people's thinking. My aim, for as long as I am able, is to remain part of the conversation.

This is one of the roles of Christianity: to engage, perhaps to influence. Never to dictate, but to put out an idea that is worth exploring.

This is not to say that individual spirituality is without importance, or that individual needs are not a consideration. This is a truth shared by the major faith traditions of the world; we all need to experience and develop an individual relationship with the 'More', the 'Greater', the 'Other', that which I and many others down through the millennia have called God. This personal evolution is necessary if we are to achieve our goal of looking beyond ourselves. Sadly, in the highly individualised societies in which we live, this is not easy to do.

We must therefore build a sustainable movement, and one of the most effective ways to successfully do this is to be an early adopter. In order to do this, we have to notice what is going on in the wider society. Many factors mitigate against this. Our everyday concerns can weigh heavily upon us and make it difficult to look outwards. If what is happening in the broader society is complex, it is tempting to look away, to tell ourselves that it is sensible and right to take the mind-your-own-business approach to living. In these public conversations, I and many others are trying to effect a shift, to begin a movement in a more moral and ethical direction.

This is critical, because it is in that gap between the individual and the group that, throughout history, evil has been permitted to flourish. Not always by actively promoting evil but by being passive when evil starts to occur around us.

WHEN WILL WE LEARN?

151

Individually, we may consider it wrong to place humans into mandatory and indefinite detention and stand back and watch while they descend into despair, madness and suicidal ideation. However, if we do not come together and condemn such behaviour, it becomes normalised. If inhumane behaviour is structured so that it occurs on a universal scale, the possibility of the individual challenging such a system becomes remote.

The integrity of a society cannot be taken for granted. The conversation around what happens in society is the responsibility of all citizens but not least those who claim to be Jesus' followers. They have a stated mission and mandate to build a society that reflects the principles and values of a world yet to come into existence. This is why Christians pray 'on earth as in Heaven'.

Technology may change, lifestyles may change, but our human quest for spiritual connection is unchanging. People's religiosity is always finding new forms of connecting. Today that quest is occurring less through conventional organised religion as it has been traditionally understood.

A good many people who attend our church are not Anglicans, and that is absolutely fine with me. I interpret their attendance as seeking something that is difficult to define and perhaps sensing that they may find it in the place where ancient faith and the modern secular world are brought together.

I sense this quest even more keenly in the digitalised world. Most of the more than 50,000 people who follow the Gosford Anglican Church on social media do not identify as Christian, yet they are deeply interested in exploring the space where the physical and spiritual are difficult to differentiate.

THE CHURCH YOU GO TO WHEN YOU DON'T GO TO CHURCH

Different people want different things from organised religion. Perhaps they want their children to be engaged in some kind of ethical framework. Perhaps they love the music for its uplifting or transcendent effect. Perhaps they love to hear a sermon that reminds them each week that they are not the centre of the universe. Perhaps they have a desire to more deeply explore their faith. All these expressions are equally valid. For me it is engaging in what Jesus embodies and personifies; the mysterious place where heaven and earth meet, where the physical and spiritual are inseparable, where the fact of science and the truth of faith meet in the embrace of wisdom.

Apart from considering what we want from organised religion, Christians need to ask themselves further questions about how they might authentically live out their faith in an increasingly secular society. One of the best known and therefore most misunderstood and misquoted texts from the Bible is from Matthew 22, 'Give therefore to the emperor the things that are the emperor's, and to God the things that are God's.' This text is often used to support the payment of taxes or the concept of the separation of church and state. Both of these interpretations miss the point of the text.

In the story there are two groups. The Herodians are essentially a political group that support the Roman-approved ruler of Israel and are allied with the occupying forces – the Romans. The Pharisees are the religious conservatives, preoccupied with doctrinal and pious purity. The two groups represent what are generally, and erroneously, seen as the two competing influences in today's society – secularism and religion.

Ordinarily, the Herodians and the Pharisees are opposing forces, but these two groups form an unlikely alliance, demonstrating the truth of the saying, 'My enemy's enemy is my friend.'

Together the two groups confront Jesus and try to entrap him with the question, 'Is it lawful to pay taxes to Caesar or not?' If Jesus responds in the affirmative to the question, he will be guilty of blasphemy, for to pay this tribute to the Divine Caesar is to worship a pagan god. If he answers in the negative, he will be guilty of treason.

Jesus' response is instructive for us. He asks the question, 'Whose image is on the coin used to pay the tax?' When someone states that it is Caesar's image, Jesus simply says that if Caesar owns the coin, then let him have it. But then he says that the lands the Romans have occupied belong to God and should be returned to the people of God.

Here Jesus models a way of navigating the delicate path that winds in and out and through the entangled web that is the life of a religious person in a secular democracy. He neither denies the reality of the society in which he lives nor does he totally collude with it or withdraw from it. This is the path of every Jesus follower; this is the path of every human being who prefers evolution to revolution.

CHRISTIAN LIVES DON'T MATTER. THAT'S THE WHOLE POINT

29

Rising Secularism

WHILE IT IS necessary to consider how we as Christians live in the wider world, there are questions to be asked about how we as a Church engage with society in the 21st century. These questions must initially be asked by those of us inside the Church tent, but the answers will most likely come from without. In a world of turmoil, it is both easier and more comforting to seek easy answers and religious and political certainty than to enter more fully into the mystery of reality.

DEAR CHRISTIANS. I DON'T HAVE A PLAN. SCARY ISN'T IT. LOVE GOD

A recent Ipsos poll found that two-thirds of Australians consider religion to be doing more harm than good.[1] It's therefore not surprising that increasing numbers of people do not identify with any organised religion. This is in line with the rest of the Western world. On 5 April 2017 the Pew Research Center published 'The Changing Global Religious Landscape', their comprehensive demographic study of religious affiliation. One of their findings was 'the growth of the religiously unaffiliated population in Europe, North America, Australia and New Zealand'. This echoed the theme of the British *Spectator* magazine's lead article for 13 June 2015. The article was headed, '2067: the end of British Christianity'.

None of this means that people are any less religious, of that I am sure, but given this reluctance about signing up to organised religion, my colleagues and I have to look to our future. How can we best serve? What can we reasonably hope to achieve?

I have no easy answers to offer, and in this I am in excellent company. In a radio broadcast in 1969, the future Pope Benedict XVI, Joseph Ratzinger said:

> *Let us, therefore, be cautious in our prognostications. What St Augustine said is still true: man is an abyss; what will rise out of these depths, no-one can see in advance. And whoever believes that the Church is not only determined by the abyss that is man, but reaches down into the greater, infinite abyss that is God, will be the first to hesitate with his predictions, for this naïve desire to know for sure could only be the announcement of his own historical ineptitude.*[2]

Speaking at the funeral of his friend Cardinal Meisner in 2017, the now Pope Emeritus, when referring to the Church said, 'The boat has taken on so much water as to be on the verge of capsizing.'[3]

These words of Benedict's are often misinterpreted as simply advocating for a smaller, purer Church. But he is far too universal a thinker for that. While Benedict and I would have much to disagree upon, I think his 1969 interview is worth a read. Ratzinger effectively declares the death of Christendom – the idea of the Church as a geopolitical force – and redefines it as a spiritual presence in the world.

To my mind, he was anticipating the current situation and pondering not so much how the Church could survive but how she could fulfil her calling to be an instrument of hope to the whole world.

What are my fellow priests and I to do amid this rise and rise of secularism? Do we wave our fists or simply shrug as more and more people opt for civil ceremonies rather than church baptisms, weddings and funerals? Or do we form an enclave with the faithful, retreat from the world with our doctrinal texts and our traditions?

There is a proclivity within the Church to do the latter. What I have detected in recent statements by both the Anglican and Catholic Archbishops of Sydney is what is called 'remnant theory'. In the face of declining numbers of adherents, the remnant response is to revert to being doctrinally pure. Their message becomes one of honouring their calling and being faithful to God. It is about institution-based religion battening down the hatches and sitting out the storm. What particularly concerns me is that the faithful with a remnant mentality, with their extreme focus on doctrine, often seem predisposed to thinking punitively. The marriage equality debate is one such storm.

There is, I believe, another option, because to me this deeply conservative approach is the antithesis of the message of Jesus. The Christianity I identify with not only accommodates movement and change, it expects it. Change. It is never quick enough for those of a prophetic voice. It can be terrifying for those of a conservative voice. What about those in the middle?

Society continually evolves, and the role of the Anglican Church has long been to participate in a constructive and thoroughgoing conversation around this evolution. If that conversation does not occur, instead of evolution you get revolution, with the chaos and instability that it entails. I see myself as fostering stability, marriage, the family – the fabric of society, in other words; an inclusive and humane society – and the ongoing discussion around how best to promote all those things.

WHAT KIND OF SOCIETY DO WE WANT TO BE?

We Anglicans have a proud tradition of seeking the middle way, the *via media*. There are three aspects to our process – scripture, which is the great narrative; reason, which is the antithesis of blind faith; and tradition, which is the lived experience of generations. Because the process of sustained conversation entails reflection and patience, in this world of the 24-hour news cycle we offer the gift of the long view, slowing things down. In fact, we think in terms of centuries.

Let me give an example of the long view. Religion has ebbed and flowed in popularity over time. Two thousand years ago, the people of biblical Palestine didn't trust institutionalised religion. What they saw was corruption, power and control. There were the Scribes, the Pharisees and the Temple hierarchy. There was collusion with the occupying forces of the Romans, and abuses of spiritual authority. A high level of mistrust was the inevitable outcome. Into this context, not altogether dissimilar to our own, came an individual who drew huge crowds, a rabbi. Jesus was, after all, a faithful Jew, a clear representative of his religion.

So, the question must be asked: what did so many people who were highly mistrustful of religion find so compelling in his words and actions?

JESUS SAID GET OVER YOURSELF

There are cries that religion has lost its relevance, and I utterly disagree. Only superficial theology and unquestioning religion can and should lose its relevance. Superficial theology is the straw man easily knocked down and quickly found wanting by active and questioning minds. But healthy theology further illuminates that questioning mind; it draws us more deeply into the mystery of our own existence. Those who seek consistency in either the Bible or the Church must always face disappointment. Both ponder too great a mystery to be able to offer mere consistency. Good science and good theology are the lovers that produce the offspring of wisdom. Bad theology and bad science spend all their energy in a fruitless argument and prove to be a barren coupling.

Theology used to be regarded as the queen of sciences, and I would love that to be revived. I feel the expression is still apt. It is for me interesting to note that the current working theory of the origins of the universe, the Big Bang Theory, was first postulated by a scientist who was also a theologian, Father Georges Lemaitre. It seems to me that it requires something of a truly theological mind to reach into the mysterious realms of universal origins. It is also interesting to note that the climate change deniers of the conservative right wing in America are beginning to be challenged from within by evangelical Christians who hold a doctrine of Creation that calls for careful stewardship of the Earth rather than exploitation.

Jesus' mission is to make manifest what he called the 'Kingdom of Heaven', to encourage people to live a more fully human life here and now in this world. His mission is to get heaven to people, not so much to get people to heaven. Sadly, the Church has all too often wanted to project that life into a heaven light years away.

This, too, has been a cosy relationship between the Church and the prevailing domination system of the day, keeping the poor, needy and marginalised in check with a promise of a better life in the next world. Once again, the antithesis of Jesus' message.

An 'evolutionary' has to have patience. Social change can take several generations to flow through. It can often start with that prophetic voice in the wilderness, be pondered by the wise ones of ensuing years and then taught to their disciples, eventually finding its way, albeit in a distilled form, into the popular consciousness. Jesus' modern-day followers partner with him in the continuation of his mission.

Take the example of Bishop John AT Robinson, who in 1963 authored a small and highly controversial book called *Honest to God*, which questioned the essentials of the Christian faith. His ideas about the birth, life, death and resurrection of Jesus sparked intense and widespread debate. To me, this is a brilliant example of a deeply intelligent and reflective theologian who was well ahead of his time; by raising new concepts Robinson successfully engaged people near and far in these provocative debates. There is no doubt that in the past ten years, Robinson's ideas have informed the thinking of contemporary public theologians such as Rob Bell, Brian McLaren and Marcus Borg.

For most people, the intricacies of such debates would be daunting, yet I believe if Christianity is to bring theological issues to a wider audience it must find ways to inject those live debates into public discourse, to make good theology accessible.

Much of the fruits Western society enjoys today spring from seeds sown in the evolutionary times of the 1960s and '70s. People speak with fluency the language Martin Luther King Jr used in the Civil Rights Movements in the United States, that Archbishop

Desmond Tutu used in the anti-apartheid movement in South Africa and Archbishop Oscar Romero and his fellow liberation theologians spoke throughout South America. But we are living in the here and now. So, what role do faith-based perspectives have in our world?

THE BIBLE HAS TEXT APPEAL

Those who feel that faith-based perspectives have no place in public discourse will argue that there are so many different perspectives that none can be taken seriously. I, on the other hand, trust our society – if given time and proper information – to discern which arguments are of value and which can be rightly discarded. While I do believe that everyone has a right to their opinion, not every opinion is of equal value. Society in general seems to be quite adept in the ultimate discernment of the difference.

It is undeniable that in our secular democracy the Church does not have the overt political power it once had. I believe that is a good thing and certainly no reason to turn inwards, to deny ourselves a role on issues of social justice. If Christians truly believe that in Jesus of Nazareth God has affirmed the human physical body, we also must therefore believe that it is wrong to collude with injustice. It is my duty – one I take seriously – to remind people of this.

I STAND FOR MERCY

My choice is to go to the 'new public marketplace', build up a following on social media, and find new means to bring home that message. No society can claim to be civilised while denying basic human rights to others. When, as a wealthy nation, we continue to oppress the poor and vulnerable, we remain nothing more than sophisticated barbarians.

This is admittedly not the perceived traditional Christian message of personal salvation; ironically this narrow, insular portrayal is hard to find in the life and teaching of Jesus as recorded in the New Testament. Rather it is a message about the salvation, which ultimately means healing, of our whole society and even our planet; this outward, expansive narrative is what informs the portrayal of the life and teaching of Jesus in the New Testament.

I have been searching for some time to find a language to articulate this expression of Christianity. In order to survive and retain any meaning, Christianity will most likely find itself much more as a movement than as an institutional Church. So as not to lose its way, though, it will need to find a mechanism through which it can continually refer to its historical roots. It was my Buddhist brothers and sisters from the Engaged Buddhism movement, also known as 'Socially Engaged Buddhism' who provided the answer.

In the early 1960s, with the Vietnam War decimating his country, Buddhist monk Thich Nhat Hanh made a paradigm shift; he moved to apply Buddhist teachings beyond the traditional emphasis on personal spiritual progress to one also aimed at reducing suffering and injustice through social and political reform. While applying this outward focus, Hanh did not abandon Buddhist teachings concerning the personal journey toward enlightenment, but actually emphasised that social change must begin with oneself. These inward and outward expressions, each interwoven and interdependent, moved Buddhist philosophy from having its being exclusively inside the tent to one of being simultaneously inside and outside the tent. Consequently, I have come to think of the work we do at the Anglican Parish of Gosford as 'Socially Engaged Christianity'.

So, now one can see that personal salvation is not the only game in town; it is subsumed in the concept of unity. To understand unity, consider, for instance, St Paul's metaphor of the body. Different parts of the body have different roles and, rather than being in competition with each other, they work in a holistic way to engage with the world. It is a compelling image. Sadly often, however, the Church's conservatives and progressives lose sight of this and fall into the trap of dualistic behaviour – declaring that one is right and the other is wrong. This is counterproductive and actively disables the Church's mission. For the Church to function productively in public discourse, it needs both theological orthodoxy and progressive engagement.

The conservatives are diminished when they cling exclusively to doctrine and dogma and see themselves as the faithful remnant. They then begin to behave more like a cult, dwelling in the shadows at the edge of society. When progressives lose sight of the anchor that is the theological orthodoxy of the second and third century, they inevitably start floating into an abyss of nothingness that leads nowhere, that changes no lives for the better, and brings nothing to humanity that will enable us to live in our fullest potential.

It is when the progressives appreciate the touchstone that orthodoxy provides and the conservatives appreciate the pathways created in the modern world by the progressives, that St Paul's 'body of Christ' walks the earth.

The expression of my thoughts regarding the future of Christianity in Western society is tempered by Joseph Ratzinger's warning that the boat, that is the Church, is on the verge of capsizing. I suggest that in forging a sustainable future for Christian expression in an increasingly secular environment, the past will not be fully abandoned, nor the new exclusively embraced. The ongoing Christian presence in Western society will, in its healthiest expression, reflect something of past manifestations but in entirely new ways.

It is not that doctrinal purity will cease to be important; on the contrary, cherished doctrines are likely to regain something of their original mystical importance and interpretation. These doctrines, I believe, speak deeply of the universal human yearning to reach its fullest expression. They are far too important to be limited to and diminished through fundamentalist interpretations, or to be used as weapons to exclude and delegitimise those who claim to be Jesus' followers but whose faces are unrecognisable to the eyes of conservatives. The human condition involves messiness; wishing things were otherwise is futile. If only we could embrace this messiness with kindness and a sense of humour.

DEAR CHRISTIANS, LAUGH AT YOURSELVES. I DO. LOVE GOD

For Christianity to reach its full potential and this ultimate destination in the manifestation of what Jesus called the Kingdom of Heaven, it will need to become an illuminating and life-giving influence in the world. For that to happen, the Church will need first to rediscover the simple and universal truths contained within its story and then develop the language to communicate these in such a way that they will resonate with the modern human heart and mind.

One of the many things that history shows us is that out of a time of religious fundamentalism and legalism there arises the influence of reforming mystics. These are people who have lived constantly and simply in the place that is created for all human beings; that place where the spiritual and the physical meet, where heaven and earth come together and divinity and humanity are seen as one.

We are beginning to see some of these people revealing themselves in popular theological and social justice culture. This gives me enormous hope. I have faith that Christianity will continue to flourish, albeit in a less institutional and intentionally doctrinal form, and that it will continue to be an influence for good in the world.

This both mystical and political dynamic is most beautifully encapsulated in the words of the writer of John's Gospel:

He was in the world, and the world came into being through him;
yet the world did not know him. He came to what was his own,
and his own people did not accept him. But to all who received him,
who believed in his name, he gave power to become children of God,
who were born, not of blood or of the will of the flesh or of the will
of man, but of God.

John 1:10–13

Here, John poetically demonstrates the interaction between the spiritual and the political. In one sentence he uses the powerful word 'cosmos', which we translate as 'world', three times in three different ways. By saying, 'He was in the world', John is illuminating the dynamic that the incarnate divine, taking on human flesh, affirms the physical realm in which we live and move and have our being. It is important to know that under normal circumstances, people of faith are meant to be in the world fully participating in human evolution and not to withdraw from it.

John goes on to say that 'the world came into being through him'. This, the second use of the word 'cosmos', refers to the entire universe, the unity of all things physical and spiritual, that it comes into being, and its existence is sustained by the very act of being to which the mystics attach the divine inscription.

John's third use of 'cosmos' refers to the domination system that is used to order the affairs of humanity. This expression of the world evokes the struggle to live productively and in a life-giving way in the place where humans are made to dwell. And yet this is the domain in which Jesus expended the majority of his energy, focus and – ultimately – his life. And therefore, this is the place in which Jesus' followers are called to engage.

The future of Christianity is messy. Its success or failure will not be measured by the number of bums on seats on a Sunday, nor will it be calculated by those identifying as Christian in the census. It will not be understood as the ability to be found innocent in an inquisition or a heresy trial. The success or failure of Christianity will be gauged by its influence in the journey of human evolution and whether it leads to its fullest expression and the clearer vision of the Divine life. This I believe will be most effective when lived out in movements such as Socially Engaged Christianity; the expression of Christianity with which I have fallen in love. It seems to be the expression of faith that is right for now, for this moment in time. It has this whole-of-society focus. As a society we need healing, wholeness, integrity; as a community we need to be able to put aside our own personal needs for the good of the whole. This incarnation seems to me to offer the best hope for justice.

IMAGINE

30

All Justice Is Social

My LIFE BEGAN in injustice.

There is no justice in a society that forces a mother who is perfectly capable of raising a child with the help of that society to relinquish that child.

That same society labelled me illegitimate. No human being is illegitimate and any society that sees one as such is also without justice. The same society remains unjust to this day because it still illegitimises humans on the grounds of social status, religion, ethnicity, gender, age and sexual identity.

All injustice is social.

By 'social' I mean the way in which we humans interact, and by 'justice' I mean the equitable manner of that interaction.

As a child, I was the survivor of relentless bullying by older, bigger and physically stronger boys. I was vilified, mocked and physically assaulted. My peers did nothing to stop this; neither did those with authority around me.

BULLETS ARE MADE FROM WORDS

I became aware of a burning anger within me as a response to this injustice, an anger that for the most part found negative and self-destructive expression during my teenage years and into my early 20s. Ironically, this often resulted in me further contributing to the injustices of society.

It began to dawn on me that to create more justice, we had to create a more just society. This of course was not a new idea.

From the dawn of human social consciousness, we have sensed that human society has the capacity to be just, along with the propensity to be unjust, and so we have attempted to fashion a more just society by implementing legislative frameworks to create a context in which humans are encouraged to interact in an equitable manner. Ironically the ultimate need to enforce such structures results in acts of injustice.

Throughout the four major paradigms of human history, there have been numerous heroic but vain attempts to create a more just society.

For tens of thousands of years, we humans lived in a paradigm that could be typified as family, or tribal. Most of the attempts from within that paradigm to curb the human proclivity towards injustice and promote a more equitable society went unrecorded. However, one such attempt has withstood the ravages of time and to this day stands as a monolith to justice: the Ten Commandments.

Ironically, the formulation of this ancient charter of justice marks the beginning of the end of the dominance of the tribal consciousness and ushers in the religious paradigm. Everything – in what was to become the Western world – would be viewed for 2500 years through the lens of faith. While for the most part during this period religion was used to order a society that was tailored to favour the wealthy and powerful over the poor and marginalised, there were remarkable attempts to create something different. Not least of all is the example of a first-century Galilean carpenter who spoke passionately about life in the age to come and was executed for attempting to live that life in the here and now.

Attempts to reform the abuses and injustice of this age came, as they usually do, far too late, and by the 18th century, the so-called Age of Reason, the Enlightenment had heralded in the era of the 19th-century political paradigms of Marxism, Communism, Fascism and Capitalism. But the Enlightenment played a terrible trick on us. It convinced us that we were rational beings and that through our own reason we could create a just society through the ministrations of the state or the market. Certainly, we are beings capable of reason, but we are not by nature rational beings, and our baser instincts of power and greed corrupted our 'isms' and led to a less rather than more just society. These paradigms came crashing down in a bloody global conflict.

The triumph of greed provided fertile ground for the fourth and most recent paradigm, the economic. Trickle-down theory promised a more equitable distribution of wealth and, ultimately, a more just society.

This deception was dramatically exposed through the Global Financial Crisis, during which what little equity the poor had flowed upwards towards the banks and their shareholders, creating further injustice. Banking reforms arrived, as usual, too late to save the paradigm.

THE RICH WRITE HISTORY SO THE POOR GET THE BLAME

About every 500 years in the Judeo-Christian tradition there is a reformation. This movement comes from the human capacity to dream of a more just society. There was King David's failed attempt to create a united kingdom in the first millennium BCE. Cyrus King of Persia returned the exiles from Babylon 500 years later. Then there was the Christ event and the ongoing process of evolution into that particular vision of 'The Kingdom'. This vision was renewed by St Benedict and the monastic movement in 500 CE – another attempt to create a just society through offering hospitality and welcoming the stranger. Five hundred years on, however, the Benedictines had become rich, powerful and corrupt. In the 12th-century along came St Francis and St Clare of Assisi with their commitment to poverty and simplicity revolutionising the way Christian Europe saw itself until, inevitably, the orders they founded became corrupted. In 1517 CE, Martin Luther sparked the beginning of another reformation aimed at standing against the many abuses and injustices that marred Christian Europe at the time.

Now we find ourselves, 501 years later, in the midst of another reformation and paradigm shift. But this time circumstances are markedly different. For the first time, we actually know that we are in a paradigm shift. The Global Financial Crisis was the beginning of the end for the economic paradigm. It may take another hundred years to crumble, but there is no doubt that it is over.

Obviously, the new paradigm is ecological: climate change will see to that. For the first time in almost 12,000 years, since the end of the last Ice Age, the planet rather than humans is in charge of the agenda. All we can do is play along in the best way possible. Because economics is the only language we know, we will for a while try to engage the issues financially, so we will try carbon taxes and emissions trading, but ultimately, we will have to find a new way of being. This reformation will not only seek to address the issues of social justice, but human survival.

THERE IS NO PLANET B

However, human survival will ultimately depend on our ability to create a just society.

So, now we know where we have been, perhaps we can see where we are going. The reality is that we have not abandoned the old ways as the new ones have come along; it's just that the new ones have become dominant. As will be the case as the climate begins to change our behaviours. All our family/tribal consciousness needs to do is to expand its horizons and help us to see ourselves as one human family.

Following the mass school shooting in Florida in February 2018, I put up a street sign and social media post asking Americans a question, one that many have been asking for some time, one that challenged one of their most extremely powerful, white, domination systems: National Rifle Association.

WHEN WILL THEY LOVE YOUR KIDS
MORE THAN THEIR GUNS?

I was trolled dreadfully and received hundreds of hate-filled posts from gun-loving Americans basically telling me to 'F&*% off' out of their business. However, I also received numerous grateful responses, and was most touched and surprised to receive a number of kind hand-written letters from American citizens. One of these was from Caitlin, and I share this excerpt with her permission:

> *I suspect many Americans who learn about your commentary on our values and politics will feel resentful, and tell you to stay out of it . . . But by virtue of being a citizen of the world, you are free to discuss*

its nations; by virtue of being a human you have more than a right
to express care for others, regardless of where they live . . . [This] is
encouraging to me as a person who wants to be the best for the people
of the world.

Thank you, Caitlin! In a few sentences you have articulated the thesis of this book and presented us with the way forward. It really is that simple and that hard.

As people choose to move away from organised religion, we have the capacity to become more spiritual and mystical and finally embrace the true meaning of religion, which is to connect over and over again. This is also a pretty good definition of society.

If we can embrace the reality that we are irrational beings with the capacity for reason, we will see our political systems not as instruments of control or oppression, but as containers and facilitators of our social organisation.

Our economic transactions are then based on social benefit, not on individual profit.

SOCIETY FIRST, ECONOMY SECOND

I am not describing a utopia but the only form of existence left open to us.

Will our grandchildren's lives begin in injustice? Or will we finally learn to love one another?

Random acts of kindness are wonderful things and incredibly powerful when juxtaposed with equally random acts of evil, but they are robbed of their influence when evil becomes intentional and systematic. This is invariably the case when society is ripe for reformation. Reformation takes place most effectively and sustainably when acts of kindness become intentional and systematic.

This has the potential to evolve into a movement, one I like to think of as a 'conspiracy of compassion'.

We have seen in recent times systematised evil in the behaviour of our financial institutions towards their powerless customers, in our government towards the marginalised and the poor, refugees and minority groups. We have seen the spiritual corruption of religious organisations that led to the abuse of vulnerable children. These realities are all symptomatic of a society whose corrupted nature has led to injustice.

The only sustainable remedy to this situation is a social reformation that leads to a just society through the intentional, systematic application of a culture that values kindness above all else. And leads to none other than a conspiracy of compassion.

COMPASSION. CHANGE THE CULTURE. HEAL OUR NATION

Climate change will make almost all of our choices for us in the coming century. But the planet cannot make this choice for us, only we can choose compassion.

FAIR GO AUSTRALIA?

31

Advance Australia Fair

EVERY MONDAY MORNING in the little, one-room, one-teacher country primary school I attended, I and the 11 other students would line up. After our hands and fingernails had been inspected for cleanliness, and, for reasons now lost to me, it had been confirmed that we were in possession of a handkerchief, we would solemnly salute the flag and heartily sing 'God Save the Queen'. I grew up with a sense that I was British but that like my ancestors I had done something terribly wrong and that I wasn't allowed to go home.

Then on 19 April 1984 everything changed, we had a new national anthem: 'Advance Australia Fair'. Although my inner Britishness was slightly offended, I did begin to discover a strange new sense of 'at homeness' beginning to slowly well up within me.

There are three words in the title of our national anthem. Each of them comes packed with history, cultural layers and imperatives. The anthem 'Advance Australia Fair' was penned by a Scotsman, Peter Dodds McCormick, and was first performed in

1878. McCormick wrote the song in his head on the way home from an event where lots of different anthems for countries were played, and he thought it was a shame Australia didn't have its own. It seems likely to me that, being a Scotsman, he displayed an early symptom of post-colonisation nationalism, which began among some, like Irish convicts, to cause resentment toward British institutions, class systems and authorities.

Peter McCormick would have hated hearing 'God Save the Queen' sung, knowing that it meant the English were still hanging over his Scottish pride with their cursed song. So, to take those words in no special order, the etymology of 'Australia' is from Terra Australis, a combination of the name of the Roman goddess of the Earth, 'Terra', and a rather contested use of the word 'Australis', which appears to have its origins in the Romans' name for the winds that blew from beyond the end of the Italian peninsular towards the inland and came to be translated as 'south'. European navigators had some idea of the existence of the 'earth in the south', or the 'south land', from around the 15th century.

However, Islamic society produced much of the technology and skills of 'modern' navigation long before that, and the navigator who directed Columbus to bump accidentally into America was actually Muslim. In fact, some of the earliest maps indicating the great south lands were drawn by Muslim cartographers more than 500 years before Columbus. Certainly, Indonesian traders have been visiting our north for over 500 years. All of this, however, begs the question of who got here second.

The Dutch have one idea about who first mapped or visited here, and some of the earliest European names, such as New Holland and Van Diemen's Land, demonstrate this. Captain Cook, of course, gets credit from the British as a navigator for mapping vast parts of the continent's coastline. But all of this ignores the perspective of the people who had been in continuous settlement of the land for tens of millennia before any of this. Australia, to generalise the perspectives of Aboriginal cultures in a way we should not do, is the Dreaming place that flows from the great Creator Spirit, who has many different names depending on where the story is told. So, any talk we have of 'Advance Australia Fair' should begin with deep respect for this story – not a story written in books, but told in song and dance, in rock carvings and painting, in ceremony and story.

The central point about the main idea of the reality depicted by the word 'Australia' is that no-one absolutely owns it. The land was being inhabited by a highly advanced complex culture for tens of millennia before Romans sniffed the winds from the south, Muslims drew maps, sailors from the great northern continent took to boats, or the British ran up flags. And even if it challenges some of the most dearly held ideas, theologically, culturally or otherwise of those of us Muslim, Christian, Jew, Buddhist, Hindu, atheist or anyone else who arrived here uninvited since, sheer politeness and basic decency demands that we all attend to learning whatever we can, with respect, from the world's oldest living culture.

LEARN THE SONGLINES OF YOUR REGION

'Advance' is another word that is highly packed with cultural inferences. What do we think 'advancing' means? Does it mean invading sovereign countries, or increasing our wealth and power individually, nationally and/or globally? Is it about pushing forward our own agendas over others who think differently, such as ensuring, whether they want it or not, our children have greater education and better jobs than us? What about the poor and marginalised, do we treat them as 'less than', trampling over them in our rush to further our own individual universes? Or does it mean that we are able to sustain human life for increasingly long times through our ability to live compassionately, mindful of the wisdom and gifts our histories provide while simultaneously holding and embracing the advancing discoveries of medicine and science?

The word 'advance' is derived from the Latin 'abante', which is literally 'from before'. I think a good deal of this meaning has been transcended in modern English to reflect linear Western thought patterns that typically tend to look forwards without too much looking back.

Of course, this is always a bad idea.

If our idea of advancing or advancement is simply about the next step forward, without any sense of what has been before, we very well could end up with a world where the Earth is unable to sustain life. That's because we would have not looked back to the wisdom of those who came before us, the warnings of science, or the discernments of our faiths, which all ask us to be careful stewards of the Earth as it reflects the beautiful complex energy of creativity. We might end up with a world where people think that social advancement is only about the next hot topic, in which old wisdoms are disrespected, distorted or ignored, leading to violence and warfare. And all of this might be enacted by our fellow brothers and sisters on our streets where we live and politicians in our parliaments.

Advancing without looking back and moving from before to what comes next generates ignorance, bigotry, anger and violence. This creates endlessly repeating cycles of never looking back to what matters and what connects us, to only ever 'advancing' selfishly toward the things that divide.

'Fair' is an odd word in the English language with numerous meanings. From a description of physical beauty, a gathering of people selling things, a sense of what is just, to the colour of skin. Could it be that McCormick was referring to how nice the country was? I'm not sure how much of it he'd seen. Although it is lovely, it is a little unlikely that he thought it was pretty. I think we can rule out any connection to trade. Was he thinking of a country built on a platform of justice? This is the contemporary understanding of the word in the anthem. However, I do wonder if perhaps he was a man of his time, and with the official White Australia Policy just over a decade away, fair refers to 'white skin'.

Regardless of my ponderings, I feel sure McCormick was not referring to the construct that has seen our national conscience colonised and deceived since the 19th century, that Australia is the 'land of the fair go'.

It is not.

ONE CONFUSED NATION

32

Captain Cook: 'May We Come Ashore?'

ONE DAY, I was riding through a paddock in the vicinity of where my grandfather and father had died. When I got off my horse to open a gate, I had the strangest experience. As my feet hit the ground I felt as though I were sinking into the earth, as if I were becoming a part of the land. It was an entirely peaceful feeling, and I stood there savouring it until it eventually passed. This was over 40 years ago and it is something I have never forgotten. This experience of connection to place remains immediately available to me whenever I call it to mind.

This, I think, began a wondering in me about what it must be like for Indigenous peoples in the lands where their forebears once walked and are buried. My familial connection to place only goes back 180 years, so what must it be like if a connection goes back 65,000 or more years? This is, for me, the crucial question if we as Australians are ever to properly engage in the deep and essential question of national identity.

When Captain Cook arrived in 1770 he should have asked the custodians of this land three questions: 'May I come ashore?', 'Tell me, please, how do you live in this place?' and 'How do you pray here?'

It's now 2018, and we still haven't asked those questions. It is disturbing that, up until relatively recently, the framework for understanding our nation's history was primarily based on the arrival of the British and subsequent colonisation. No looking back, just forward. This is a narrative embedded in the lie of *terra nullius* – that when the Europeans landed on Australian soil it was nobody's land. It has been a lie fed to and thoroughly digested by successive generations of Australians, and one that has shaped and impoverished our national identity, culture and consciousness.

POOR FELLOW MY COUNTRY

The Australian government website falls into this trap. Although it does mention – though falls short of celebrating – pre-European Indigenous culture, it does so in reference to the dominant post-European interaction. Not that I want to suggest that we should view Indigenous culture as static and frozen in a time pre-settlement; in fact, I would suggest precisely the opposite. We as a nation will benefit from understanding and appreciating 65,000 years of civilisation as a continuum of dynamic human interaction with a land rich in diversity and proven ecological sustainability. We still await such a day.

As a primary-school student my introduction to First Australians was through pictures on matchboxes. One image comes easily and vividly to mind. It is of the 'noble savage' as we were taught to label him, dressed in a loin cloth, standing on one leg while leaning on a spear, with colonial cottage, smoke wisping from its hearth, in the background. The message was unmistakable: Australia's First Peoples were one of the least evolved of all people, and nothing more than a curiosity for their 'superior' European interlopers. We were led to believe their primitiveness would ensure they wouldn't be around for long.

As an adult I have become increasingly aware of many of the contemporary issues facing First Australians, including some of the horrors of colonialisation, however it would be 40 years on from the matchbox image before I began to deeply discover a different national history to the one I was taught, helped immensely by Kerry's undertaking of a degree in Australian Modern History. It wasn't that I believed the whitewashed historical narratives, it was just that I never had the opportunity to access academic evidence offering the gift of greater awareness.

And so began a search for new truths; the more I read the more shocked I became. I accessed catalogues of historical records, reviewing evidence from historians, colonial officials, settlers and traditional owners, and it was here that massacres, slavery and mass scale biological programs to bring about extinction revealed themselves. Controlled lives, restricted marriages, forced movements, stolen children, pilfered lands, unpaid wages and curfews; First Nations peoples suffered genocide, abuse, torture and every imaginable deprivation. This information was not only available in multitudes of primary sources, but also credible academic research. Now I could finally begin to appreciate in my deepest inner knowings why European settlement caused such a deep brokenness in this nation.

Nevertheless, I also discovered men and women of resilience, courage and bravery, heroes whose names in some cases I had not heard before. I found myself reflecting on the further tragedy that most Australians, certainly of my generation, do not know these people or their stories of sacrifice, tenacity and audacious resistance.

I would like to give acknowledgment to some of the incredible First Australians I have met in this journey of learning.

Initially, following the arrival of the British, the fight represented a long and sustained guerilla campaign in defending lands. These battles are now known as the Frontier Wars, and one of the fiercest was the Black War in Tasmania 1824–31, which saw Tasmanian Aboriginal resistance fighters defend their lands with spears and clubs against increasing settler numbers armed with superior technological weaponry. For seven years they fought until barely two dozen remained, led by heroes such as Tongerlongerter, who, following a devastating injury from a bullet, amputated and cauterised his own arm.[1] And Pemulwuy, a member of the Eora people, who carried out an orchestrated 12-year campaign of resistance against the British around Botany Bay before being shot by settlers in 1802. Following his death Pemulwuy was decapitated and his remains transported to England – to date they have been unable to be located or repatriated.

From the early 20th century First Nations Australians began to rise up in engaged and organised political and social activism, however it would be in the second half of the century that significant gains began to be made. Faith Bandler actively campaigned for the 1967 Yes referendum case to remove two discriminatory references to Aboriginal people from the Constitution, to which 90.77 per cent voted in the affirmative. Charlie Perkins and Gary Williams instigated the 1965 Freedom Ride throughout western NSW to illuminate the Aboriginal cause. Perkins went on to become a high-profile activist and held significant roles in the arts, media and sport. In 1984 he was the first Aboriginal Australian appointed to hold a government bureaucratic position. Eddie Mabo fought for recognition of native title, which, following a 10-year campaign, was enshrined into Australian law in 1992, replacing the 222-year-old doctrine of *terra nullius*. This ruling came just over four months after Mabo died from cancer.[2]

Albert Namatjira – artist, Neville Bonner – politician, Evonne Goolagong-Cawley – Wimbledon champion, Cathy Freeman – Olympian, Professor Marcia Langton – anthropologist, geographer and academic, Noel Pearson – lawyer, academic and activist, Stan Grant – television and political journalist . . . my esteem for these my fellow brothers and sisters has grown immensely since educating myself about their ancestral struggles which continue to this day. More of that soon . . . I'd like to return briefly to the colonies.

Looking back, I can now understand that the colonial mindset allowed settlers to see First Australians as 'the other', giving permission to treat them with contempt as subhuman. This is clearly illustrated in 1838, when 11 settlers were accused of perpetrating the Myall Creek Massacre in which at least 28 Aboriginal men, women and children were violently murdered and then their bodies burned; however, the number of victims may have been much greater. A jury took 20 minutes to deliberate their judgment and acquit the accused. One of the jurors was reported to have said, 'I look on blacks as a set of monkies [sic], and the earlier they are exterminated the better. I knew [the accused] were guilty of murder, but I would never see a white man suffer for shooting a black.'[3] At a subsequent trial, seven of the men were found guilty and hanged that same year.[4] This was the first time in Australian history that white men had been executed for killing Aboriginal peoples.[5]

Slavery was rife. The pearling industry in northwest Western Australia was underpinned by Aboriginal bondage. For 36 years from around 1850, wealthy graziers and professional pearlers used Aboriginal divers on pearling boats to collect the rare mother-of-pearl shell. Many had never seen the sea, possibly could not swim, and had been removed from their traditional lands. Graziers used or sold their Aboriginal station labour for five pounds, while professional pearling operators often kidnapped their workers.

Upon capture, men and boys were chained together and marched in long lines to the coast, their women and children made to follow as food gatherers for the men and their captors. On reaching the sea the captives were placed on boats and taken up to two kilometres offshore, forced to dive naked for shells and then imprisoned in hulls or left on desolate islands for days at a time.

Pregnant women were prized capture because their lungs were believed to be of especially large capacity. Many died from shark attacks, pneumonia, influenza and the bends. Pearlers and graziers considered it a satisfactory outcome if a diver lived for three months, and the fatality rate has been estimated at 50 per cent. The second half of the 19th century has become known by Aboriginal people as 'the shelling times' in memory of the men, women and children enslaved by the pearling industry.

Murder, kidnapping, forced removal from traditional lands and slavery; these two stories offer just a minute glimpse into the realities of our colonial history.

NO TREATY. NOT SETTLEMENT. INVASION. SIMPLE AS!

And the children. The stolen children. As a father and grandfather it is beyond my capability to imagine what it must be like for children to be rounded up like cattle, taken far from all familial relationships and then abused, exploited and used as slave labour.

In 1997, the Human Rights and Equal Opportunity Commission released 'Bringing Them Home: Report of the National Inquiry into the Separation of Aboriginal and Torres Strait Islander Children from Their Families'. One of the findings was that between one in ten and one in three children were forcibly removed from their families from 1910 to 1970 and sent to church missions or other institutions or else fostered or adopted into white families. Vulnerable children were placed at risk of physical and sexual abuse; many experienced unspeakable suffering. Welfare officials failed in their duty of care to protect these children.

According to international law from c.1946, the forcible removable of children from their families amounts to the crime of genocide, and from 1950, Australia's laws regarding Aboriginal children were deemed to be racially discriminatory.

Why, as a nation, can we not begin to corporately imagine the horror of these acts? Why, as individuals, can we not imagine how we would feel if these crimes were perpetrated against us: our husbands, our wives, our parents, our children, our grandchildren.

In an astonishingly devastating policy decision in 2015, the Federal government began to explore the possibility of closing down remote Indigenous communities because of the high cost of providing services to what is usually small numbers of individuals. I was horrified to hear Prime Minister Abbott at the time say, 'What we can't do is endlessly subsidise lifestyle choices.'[6]

CULTURAL IDENTITY IS NOT A LIFESTYLE CHOICE

From previous examples of forced closure of communities, it is known that when displaced from their country the residents feel cast adrift, and the social outcomes are typically poor. There was an element of social injustice about the proposal that disturbed me, but there was something deeper that concerned me. I felt that there was a potential loss, not only for each affected Indigenous community but also for the nation as a whole.

The quest today is not just for the preservation of remote communities, as important as this is, but for the very soul of this land and its people. We cannot do that honestly without admitting, owning and compensating for the illegality and cruelty by which we have arrived at this point.

It appears we are far from that particular destination, because in the same year Tony Abbott was proposing the closure of remote communities, Adam Goodes, Australian Football League hero and Australian of the Year, committed a 'crime'. The Sydney Swans player dared to display his Indigenous culture on the football field, in, by the way, the AFL Indigenous Round. Goodes performed a post-goal celebratory Indigenous war cry that imitated throwing a boomerang. I acknowledge that some within the media and AFL fan base felt that Goodes' act mimicked the raising of a spear in an aggressive act toward opposition fans.

This was a dance taught to Goodes by a group of 15-year-old Indigenous AFL players some years before, at which point Goodes, a powerful role model to the boys, thanked them for being the first to teach him an Aboriginal dance. While Adam Goodes was crucified for displaying his cultural pride,[7] celebratory rituals are commonly and publicly carried out by players in all sporting codes to the cheers of adoring fans. Nonetheless, this one was apparently unforgiveable, and white Australia was outraged. This hypocrisy was astonishing.

BOO THE BIGOTS. WE STAND WITH ADAM GOODES

Consequently, this began an ugly episode in Australian sport, which drifted into the media and wider society; everybody had something to say, and much of it was unedifying about Goodes. In the face of this overt racism and bigotry a courageous Goodes continued to call out the racists and bigots. To our nation's shame the booing of Goodes during games became an appalling national phenomenon, and the justifications for it were incredible. Goodes' behaviour was 'provocative', his accusers said. An incredulous Tracey Holmes, ABC journalist, wrote in a piece for *The Drum* at the time: 'Provocative? In a way that booing isn't? In a way that *terra nullius* isn't? If provocation means holding up a mirror to see what's really there, then I, for one, am all for it.'[8] However, getting hold of that mirror is elusive.

As a priest I have learned that personal psychological healing cannot take place until truth and reality is faced and embraced. The same dynamic applies to a nation. While in reality it could be said little has been achieved toward embracing and facing our colonial past, I do believe it is important to acknowledge those efforts toward Aboriginal peoples that have been made as acts of restitution and goodwill, of which I would include Prime Minister Gough Whitlam's symbolic pouring of earth into the hand of Gurindji leader Vincent Lingiari to signify Indigenous land rights in 1975, and Prime Minister Paul Keating's 1992 Redfern Speech.

The reconciliation process began, at least for me, on 13 February 2008. Members of the local community had gathered at the Central Coast Regional Art Gallery to watch Prime Minister Kevin Rudd apologise on behalf of the nation to the Stolen Generations. It was an outdoor event, and as the Prime Minister started to repeat the words, 'We say sorry', the heavens opened and torrential rain began to fall upon the gathering. No-one moved or ran for cover; a few umbrellas went up but mostly people simply stood and listened in solemn and respectful silence, allowing the rain to wash us clean from the sins of the past.

This was a profound event and there was a certain earthy spirituality to the experience. It was an absolution and a baptism, an opportunity for rebirth and a new beginning. It has been validly argued that the Apology to the Stolen Generations has not precipitated better outcomes for Indigenous people. While that is true, I like to see the Apology as an important event in the long and arduous process of restoration – of ensuring Australia is truly a place for all Australians.

Our shared experience in the rain that February morning, where collectively we attributed meaning to a natural occurrence, had resonance with the human interaction with this land over the course of 65,000 years. That for me was the essence and efficacy of the occasion. Looking at the Apology through the lens of Christian tradition, it seemed that the Prime Minister had voiced our confession for us and the land had pronounced the absolution.

SORRY DOESN'T MEAN GET OVER IT

This hasn't been an easy chapter to write, because it is a very important one for me. Why? Because, for me, respect for the spirit of the land underpins everything about Australia's First Peoples. I believe it is essential to explore this subject with them at the forefront, and that this exploration must be the foundation upon which a modern Australia is built. Australians, who have come from an incredible diversity of lands and cultures, have two things in common: our humanity and the fact that we now walk together on the same ground. This is the only possible starting place for a conversation on Australian identity.

I believe two steps are integral to begin our journey into healing. Firstly, we must change the date of Australia Day. In order to articulate the argument for this, the best analogy I can think of is this: imagine if some alien force invaded our land . . . today. Imagine if they arrived with the perception of themselves as superior beings and committed systematic genocide against us. Imagine if they massacred our friends and family, used us as slave labour, stole our children, chained us like animals, and drove us into places where we could not sustain our living. Imagine if they enforced these oppressions upon us for hundreds of years, and in doing so chose a national day of celebration as the date of their arrival. I rest my case.

Recently, Kerry and I were in the Pilbara in Western Australia visiting our children and grandchildren. While I was waiting for Izzy at her dance class at the local community centre I met and had a conversation with three children: Matthew, Kyle and Jeffrey. The boys' first language is not English, but Martu. Because of their remoteness the Martu were some of the last to contact European settlers, remaining on their traditional lands until the 1950s. This has meant that elders who are alive today have lived traditional lives and are able to communicate incredible ecological and cultural knowledge to their younger generations.

As we chatted, I became slightly embarrassed at my own monolingual status; however, I rejoiced in learning from these engaging nine-year old boys the words for water, lizard and sky.

It was a wonderful chance encounter; however, it did occur to me at the time that celebrating our current national day would make no sense at all to these young Australians who spoke one of the oldest living languages in the world. I do not know what an appropriate date for a national day would be, but it is clear it is not 26 January. It is heartening to see that there are the beginnings of a paradigm shift in the Australian psyche. As I write this book, on 26 January 2018 we witnessed tens of thousands of Australians march in support of changing the date of Australia's National Day.

STRAYA DAY. CHANGE THE DATE MATE

The second step that must be taken is full and abiding acknowledgment of the traditional owners of this nation. On 26 May 2017, the First Nations National Constitutional Convention released the Uluru Statement, some of which said:

> *In 1967 we were counted, in 2017 we seek to be heard. We leave base camp and start our trek across this vast country. We invite you to walk with us in a movement of the Australian people for a better future.*[9]

The guiding principles the statement listed were clear and dignified:

1. *Does not diminish Aboriginal sovereignty and Torres Strait Islander sovereignty.*
2. *Involves substantive, structural reform.*
3. *Advances self-determination and the standards established under the United Nations Declaration on the Rights of Indigenous Peoples.*
4. *Recognises the status and rights of First Nations.*
5. *Tells the truth of history.*
6. *Does not foreclose on future advancement.*
7. *Does not waste the opportunity of reform.*
8. *Provides a mechanism for First Nations agreement-making.*
9. *Has the support of First Nations.*
10. *Does not interfere with current and future legal arrangements.*[10]

Here was the road map! On 27 May 2017 I was hopeful . . .

In this eloquent statement the delegates of the Uluru Summit have shown us in a clear and simple manner the way forward to understanding the essence of living in this ancient land. I hope and pray that we can now learn from those who have lived here for 65,000 years about how to flourish in this place not only materially but also spiritually.

The next step was to establish the Makarrata Commission. Despite the years of effort that had gone into the Uluru Summit, negotiations with the Turnbull government broke down at the end of 2017. Opposition from within the LNP cabinet at the proposed reforms revolved around the 'inequality' of Indigenous people having a voice in the parliament that the remainder of the country did not have. Noel Pearson, in a scathing article on the government's about-face on reform, wrote in *The Monthly*, 'It was staggering. I thought of the people out in the red dust of Mutitjulu and these privileged, powerful, white cabinet ministers complaining about inequality.'[11]

SUPPORTING CONSTITUTIONAL ACKNOWLEDGMENT OF FIRST NATIONS

The day must come when we are a healed and healing nation, a nation of people who truly understand, who are alive to the spirit of this land. To reach that place we will attribute meaning to the natural environment and from that meaning draw a common identity. It is only then that we will have become part of this land, and the lot of the First Nations people will not only have been restored, but the primary culture of this place will be respected and drawn upon for the good of all Australians. Any other foundation will be like a house built upon the sand: 'And the rain fell, and the floods came, and the winds blew and beat against that house, and it fell, and great was the fall of it' (Matthew 7:24–27).

The songs and wisdom of the pre-European culture of this land call every Australian to an understanding that is potentially life-giving. I want to qualify what I mean by the word 'understanding'. I am not talking about a capacity to articulate a certain view or doctrine on this subject, but to enter into the experience of it. In the New Testament, one of the words we often translate as 'understand' literally means to 'send together'; it is as if true and abiding understanding can only come from common experience; this is a journey we must take together. We still have so far to go.

33

XX and XY

In 2018 GENDER inequality remains a significant issue. As a man I am advantaged in countless, multifaceted, overt and covert ways women are not. Because of this it feels wrong to me, actually that I am colluding with the male domination system, to write about gender issues that, due to my male privilege, I have no way of comprehending in my lived experience. I feel completely out of my depth on this issue. However what I am completely sure of and committed to, without hesitation, is that a just society cannot tolerate gender gaps in any aspect of its life and living, whether it be in pay, opportunity, empowerment or physical and psychological safety.

WE REJECT CHAUVINISM

I belong to an organisation that has had little to be proud of in recent years but on this one issue I believe we have made significant steps forward. Dioceses in the Anglican Church in Australia, except for several notable exceptions, now have women clergy at every level of ministry including the world's first Archbishop. We are intentional in gender balance on governance boards and ministry teams; this has enhanced our ability to see clearly into issues of spirituality and community life in a way that has not previously been available to us. I am still in the process of attuning my ears to hear the female perspective, and I have been significantly facilitated in this by my wise and patient women colleagues who have assisted me in letting go of a framework that belonged to the destructive and debilitating male domination system.

I have benefited from the modelling of my mothers, who having been formed in the male domination system, have refused to allow it to render them powerless. Our daughter and daughter-in-law have challenged my prejudices, as does my eight-year-old granddaughter who has enabled me to rejoice in the unbridled expectation that she will one day be an astronaut. But above all else it has been the interdependent partnership between Kerry and me that has, not without pain and conflict, enabled me to begin the journey in moving beyond the deeply entrenched gender aspects of our society.

With Kerry's permission I share with you her experience of that system:

I am the daughter of a woman defined by a gender system that told her, regardless of her many gifts, that she would never rise to the management level she was more than capable of achieving because it was strictly a male domain . . . nor that equal pay was her due, neither was keeping her job after marriage, and she should most certainly never take it upon herself to imagine she could work during pregnancies. She was however able to experience sexual harassment in the workplace, at the whim and without constraint of the perpetrators. She had a clear understanding that she had no right to divorce her husband, and if she dared challenge the status quo she would end up homeless. She was told by her male bank manager that her name wasn't required on the title deeds of her home, nor on other assets of value.

I imagined my experiences to have been so much better . . . however on consideration of my life as a younger woman, placed somewhat in the context of current gender inequality statistics, I realise that for half my life I lived a similar existence:

I am the girl who was groomed, both by my family and my society, to expect less, strive for less, and demand less.

I am the teenager who experienced the disconnect between Helen Reddy's feminist anthem 'I Am Woman' with the reality of being judged worthy or not by the size of my breasts, the length of my legs and how I looked in a bikini.

I am the school leaver who chose a basic, gendered job, regardless of my gifts, based specifically on the merit of being a stop-gap between leaving school and getting married.

I am the young woman who was told only whores have premarital sex, while my single, male peers rabidly pursued as many sexual 'conquests' as they could manage.

I am the woman who was always the subordinate in my workplace because all management positions were filled by men.

I am the woman whose wages and salaries were always less than my male peers, regardless of my talents and/or performance.

I am one of the one in two women who experienced discrimination due to pregnancy in my work places.[1]

I am the woman who was told working mothers were disgracefully derelict in their duties as a parent.

I am the woman who worked a day job, managed the household and provided the primary care of my children.

I am the woman heading to retirement with very little superannuation.[2]

I am the woman who needed a husband to get a bank loan, and a guarantor to rent a house.

I am one of the one in two women who has experienced sexual harassment.[3]

I am one of the one in three women who has experienced physical and sexual violence since the age of 15.[4]

On average at least one woman a week is killed by her intimate partner or ex-partner.

ANOTHER WOMAN MURDERED. WHAT ARE WE GOING TO DO?

Women are five times more likely to fear for their lives, and need hospitalisation, than men following partner violence. Sexual abuse and violence is also perpetrated against women by strangers, with 300,000 women assaulted annually, often sexually, and a 2015 report revealing that eight out of 10 women between the ages of 18 and 24 had been harassed in public in the preceding year.[5]

Kerry's story is sadly still all too common. This is a hideous indictment on our society, a failure on the part of those of us within the male domination system to realistically, and with commitment, make gender inequality a thing of the past. I want to be part of a community where this story is only told as an historical remembrance, and a way of celebrating how far we have come in being a truly just society for all women and girls.

34

I Do . . . or Don't

I BELIEVE IN marriage. I believe that marriage is one of the corner-stones of our society. I believe that an equitable, stable, culturally and legally sanctioned relationship is the best environment in which to nurture children.

I was somewhat bewildered when both the Anglican and Roman Catholic Archbishops of Sydney were encouraging people to vote 'No' during the marriage equality postal survey. Clearly they both believe in marriage. Clearly they both believe that marriage is one of the cornerstones of our society. Clearly they both believe that a stable, culturally and legally sanctioned relationship is the best environment in which to nurture children. And yet they also clearly believed that these benefits should not be available to some citizens.

Why they would want to deny some families the stability and protection of the law and the support of the culture that marriage can bring is difficult to understand. I believe that the Archbishops have the right to hold, teach and proclaim that Holy Matrimony is the union between a man and a woman. And as obscene as I find it, I uphold Archbishop Davies' right to throw $1 million at the 'No' campaign.[1] That does not, however, give anyone the right to deny someone else's civil rights.

LGBTIQ PEOPLE PLEASE FORGIVE US

Could it be that the Archbishops learned nothing from the recent Irish referendum experience? The Irish referendum taught us many things, one of which is that the 'Church' does not oppose marriage equality; the institution of the Church may, some bishops and leaders may, some doctrinal gatekeepers may, some Christians may, but the majority of the Irish people did not, and the majority of Irish people identify as Christian. The Church, after all, in its purest definition, is the people.

What was seen by secular commentators as a decisive victory against the Church was in fact a decisive victory for ordinary Christians. These people have lesbian, gay, bisexual, transgender, intersex, queer and asexual children, grandchildren, nieces, nephews, brothers, sisters, friends and lovers, and they were unwilling to stand by and allow them to be treated as second-class citizens. An ancient and venerable decision-making paradigm for Christians is the *sensus fidelium*, the agreement of the faithful; and in Ireland the faithful agreed.

Society is evolving as it always has, and we are continually learning about more comprehensive ways of being family and growing into a more honest community. The Church has a choice to make: it can either retreat into a cult mentality, dwelling in the shadows at the edge of society, or it can do what Jesus instructed us to do – fill the world with justice like light fills a room, permeate our culture with compassion like yeast infuses bread, and fan the spark of life in every human being until it bursts into the flame of its fullest potential.

In Australia, as in Ireland, the majority of Christians ignored their institutional leaders and doctrinal gatekeepers and supported marriage equality; they blessed and affirmed and said Yes!

LET THEM EAT CAKE

Existing Australian laws restrict our ability to discriminate on the grounds of sexuality. The Church, however, has some limited dispensation from anti-discrimination laws. Therefore, it will remain legal for the Church to teach that Christian marriage is between a man and a woman, but not legal to vilify LGBTI people in order to promulgate that teaching.

My own community, the Anglican Church, defines marriage as being between a man and a woman. The Anglican Church is unlikely in the foreseeable future to be able to change its *Rite of Marriage* so that, even under the new legislation, we would be able to conduct a legal marriage between two people who did not identify clearly as a man and a woman. This is because the Attorney General only authorises religious ministers to officiate at marriages according to the rites of their particular religious organisation. The change in legislation does not affect what we Anglicans know as Holy Matrimony. However, there are Christian Churches that will be able to more easily make those changes and will be willing to do so.

Likewise, faith-based schools have responsibilities, especially if they receive public funding, to adhere to a curriculum. For example, in a civics class, a responsible educator should be required to inform students that the Marriage Act allows for same-sex unions. While in the same school, in a class on religion, it would be perfectly acceptable to teach that that particular religion holds that marriage is between a man and a woman.

Current anti-discrimination law prevents commercial businesses from discriminating on the grounds of age, race, religion, gender or sexuality, and there is really no viable legislative architecture that could provide exemptions from this requirement. For a commercial operation to be able to lawfully discriminate against a person on the grounds of sexuality opens the door to discrimination on the grounds of race, religion, gender and age and therefore is to deny far more abiding freedoms. This must be strenuously opposed by all people of goodwill and not least of all by Christians. It is ridiculous to suggest that an atheist baker could refuse to sell me a cake if she were to reasonably believe that I might say grace before I ate it. One person's religious rite is also another's civil right, and in a secular democracy like Australia they must be able to coexist. In fact, if we cannot protect each other's rights we cannot protect our own. Ultimately all civil rights are interdependent.

Freedom of speech is essential for a civil society but so are the reasonable limitations of what we can say, but more importantly, how that can be said. Likewise, freedom of action is essential and is self-reliant on the lawful limitation of certain acts. Those who, only several years ago, opposed the introduction of a Bill of Rights have now turned the debate toward the issue of religious freedom. While religious freedom is enshrined in the Australian Constitution, freedom of speech is not. There are conventions that support the concept of freedom of speech and expression, as well as anti-discrimination laws, which restrict and govern those very freedoms.

Marriage equality legislation is not and should not be a question of religious belief. This is simply a matter of a secular government enabling the proper enjoyment of a human right as clearly endorsed by the United Nations.

EVERYONE HAS THE 'RITE' TO BE MARRIED

In 1948, a former curate in the Parish of Gosford, Ernest Burgmann, by then Bishop of Goulburn, travelled to Paris with HV Evatt to participate in the formulation of the Universal Declaration of Human Rights, in which Article 16 states:

(1) *Men and women of full age, without any limitation due to race, nationality or religion, have the right to marry and to found a family. They are entitled to equal rights as to marriage, during marriage and at its dissolution.*

(2) *Marriage shall be entered into only with the free and full consent of the intending spouses.*

(3) *The family is the natural and fundamental group unit of society and is entitled to protection by society and the State.*[2]

While it cannot be inferred that in its historical context this Article is referring to what we would now understand as marriage equality, it can be argued that interpreting this to support such equality in the contemporary context is valid and entirely reasonable. This understanding is particularly judicious when interpreted in the light of Article 1:

All human beings are born free and equal in dignity and rights. They are endowed with reason and conscience and should act towards one another in a spirit of brotherhood.[3]

In relation to human rights, the phrase found in Article 2 of the Declaration, 'without any limitation due to race, nationality or religion', now inevitably includes, 'or any other status, such as age, disability, health status, sexual orientation or gender identity'.[4]

Marriage is a human right. To deny marriage to an adult person who identifies as lesbian, gay, bisexual, transgender, intersex, queer or asexual is a blatant denial of that fundamental human right. This also reduces the idea of holistic human relationships to a narrow and now discredited binary understanding of sexual identity.

Children are being raised in committed relationships other than those understood as 'traditional'. Denying the status of marriage to the parents of these children is obviously depriving them of the protection of society and State that is their right. We are lucky to live in a secular democracy. We benefit from a system of government that respects that citizens have a variety of religious practices, beliefs and traditions – or none at all.

The government doesn't infringe upon the various individual beliefs and does not impose any religious beliefs upon any citizen. People of faith are free to live out their private religious traditions under the rule of law. If personal religious practices infringe the law, then the faith practitioner must be willing to pay the penalty prescribed by the law.

The marriage-equality debate has vividly raised the issue of the imposition of a certain religious view upon unwilling citizens who are, to all intents and purposes, living entirely within the rule of law.

In a secular democracy, legislators cannot legitimately be motivated by their personal religious convictions to deny a right to one group that is afforded to another. Religious special interest groups, and any other group for that matter, have the right and even responsibility to inform legislation, but not the right to form it.

The Churches have every right to lobby the legislature to be exempt from performing same-sex marriages as a matter of conscientious objection, primarily because under section 116 of the Constitution, the State cannot dictate the rites of the Church.[5] The secular government then has a responsibility to allow the Churches to discriminate on certain matters of conscience. The advantage of a secular democracy is that it can allow for limited discrimination within the rule of law, while simultaneously protecting the rights of diverse groups of citizens.

To enshrine in law the denial of a secular civil right creates a precedent that could, in the fullness of time, be used to deny the rights of other groups. Australian statistics show Christianity is losing its adherents, and if current trends continue there is no doubt that at some time in the future Christians will become a minority group in Australian society. Until then, it is difficult for them to fully appreciate the ramifications of their campaign to deny marriage equality to people identifying as LGBTI.

Thankfully, we as a nation chose to abandon the idea that marriage was only between a man and a woman at 10 am on 15 November 2017, when the Australian Bureau of Statistics revealed the result of the postal survey on marriage equality.

YES YES YES YES YES YES YES YES YES YES

The result was that just over 61 per cent of those who participated in the survey believed that all consenting adults, regardless of their sexual orientation, should have the right to civil marriage. I am a part of that 61 per cent, as in fact are the majority of Christians.

The journey began in earnest for me when, as previously discussed, I was asked to administer the last rites to a dying gay man. I had also noticed at funerals over the years that the surviving partners in same-sex relationships were not treated with the same dignity and acknowledgment as opposite-sex partners. They were often sat in the second row and if acknowledged at all it was as 'Steve's friend' or 'Alice's companion'.

It occurred to me that if I did not try to do something about this injustice I would not be faithful to the fourth of the five marks of mission in the Anglican Communion: 'To transform unjust structures of society, to challenge violence of every kind and pursue peace and reconciliation.'[6] And so, I became a vocal advocate for marriage equality.

This has been a controversial issue within the Christian community, with different expressions of the faith basing views in varying interpretations of scripture and dearly, deeply held and passionate views about human sexuality. These conversations will go on for some considerable time.

The text most used by the opponents of marriage equity is Leviticus 18:22. This lies in the midst of a long list of dietary, cleanliness and moral laws, the breaking of most of which is commonplace in modern society, and rarely raises an eyebrow. Romans Chapter 1 is also a favourite but here the Apostle Paul also assumes that what we know as heterosexuality is the absolute norm. 'Their women exchanged natural intercourse for unnatural, and in the same way also the men, giving up natural intercourse with women, were consumed with passion for one another' (Romans 1:26–27). It is not clear why a few short verses on human sexuality have taken on such enduring primacy, although the findings of Sigmund Freud, Alfred Kinsey and subsequent studies can be instructive. The question remains: can a pre-scientific understanding of sexuality be used to inform 21st-century legislation?

THE BIBLE HAS NO SAY ON GAY

The reality is that no biblical text speaks about homosexuality, because this is at best a 19th-century concept. Biblical writers have no notion of what we now understand as the spectrum of human sexuality; they are only aware of what we would now call heterosexuality. Therefore, any variance on that theme is seen as departure from the norm and, in religious terms, an abomination. In reality, all the Bible says in this regard is that straight people shouldn't have gay sex.

We hear a lot today about safeguarding 'religious freedom'. Sadly, those raising these issues have no concept of what religious freedom truly means. They seem for the most part entirely imprisoned in their own fears and anxieties.

A truly free human does not discriminate. That's the whole point of being free; you don't see others as a threat and therefore don't experience the need to exclude or control.

TRUE RELIGIOUS FREEDOM DOES NOT DISCRIMINATE

I often wondered why I feel a deep resistance to people who call me up and want to vilify LGBTI people. I have discovered that it isn't simply what they say that I am resistant to, it is their feelings of fear, loss and anxiety. It is as if they are in a prison and are trying to drag me in with them.

It is important for us Christians to remember that perfect freedom is found in the ability to serve others, especially in the provision of a just and compassionate society for all, regardless of their age, race, religion, gender or sexuality. The Christian bias must always be towards those who are vulnerable to discrimination rather than in favour of those who have the power to discriminate.

When I consider the idea that marriage should only be between a man and a woman, I am convinced that it continues to be a very superficial understanding and one that has sacrificed justice to the integrity of human diversity. Therefore, I believe in marriage as a civil right for all consenting adults.

I said Yes because I believe in marriage.

I said Yes because I believe in civil rights.

I said Yes because I believe in a just, loving, compassionate, free society.

While I passionately believe in marriage, I do not believe that any person should stay in a relationship that is unhealthy or that has failed to be life-giving for one or both parties.

As we know, the religious have much to say about marriage. This is also the case when it comes to divorce. A theological interpretation of scripture placing male headship within marriage, disallowing women equal rights, and forcing them to remain in abusive marriages are, to my shame, still found in contemporary Christian teaching in this country.

BRIDES DON'T SUBMIT HERE

When marriage breaks down irreparably, divorce is devastating and painful, even when done amicably. When Kerry married as a young woman she did so with every intention that it was for life. When Kate and John were placed in the middle of a painful divorce it was incredibly damaging. The valley of tears in this story belongs to Kerry, Kate and John. Hopefully, as was the case for them, there can also be, in the fullness of time, forgiveness, acceptance and peace.

But what happens when a priest falls in love with, and chooses to marry, a divorced person? When I proposed to marry Kerry, there were those who warned me that it would be a career-limiting move, and this is still true. Back then, while the Church had agreed to marry divorcees, there was still an expectation by some that clergy would be above this. There are some dioceses within this nation today who would not accept me because I am married to a divorced person, and therefore considered to be an adulterer.

This is wrong in so many ways. It is wrong because it is based on a fundamental misunderstanding of the essence of marriage. When Jesus is questioned on this issue in Mark Chapter 10 he goes right back to basics. He reiterates that it is not religious authorities that make people married, but the very essence of their being that binds them together, and he uses the agricultural metaphor of the yoke, which binds two oxen together to emphasise the essence of marriage.

Being raised in the bush I am just old enough to remember working bullock teams. I can remember the bullock drivers hitching up their teams and me wanting to be an eager helper. I recall the bullocky shouting at me, 'Don't put those two together, they'll kill each other!' He knew from bitter experience that some beings are just not made to be together, and no matter how heavy the yoke used to bind them, it will never work. He also knew there was more to it than beings just not getting on; there is no sense in yoking two bullocks of different size, strength or stamina, because one will end up a burden on the other, dramatically increasing the load needing to be borne.

For so long society thought that it was the Church that made people married, and the Church was more than willing to allow that misconception to continue. This led to untold abuse and suffering for people trapped in marriages that should never have been. This is what happens when the Church colludes with the state for the purposes of social control.

To some extent all marriages are civil marriages – they are entered into with the intention of being to the exclusion of all others and for life. It is a civil contract between two people who – we hope – love each other, and it recognises the relationship as a legal entity for the good order of society. But people change, things go wrong and sometimes get broken, and it is then that civil law needs to provide a mechanism for that contract to be renegotiated or dissolved.

Faith-based marriages introduce an extra element. For Christians, the essence of marriage is exemplified not just in the essence of the two being able to become one, but also in the very nature of that becoming. Christian marriage is, or at least is supposed to be, modelled on the relationship between Christ and the Church, based on the present and continuing reality of mutual self-sacrifice. Both these elements are needed for a Christian marriage to exist and, if one of them is missing, there is no marriage and the parties should be free to go their own way. The Christian Church will need to continue to debate the essence and substance of marriage, and therefore the meaning of divorce, for the foreseeable future.

There is also no doubt that Jesus condemned divorce but it also must be recognised that he was doing so in the context of hard-heartedness. It was very easy for a man to divorce his wife (note: not the other way around) in Jesus' culture, as it is in many Middle Eastern cultures to this day. This would often leave the woman culturally shamed and without financial or social support. This was the kind of divorce Jesus condemned, and so should we. This was society at its most unjust and it was intolerable to him. Again and again he condemned injustice and taught the way toward a more just society.

On the night I was inducted into the Parish of Gosford, I overheard one of the more conservative parishioners ask his friend, 'Are you sure he's okay; you know she's divorced, don't you?'

On the same night a woman in the parish pulled Kerry aside and whispered, 'I'm so glad you're divorced. So am I. I have always felt so ashamed and have never been brave enough to tell anyone for fear I would be judged harshly, or worse, ostracised.'

35

Asylum Seekers

WHILE I WAS raised in a loving family and caring community, being an adopted person meant that I grew up, at least psychologically, on the edges of my society. In the valley where I lived, everyone was related to everyone else, meaning there was a high degree of familial identity. While I was mostly not excluded from this identity, I always felt that totally embracing it would require a lack of integrity on my part, as I truly doubted that I was who I said I was. This, I believe, is an important factor in my strong identification with the outcast, the marginalised and the refugee. Australia's asylum-seeker policy was the tipping point for me. I began to become concerned not only for the human beings fleeing the persecution of corrupt and brutal regimes overseas – which was distressing enough in itself – but also for Australians.

I began to understand that as a nation we were capable of creating a morally corrupt and brutal regime, and that the Australian people were capable of standing by and allowing this to happen. In the process, we were allowing our own corporate soul to be sold to the devil. We were allowing ourselves to be diminished in such a way that would lead to the self-destruction of our own society. I could no longer actively collude with such a process, nor could I stand by silently and allow it to happen.

With this formative blueprint, it is not surprising that the fight for asylum-seeker and refugee rights in Australia has consumed me since 2013.

TONY. PLS STOP CALLING ASYLUM SEEKERS ILLEGALS. I DON'T LIKE IT. GOD

The people who head for Australia by boat are not illegal. They are acting within their rights. That such displacement and desperate behaviour occurs reflects a simple fact: situations in some places around the world are so intolerable that the risks associated with fleeing are better than the risks of staying put. Part of what makes us human are things like our instincts to have a home and to belong. These are powerful forces. Human beings don't leave everything and everyone they know, literally risking their lives, if the risk of staying isn't worse.

Often, I've heard Australians say that they would never put their families onto a dodgy boat, or, worse, that to put a child in a boat is paramount to child abuse. How can they be sure about that? If someone was on their way to your house to kill you and your children, wouldn't you do whatever you could to get to a place of safety?

JESUS, JOSEPH AND MARY WERE ASYLUM SEEKERS

Not only do I connect with this issue with my heart and my head, I now connect with it in a much more personal and immediate way, and that is face-to-face. In November 2013 a message came through our Facebook page for us to visit Villawood Detention Centre.

Kerry and I accepted. Here we had the privilege of meeting people who, in their second and third year of illegal detention at the hands of the Australian government, still exemplified the greatest dignity. I have never been offered such hospitality; so many cups of tea . . . so many sweets . . . so much fruit. So much kindness. So much grace.

The absurdity of the incarceration of these people was illuminated powerfully by those who courageously shared their stories with us. Harrowing lives, terrifying escapes, smuggled through Indonesia, the sea journey . . . destination reached. Australian detention. The loss, the grief, the confusion, the fear, the sorrow . . . the palpable pain and anguish.

It was one of those moments when truth flies down and slaps you in the face, and I was left staggering in a haze of bewilderment and denial that we as a nation could be incarcerating such inspiring and courageous human beings. This visit was a watershed moment, and left such a deep impression on us both that on the drive home, when sharing our stories of those we had met, we wept.

This was my introduction to the Australian government's detention-centre regime. But it would get worse than this, in ways I could never have imagined.

Australia as a nation signed the UN Refugee Convention in 1954 – we made a promise to protect refugees, and then, when it didn't suit us any more, we broke that promise. We did it in a non-partisan way: LNP and ALP governments alike. For a long time, differences in policy between these two major parties have been minimal.

While successive governments since the 1970s have continued to vilify asylum seekers arriving by boat, 2001 was a pivotal year.

Then Prime Minister John Howard declared on 28 October, 'We will decide who comes to this country and the circumstances in which they come.'[1]

This followed the August incident where the Australian government refused permission to the Norwegian cargo ship MV *Tampa* to enter Australian waters to disembark 433 asylum seekers rescued from their sinking vessel near Christmas Island. After 48 hours with sick asylum seekers on board, and following numerous unsuccessful requests to the Australian government, the captain chose to enter Australian waters without permission. Immediately the government ordered 45 Special Air Services personnel to board the vessel to prevent it travelling to Christmas Island. An eight-day stand-off ensued before New Zealand and Nauru agreed to take the stranded asylum seekers.[2]

Then, in October, images of children in the water at the time of the sinking of another asylum-seeker vessel were used by the Howard government to accuse asylum seekers of 'throwing their children overboard' to ensure entry into Australia. Although this story was later found to be untrue, it remains a powerful myth in the nation's psyche. These two incidents fractured the nation over asylum-seeker policy and were significant in winning the Howard government another term in office with a 3 per cent increased majority in the November election.[3] The new government opened asylum seeker processing centres for those arriving by boat on Nauru and Manus Island, in what came to be known as the 'Pacific Solution'.

Howard lost the election to Labor in 2007, and in 2008 the Rudd government closed down the off-shore processing centres. In 2009 Tony Abbott, a hard-right-wing conservative, became leader of the Opposition, and with boat arrivals increasing under

Labor's watch, Abbott began relentless attacks on the government for their failures to secure our borders. His dog-whistle attacks on asylum seekers, aided and abetted by his bombardment of the electorate with his three-word slogan, 'Stop the boats', was winning hearts and minds. In an attempt to claw back votes, the Labor government, now led by Julia Gillard, reopened the Pacific Solution in 2012.

By 2013, Australia was facing an increasingly volatile period in Australian politics. In one term of government the Labor Party had changed leaders twice: Rudd/Gillard/Rudd. Staring down a landslide defeat in the looming September election, Rudd expediently signed an agreement with Papua New Guinea on 19 July which determined that all asylum seekers arriving in Australia by boat would be processed offshore. At the joint press conference between both leaders, Rudd said, 'From now on, any asylum seeker who arrives in Australia by boat will have no chance of being settled in Australia as refugees.'[4]

LABOR SELLS ITS SOUL ON REFUGEES

Once again, the political pawns and scapegoats of the Australian parliament fell victim to shameful, self-serving politics in a shared race to the bottom of the barrel. The Rudd government was not as fortunate as Howard in 2001; however, this outrageous policy did salvage some of their projected losses, the election victory falling to the LNP ably assisted by Abbott's mantra, 'Stop the boats.'

I have viewed video footage of the first asylum seekers arriving on Christmas Island following the execution of the PNG agreement. It is extremely distressing to watch; groups of men, women and children sitting on the floor in a large room sobbing and trying to comfort one another after being advised by Australian

Immigration officials they will never settle in Australia. This great, wealthy, under-populated nation has no heart for the vulnerable stateless person. As the clip went on to show workers packing up plastic bags containing the asylum seekers' meagre belongings, I found it difficult to sustain my gaze.

To this day, I am so ashamed that this is my country's response to a few thousand vulnerable, frightened people. I cannot imagine their anguish after embarking on a journey from the other side of the world, fleeing war or a deadly regime, leaving everything behind, often including close family members, handing over every last cent they own to get on a leaky old boat with a 50 per cent chance of not making it alive to the other shore. To then arrive, if lucky, after days at sea crammed in like sardines, seasick, covered in faeces, vomit and urine, and be taken to a room . . .

THERE IS NO QUEUE TO JUMP

If we thought things had been bad up to this point, we had no idea how much further we would allow our politicians to go. In 2013 Operation Sovereign Borders commenced under the direction of the LNP Minister for Immigration, Scott Morrison, who vowed to protect our nation from evil people smugglers and hordes of 'illegals' arriving in boats.

The Howard Government had initially introduced the term 'Illegal Maritime Arrival'. Morrison revived the label and further reduced it to the more dehumanising 'IMA'. Along with this change in language, asylum seeker 'clients' were labelled 'detainees' and were called by their boat number. Australians moved from the idea of vulnerable human beings fleeing persecution to a hoped-for sanctuary, to these very same people being seen as criminals who could be rightly and justifiably incarcerated. These labels have very effectively served to dehumanise asylum seekers. Language is every-thing . . . it was the beginning of the end.

The justification for the return to the Howard-era policies of turning boats heading for Australia around at sea and forcing them back to Indonesia was supposedly to 'stop drownings at sea'. This policy is not only a violation of people's human rights, but also international maritime law.

IN THE OCEAN NO-ONE CAN HEAR YOU SCREAM

Morrison also instituted media restrictions so that the topic of asylum-seeker boats was largely taken off the radar – out of sight, out of mind. Within four months, Operation Sovereign Borders' weekly media briefings by the minister and Defence Force person-nel were moved to 'as needed', becoming rarer as time went on. Even when a press conference was held, journalists were frustrated at the lack of transparency and refusal to answer – or evading – questions due to secrecy around 'operational matters', deemed necessary in the public interest.[5]

During his tenure the minister also introduced a raft of legis-lation eroding the human rights and rights of appeal of asylum seekers, including, but not limited to, removing references to the Refugee Convention and Australian law, fast-track processing of asylum seeker applications including while 'on-water', the reintro-duction of Temporary Protection Visas, and increased powers and secrecy for the department.[6]

The government's propaganda campaign was initially incred-ibly successful, but by 2014 cracks were beginning to appear in their asylum-seeker regime. In November 'The Forgotten Children' report by the Australian Human Rights Commission on the status of children in detention was forwarded to the Attorney General,

George Brandis, however the government sat on the report until mid-February 2015. The report documented hundreds of physical and sexual assaults and incidents of self-harm, anxiety, stress and deteriorating mental health, calling for a Royal Commission into children in detention, and for all children to be released from mandatory detention.

Instead of the government focusing its energies on addressing the report, it attacked, discredited and vilified Gillian Triggs, the President of the Australian Human Rights Commission. Triggs, however, surprised politicians and commentators alike by resolutely and courageously standing her ground against shocking personal and professional attacks.

#I STAND WITH GILLIAN TRIGGS

The President's position was clear:

> *It is imperative that Australian governments never again use the lives of children to achieve political or strategic advantage . . . The aims of stopping people smugglers and deaths at sea do not justify the cruel and illegal means adopted. Australia is better than this.*[7]

Sadly, we weren't . . .

In December 2014 the immigration baton was handed to Peter Dutton, and as 2015 dawned the writing was on the wall for asylum seekers; their fragile positions were to become even more precarious and fraught with danger.

Released in March 2015, the Moss Review had been commissioned in October 2014 by Scott Morrison. Former Integrity Commissioner Philip Moss was appointed to conduct a review specifically on conditions within the detention centre on Nauru in response to allegations of misconduct by staff and contractors. These included allegations of the rape of a child, the rapes of two women, women being forced to expose themselves to guards in order to be allowed to take a shower, trading marijuana in return for sexual favours, and consistent reports of children self-harming by sewing their lips together, hanging and self-wounding.[8]

Again the government sat on a significant report, this one for six weeks, releasing it on a Friday within hours of the announcement of the death of Malcolm Fraser, leading some to speculate the government tried to bury it in the media frenzy surrounding the former Prime Minister. In response to the damning report, Prime Minister Tony Abbott, in an interview with 2GB broadcaster Ben Fordham, said, 'Occasionally, I dare say, things happen . . . Because in any institution you get things that, occasionally, aren't perfect.'[9]

NO MR ABBOTT. WE ARE SICK OF CRUELTY

One of the most galling and corrupt events of 2015 occurred when Amnesty International revealed the Abbott government had paid people smugglers to turn their boatload of asylum seekers back to Indonesia.[10] Abbott, master of the inane three-word slogan, should have changed his mantra from 'Stop the boats' to 'Pay the smugglers'. Here we were being told as a nation that the evil people-smuggler trade must be stopped, yet our government was engaged in those same illegal activities with said criminals.

And apparently that double standard was okay for the majority of our nation, too, whose brainwashing into blind ignorance, racism and hatred for asylum seekers provided the government with vindication for using whatever means necessary to keep them out. It was a costly day; the money paid to the people smugglers, the loss of our international reputation, and the ongoing sacrifice of the soul of our nation. In a rare show of frankness, the LNP government admitted to having turned back 20 boats with 633 asylum seekers on board over a 20-month period, although it was obviously above the pay grade of tax-paying Australians to know how many more 'evil people smugglers' might have been financially paid off by our own government.

When in September 2015, Tony Abbott lost the leadership of the Coalition government to Malcolm Turnbull, again we dared to hope . . .

HOPING FOR A NEW ERA OF DECENCY IN POLITICS

Many, myself included, believed Turnbull to be a centrist who offered the chance for more humane asylum-seeker policies post-Abbott. Sadly, however, Turnbull failed miserably to deliver. Held hostage to a nation well drilled in 'otherising' asylum seekers – somehow making them seem like a lesser category of people unworthy of humanitarian responses – and powerful, hardline conservative political backers, he ensured it was groundhog day.

Twelve months later I wrote of Turnbull in a meme:

> *Australia has a weak and frightened Prime Minister promoting legislation on refugees that portrays us as a weak and frightened nation. We are better than this and we deserve better than this.*

Sadly, we weren't. We still aren't.

It is devastating to have to admit that despite years of struggle on the issue of asylum seekers, a struggle I have shared with many good Australians, we have achieved but naught in halting the escalation of draconian policy decisions implemented by the previous and current governments.

This is not to say heroic efforts haven't been, and continue to be, made. Advocates working 24/7 to assist asylum seekers with their cases, grandmothers staging weekly vigils, children donating their pocket money, ordinary citizens marching and writing letters to parliamentarians, the religious conducting sit-ins in politicians' offices, and medical staff protecting sick, vulnerable people from return to off-shore detention. But just not enough of us care.

DOCTORS RISK JAIL TO PROTECT ASYLUM SEEKERS

Inevitably, during this battle, and I do see it as a battle for the soul of our nation, I have had some high-profile clashes regarding this issue on social media.

In September 2017 I posted to our Facebook page an image of our church street sign that again caused a furore. It was not without much consideration, nor some level of discomfort that I put this sign up. Yet when Peter Dutton suggested that the world's biggest collection of Armani jeans and handbags awaited collection on Manus Island and Nauru I couldn't bear the lies, deceit and evil of my elected representative any longer.

DUTTON IS A SODOMITE

I was very clear that I was not making any suggestions about the Minister for Immigration and Border Protection Peter Dutton's sexuality. As I have explained, I was making a point about his inhospitable treatment of the marginalised, a topic that is directly addressed in the biblical story of Lot.

The story of Sodom and Gomorrah reaches back into the mythological roots of the biblical text. Like all mythologies it is open to interpretation, and therefore misinterpretation. Just as the story of Adam and Eve has been erroneously used to brand women as temptresses, the Sodom story has been used to vilify homosexuals.

Mythologies often evolve to explain major events, such as natural disasters or social upheaval; they often contain political propaganda or commentary on what is considered to be a social ill. Therefore, mythologies can be incredibly powerful tools for reflecting on, and coming to an understanding of, the human condition. Sodom and Gomorrah is a classic mythology that evolved to illuminate the issue of hospitality and its importance in Eastern culture. It also deals with the evils of military rape: the practice of the sexual degradation of the conquered, designed to destroy the morale of the vanquished and establish the dominance of those in power. Recent examples include the behaviour of US Forces personnel at Abu Ghraib Prison during the Iraq War at the beginning of this century, and Australia's endangerment of asylum seekers on Manus Island and Nauru.

The biblical narrative is set in the ancient Near East, where the obligation of hospitality is one of the highest moral imperatives. The story goes that Lot, himself an alien resident of Sodom, receives two guests into his house, honouring them with a great feast. During the night, the men of the city surround Lot's house and demand that the visitors be brought out. This demand is made with malevolent intention: the sexual degradation of these strangers. The men of Sodom fear these visitors and intend to send a message through them to those in power from where they have come. The Sodomites' intention of forcing the visitors into a submissive position through sexual violation is not in any way about homosexuality – it is about domination for the purposes of sending a message of political power in order to discourage any further visitations to Sodom. In a nutshell, the message is, more or less: 'You're not like us; go away and stay away or we will hurt you very badly.'

The wrestling with the moral and ethical issues at play in this mythological story has continued to echo since the biblical narrative was constructed. And yet, more than 3000 years later, we allow the sort of behaviour that condemned the Sodomites to a fiery end to go unchallenged. Australia's treatment of asylum seekers has been nothing less than the degradation of human beings for political purposes. This has included exposing them to rape, beatings, torture and murder. This has been accompanied by such a deterioration of mental health that for some, suicide is seen as the only viable option. The allegory of Sodom is not only fitting, it is entirely warranted.

In October 2017, when I began to use the Sodom and the Gomorrah narrative to reflect upon and illuminate the plight of asylum seekers in Australian detention centres, the former prime minister Tony Abbott was immediately wheeled out by the right-wing shock jock Ray Hadley to counter my argument. However, Abbott's inability to change his narrative merely illustrated the veracity of my position. Neither he nor Hadley could resist referring to asylum seekers as 'illegals', diminishing their humanity for political purposes.

WE NEED TO REPENT OF OUR ASYLUM-SEEKER POLICY

Abbott and Hadley labelled me as 'extreme', 'hateful', 'sly', 'unchristian' and 'left wing'. I guess that's just what they do. Then there were attacks on asylum seekers' morals, parenting abilities and personal hygiene, accusations of lawlessness – you name it, nothing is out of bounds; denigration is a tactic commonly employed by right-wing tabloid commentators and politicians alike. Ironically, Abbott, having attended the seminary, would have been well aware of the truth of the Sodom narrative.

Following the 2017 Good Friday shooting rampage against asylum seekers by PNG military personnel on Manus Island, Peter Dutton suggested that the anger in the community was in response to refugees leading a young boy into the camp for nefarious reasons, when in reality they were responding to a request from the boy for food. In an interview with Sky News six days after the incident, Dutton could not substantiate his claims. However, he continued, as did the mainstream media and his shock-jock mates, to perpetrate this abhorrent lie.[11] Dutton turned a gracious act of charity into something evil, and many Australian people chose to believe him. In an all too common twist of irony Dutton was accusing the asylum seekers of doing what he was doing himself; degrading humans for the purpose of power.

PROPAGANDA: THE FREEDOM TO BE DECEIVED

All this dehumanisation is an immense evil that is being perpetrated in the name of the Australian people and, up until this point in time, with the compliance of the majority.

I have observed over the years that evil is usually self-deceiving while at the same time has a proclivity for scapegoating others, usually the powerless and vulnerable. This is never more dangerous than when it is mixed with and enabled by political power, which also gives it legitimacy. This cruel and inhumane system continues to be used for political purposes and for these purposes alone; no reasonable person could maintain that these policies contain any humane or economic value, let alone a shallow and insincere mantra about stopping drownings at sea.

In the case of the aforementioned politicians, their behaviour speaks for itself. All criticisms of their policy are met with blanket disbelief and denial. Only someone who is totally and wilfully unconscious of the reality of others, and deeply embedded in chronic pathological narcissism, could make such statements and expect to be taken seriously.

Furthermore, legislation passed by the Senate granted unprecedented powers to the Minister for Immigration and Border Protection, placing the Minister's decisions out of reach of the courts and giving permission to act contrary to international law.

In 2015 The United Nations Special Rapporteur on Torture suggested aspects of Australia's asylum seeker policies breached the Convention Against Torture and Other Cruel, Inhuman or Degrading Treatment or Punishment.[12] Over the years the UN has referred to Australia's policies as: breaching common decency, alarming, concerning, dire, untenable, immensely harmful, torture, significant shortcomings, do not meet international standards, excessive use of force, torture and harassment, dismaying.[13]

SCOTT MORRISON, PACK YOUR BAGS FOR THE HAGUE

Evil is a strong word, but it is the only word that is fitting to describe this parliament's behaviour. While Labor Immigration Ministers in the Rudd/Gillard/Rudd government should not escape scrutiny, both current government Coalition Immigration Ministers, Scott Morrison and Peter Dutton, have been charged with a portfolio dealing with the most fragile lives, and both these men have proven over their period of government to be deficient in the moral competency to hold such a ministry. No reasonable Australian could continue to condone this morally bankrupt policy, or to consider Scott Morrison or Peter Dutton fit and proper persons to function as Ministers of the Crown.

The city of Sodom burned to the ground, so we too risk our own destruction. For the Australian people the asylum-seeker issue is complicated by the smoke-and-mirror tactics employed by successive governments over decades; none of us ever get to see any more than one piece of this particular puzzle; the vilified boat-people piece. Yet, in 2013–14 51.5 per cent of people seeking asylum arrived by plane. What a difference the mode of transport makes. Asylum seekers who arrive by air are never demonised by politicians or the press, and certainly never singled out for manda-tory detention, or – worse – transferred to Manus Island or Nauru. Most asylum seekers who arrive by plane have a visa and request asylum after entering Australia. However, they are far less success-ful in achieving refugee status. From 2009 to 2014 approximately 45 per cent of plane arrivals were found to be refugees against 94 per cent of those who arrived by boat in that same period.[14]

In addition, there are people living in Australia who are here illegally – genuine 'illegals'. As of mid-2017 there were estimated to be 64,000 visa overstayers, some 12,000 of whom have been in Australia for over 20 years. These individuals are predomi-nantly from Malaysia, China, the United States and the United Kingdom.[15] The puzzle is why the huge disparity between how we treat each group of people, and why do so few of us not notice or care that those who arrive by boat are disappeared out of our sight?

XENOPHOBIA DICTATING IMMIGRATION POLICY

Surely this information must lead us to ask some serious questions of ourselves. Why are we so afraid of people in boats? What is it about them that we find so terrifying? Is it because they represent the weak and vulnerable in us? Are we too afraid to ask, 'What if that was me?' Is it because we Australians of European heritage reject our own 'boat people' origins? Do we suffer from the 'sensitivity of thieves' – a term coined by academic Ghassan Hage[16] – too afraid to look at what we did when we illegally invaded another nation and committed genocide against its peoples? Could it be that we are still too formed in our White Australian colonial psyche, too afraid to grow beyond our colonial forebears' white, elitist paradigms? Or are we held hostage to tribalism in preferring an English-speaking asylum seeker arriving by plane to a non-English speaking person of Middle Eastern appearance arriving by boat? Are we too afraid to look beyond our own racism and bigotry?

The Australian government has told us that this treatment of asylum seekers is designed to send a clear message to those who would seek asylum by boat from Indonesia. However, the real intention is not to send a message to those contemplating paying a people smuggler, but to demonstrate that the government of the day is more than capable of protecting us, the Australian people, from those we have come to believe to be a threat to our national sovereignty. The immigration policy in place in Australia is entirely the product of the shift to the right in the domestic political landscape; it has essentially nothing to do with border protection.

How did we allow ourselves to be so pathetically brainwashed? It worries me that so much misinformation has been swallowed whole. Surely Australians could not be so gullible?

MANUS. AN INTENTIONAL EXPERIMENT IN HORROR

For 25 days, from 31 October to 24 November 2017, a standoff took place between the Australian government and 600 male asylum seekers and refugees, illegally detained on Manus Island for over four years. During this time the men had all food, water, medical and electricity supplies cut off. The stalemate ended when the men were forcefully removed from the decommissioned detention centre and transferred to accommodation in the nearby town of Lorengau. The men were refusing to move to the new accommodation as it was not completed, nor was it fit for human habitation, nor was it safe from potential violence from locals. These claims were backed up by independent service providers and human rights organisations on the ground on Manus Island.

Never could I have imagined, as I watched this tragedy unfold, that in a First World country like Australia I would ever experience someone personally begging me for a cup of water.

At 8.18 am on the morning of Sunday, 5 November 2017, a tweet came in addressed to me from one of the beleaguered refugees, a man named Ghulam Mustafa. This is what he tweeted:

Father, we are begging you let us arrange water. Navy is not letting us to get anything in from outside. Please help us please.

This haunted me. I shared it with my colleague, who used it as the core of his sermon. Father Chris had the tweet up on the church screen. These words hovered over me, goaded me and accused me. Because here was a real human being – someone named to me – begging me for a glass of water. It was extraordinarily personal.

I tweeted him back:

I want to give you a glass of water but I cannot do it alone. I need the help of the majority of the Australian people.

And that is the truth. There are just over 16 million people in the Australian electorate. I needed them to tell both major parties that Australia's treatment of asylum seekers is no longer politically sustainable. Literally, it would take just over 8 million people to give this man a glass of water.

It hit me so deeply: there was nothing I could do other than to keep chipping away and continue to be part of the voice that attempts to change people's minds.

Something has changed. Something has changed in the Australian people that we could have had men begging for water on Manus Island because we had denied them the very essence to sustain life.

What have we become?

MR DUTTON, YOU CAN'T WASH YOUR HANDS OF MANUS

That very day from the parallel universe of Canberra, Australians were being distracted by a parliamentary debate about extending religious freedoms and a new White Paper telling us how scared we all must be of the big bad boogiemen out there in the world. However, we were naïvely abandoning more abiding liberties and missing the point that the scariest big bad boogiemen reside within this country, in our parliament and in our nation: haters, racists, power-hungry individuals who will stop at nothing to ensure their grip on the reins of power.

Another tweet that day from Ghulam:

Australian government has dropped nuke of atrocity on us today. The black day of human's history. Australia has lost the tiny respect was in our hearts for that country.

I too had lost respect for my country. My only contribution was to live-tweet, share photos and videos, bear witness. I am reminded of the words attributed to President Eisenhower as the Allies liberated the German death camps in 1945: 'Get it all on record now – get the films – get the witnesses – because somewhere down the road of history some bastard will get up and say that this never happened.'[17]

The struggle with the Australian government over asylum-seeker policy is also about the morality of economics. We have surrendered our hard-earned income tax to the tune of nearly $10 billion since 2013 to fund these inhumane asylum-seeker measures.[18] This nears the 2017 annual UNHCR budget for the care of over 22.5 million refugees at US$7.7 billion. We, however, instead of taking care of millions of refugees spend those funds to incarcerate a couple of thousand in indefinite detention in intolerable conditions, all the while denying their basic human rights.[19]

By 2014 the government was looking for new Third World countries to shower with millions of our hard-earned tax dollars as a bribe to take our unwanted human cargo. A deal was inked with Cambodia allowing settlement for those from Nauru. We paid the Cambodian government $55 million to resettle four asylum seekers,[20] and again too many Australians didn't seem to mind so much.

$55M CONDEMNS 4 REFUGEES
TO POVERTY IN CAMBODIA

In July 2014 it was reported that between them Scott Morrison and Tony Abbott employed 132 spin doctors at a cost of $12.3 million to the Australian taxpayer.[21] My outrage at budget cuts for the most vulnerable was barely containable.

132 SPIN DOCTORS. $12,300,000
A YEAR TO TELL US NOTHING

It is extraordinary that Mr Abbott and Mr Morrison are spending $12.3 million per year on 132 spin doctors to make sure we get no information whatsoever. All this while our pensioners, those living with disabilities and the unemployed suffer to save us from the 'budget emergency'. When are the Australian people going to say . . . enough of this evil!

And still not enough people cared, not even when pensioners, the unemployed and those with disabilities were being vilified, dehumanised and punished into living ever further below the poverty line. There is no doubt that in a climate where people are feeling afraid of an imaginary threat, it is easy to gain political power by promising to protect people with secure borders at the cost of all else.

WHAT WOULD WE DO IF WE WEREN'T AFRAID?

Both sides of politics have contributed to this lie, and both are now trapped by its success. But they are trapped in a policy that will ultimately be proven to be economically, socially and politically unsustainable. The question is: who will blink first?

One of the apocryphal stories from the Watergate scandal concerns *Washington Post* reporter Bob Woodward, who was told by his cagey informant to 'follow the money'. It's not bad advice. If we follow Operation Sovereign Borders money it leads us to the 'custody management services' providers Wilson, Serco and

Transfield, the latter now known as Broadspectrum, and the latest government beneficiary Canstruct. Extremely lucrative contracts have been awarded to these companies to manage, at arm's length from the government, the fabricated foundations on which their propaganda rests. In 2012 the government awarded the first contract to Transfield Services to run all its detention centres, both mainland and offshore, the three-year contract estimated to be worth $1.5 billion.[22]

These corporations are not bad in themselves; they employ many good, hard-working people in a variety of legitimate enterprises. However, they do collude in the immoral, mandatory and indefinite detention of vulnerable people who have committed no crime, people who are no threat, other than to political manipulation and propaganda. The only way we can help the asylum seekers is to make mandatory, offshore detention politically unsustainable for both Labor and the Coalition, and economically unsustainable for companies like Transfield.

The very public 'No Business in Abuse' campaign attempted to achieve both those ends by changing public opinion, and it did that by changing the narrative.

HESTA DIVESTS TRANSFIELD. GOOD ON YA!

Ultimately, HESTA superannuation fund sold its stake in Transfield Services once it had been confronted with the documented human rights abuses on Manus Island and Nauru under Transfield's watch. Transfield was forced to change its name to Broadspectrum after the founding Belgiorno-Nettis family withdrew the company's rights to use the name Transfield Holdings, and sold all of its stake in the company. This was alleged to be in part over anxieties over the company's running of the detention centres.[23]

BROADSPECTRUM EVIL BY ANY OTHER NAME IS STILL ROTTEN

The key to this is always the media. We must not accept the narrative that asylum seekers are illegal; this is a blatant lie. We must not allow our politicians, corporations or the media to get away with peddling this untruth. We must continue to make them accountable in every way we can, whether it be a vote at the ballot box, at the annual general meeting of shareholders, or whichever newspaper we subscribe to. We must never underestimate the power of ordinary people in changing history.

Richard Flanagan, *The Guardian*, 24 November 2017:

> *The shame of this time will outlive us all. Our children and grandchildren will have to remake the broken trusts, the sacred freedoms, the necessary liberties that we traded away in our ignorance and our gullible fear. They must rekindle as necessary national virtues kindness and compassion to the weakest.*

Those who know me will understand that I have never been one of those 'the end is nigh' preachers; biblical texts of a dire, unsettling nature emerge from times of great social stress. Now, however, I am beginning to understand from personal experience why my Christian forebears may have felt the need to use such graphic and descriptive language. Recently I have found myself using the language of the Hebrew prophets, which was designed to point out the destructive nature of some human behaviour on society and its devastating consequences.

I join with Martin Luther King Jr echoing the voice of the prophet Amos (5:24), who puts these words in the mouth of God: 'I have no interest in your wealth or your words but let justice roll down like waters, and righteousness like an ever-flowing stream.' What I am trying to impress upon those who will listen is that if the country we love and the people we love are to not only survive but to prosper, then we need to be less focused on protecting our imaginary borders and become more focused on being a people of justice and doing what is right in the world for the poor and marginalised.

I am writing this chapter at the height of the Manus Island Detention Centre crisis, and I felt sure that there were only two things that could happen for the Manus men: they would be evacuated or they would die. Fortunately, the latter did not occur, although the situation remains unresolved and tragedies at any time could be reasonably expected. It seems, however, that the death of Australia's heart and soul is fast approaching – just as death stalked the Sodomites as they assembled outside Lot's house.

MR DUTTON, STRONG BORDERS DO NOT REQUIRE HUMAN SACRIFICE

Perhaps, however, it is not too late. Can we stop these egregious breaches of human rights? Can we be quick enough? Can we be brave enough? Can we be gracious or hospitable enough? Only time will tell.

To achieve this enough of us will have to demand more from both our major political parties in advocating for sensible and ethical policies such as, just to name three:

- *Use part of our current expenditure to increase our annual refugee intake to 30,000. This could include 10,000 from*

*UNHCR camps, 10,000 from that year's global hot spot,
and 10,000 who, having fled their homeland, have found
themselves trapped in the Asia Pacific.*

- *Use part of our current expenditure to well resource the
  UNHCR presence in Indonesia.*
- *Work on a long-term solution to be arrived at between our
  Asia Pacific partners.*
- *And . . . based on current budget costs, we would still have
  billions left over.*

Can we do it? What will we tell our grandchildren that we did
while the Manus men were risking their lives, or the children
on Nauru were attempting suicide? Are we destined to continue
to repeat the Sodom and Gomorrah story because of our own
national hard-heartedness and lack of hospitality? How we answer
this question will determine who we are as an Australian people for
decades to come.

Yet I hold grave fears for the few thousand people still being
held by Australia in illegal, indefinite detention, including children
on Nauru, because it appears current policies will remain in place
until at least 2019 should the Abbott/Turnbull government survive
its full term. Our journey out of Sodom seems a long way off.

BOAT NUMBER 'ZEB037' IS NO NAME FOR A CHILD

36

Australian Muslims

As WE SAT glued to the television on that fateful day in September 2001, watching the Twin Towers come down over and over again, as if the replays would confirm in us a reality that was by any other means inconceivable, I began to wonder what effect this event could have on the Muslim community as a whole, and the locals in particular.

My involvement in interfaith dialogue began in earnest on that day as I encountered the beautiful, gracious, fragile and, at that time, fearful Muslim community. We did not know what would happen in those few hours and days after the attacks on the World Trade Center in New York. We did not know what reactions or overreactions informed leaders might make, and even less what the uninformed, or even worse the ill-informed, might do. That afternoon I phoned the local mosque and spoke to Imam Thanvi to offer my friendship and support.

The following day I visited him and he offered me hospitality; over tea he took a biscuit, broke it and handed half to me. We both knew, in our own way, the depth of meaning contained in this action. For just a moment we sat in the profound silence of pure knowing; knowing that all the pain, suffering and brokenness, the un-forgiveness, recriminations and perpetuation of anguish could find healing, wholeness and peace in this one simple action. We did not speak any more that day of the terrible events; we spoke rather of our families, of those we love.

We were no longer a Muslim and a Christian, but just two fathers in a moment of anxiety refusing with every fibre of our being to give up on our hope for a peaceful future for our children. On that day and on many days to follow we would overcome terrorism with friendship, meet division with unity, and hate with love.

A decade later, enabled by the election of the Abbott government in 2013, anti-Muslim sentiment was beginning to take hold in Australian society. It was then I made a conscious decision to use our significant social media profile to send positive messages of friendship to the Islamic community, to build bridges and to do everything I could to minimise the devastating effect that conservative wedge politics was having on the lives of Australian Muslims.

This laid the foundation for further interactions with the Muslim community and led the Grand Mufti of Australia, Dr Ibrahim Abu Mohamed, and other Islamic leaders to make contact with me. Subsequently, new associations were formed in our respective communities, and friendships flourished.

I first met the Mufti in Gosford, having arranged several months earlier for him to visit for an interfaith event. The Mufti was jetlagged and fresh off a plane from Jakarta where he had met with the Indonesian President to plead for the lives of Australian drug traffickers Andrew Chan and Myuran Sukumaran.

I was, I have to admit, a little anxious about the meeting, being careful to offer culturally sensitive hospitality and appropriate words of welcome. I need not have worried. I was overwhelmed by the graciousness of this wonderful man; his warmth and humour broke down any barriers that may have been imagined. We struck up an immediate and enduring friendship and continued to hold joint events, building bridges and strengthening relationships.

The following December a tragedy unfolded in the Lindt Café in the Sydney CBD which shocked the entire nation. A mentally unstable man took 18 hostages resulting in the death of two innocent people. There are always those who will use such tragedies for their own political purposes, and the Islamophobes sprang into action, vilifying an entire community on the basis of the actions of one individual.

ISLAMOPHOBIA. WE MUST BE BETTER THAN THIS

The anxiety many of us shared for the Muslim community at that time gave birth to movements such as #illridewithyou, where people of goodwill began reaching out locally and nationally to Muslims: to walk beside them in public spaces, sit next to them on the train, to stand in solidarity with them to create a more harmonious society. This was significantly symbolic, because in these situations, symbolism is not only powerful, it is essential.

This was never demonstrated more poignantly than when on the following Saturday a bride wearing a hijab turned up at the makeshift flower memorial outside the Lindt Café in Martin Place. As the bride and her anxious-looking husband made their way along the ever-growing collection of flowers the crowd fell silent and began to part in order that they might get through. Then the bride, on what was meant to be the happiest day of her life, laid her bouquet at the memorial of the dead. The crowd wept and clapped at the same time in deep appreciation for this heartfelt and deeply reverent gesture. This was symbolism at its efficacious best; it was powerful in its consequence. There was no amount of hate that could conquer this act of love.

Instructed by this and other moments of rich and powerful symbolism I continued to put up signs reaching out to the Muslim community and sending messages of inclusion to counter other groups that sought to marginalise. In June 2015 I publicly wished the Muslim community a Holy Ramadan, which received 600,000 views on Facebook. There were the usual haters; however, overwhelmingly the interactions of goodwill and grace between Muslims and the wider community were quite something to behold.

On 2 October 2015, a radicalised 15-year-old boy shot a police employee dead in front of Parramatta Police Station in Sydney, in what was quickly recognised as a terrorist attack. Calls came from the tabloid media for the Muslim community to condemn the attack. The Grand Mufti of Australia immediately issued a press statement, expressing sympathy to the family of the victim, and calling for the community not to stigmatise all Muslims because of this act.

This response was widely condemned by the tabloid press as a refusal by the Grand Mufti to condemn the shooting as a terrorist act. Again a media storm ensued. Furthering their attacks on Dr Ibrahim, some called for him to be stood down from his position. Character assassinations went further, with judgments made about his lack of 'integration' and his legitimacy as a 'true Australian' when dishonest reporting accused him of not being able to speak English. This of course is a blatant lie; Dr Ibrahim speaks conversational English, though when representing his faith in a complex public forum he chooses to use an interpreter, for fear he will make an ambiguous statement, or be misquoted.

And so events deteriorated further with the ugly descent of the media into hysteria and tabloid-trash commentary. A further press conference was called, this time including myself and community and interfaith leaders standing in solidarity with the Grand Mufti and other Islamic leaders. The standing together of religious leaders in a time of crisis was the culmination of a significant journey together in a relationship of ever deepening trust.

STANDING WITH THE MUFTI AGAINST TERRORISM

The Grand Mufti, who is often also criticised by Islamophobic elements of the community, felt welcomed, and accepted a number of invitations to generously share his Islamic scholarship with gathered Christian communities, fostering understanding and resulting in the dissolution of perceived barriers. This evolving bond of affection enabled a safe environment in which people of faith were able to explore and articulate their beliefs in an atmosphere of mutual respect and genuine interest.

While all this was going on Kerry was also building deep relationships with Muslim women, working in partnership with their leadership to promote community harmony. It is our belief that the leadership of women in the community is essential in building strategic relationships that provide an ongoing generational element to cross cultural and interfaith dialogue. This facilitates a 'whole community' dynamic, which extends beyond the boundaries of polite, well-ordered meetings and conferences, to one of sharing more relational-based conversations and experiences.

WE JOIN OUR HEARTS TO OUR MUSLIM BROTHERS AND SISTERS

It is a context such as this that best affords not only professional theologians but also people of faith from all walks of life, the intellectual freedom and security to practise, articulate and grow in their faith. These evolving relationships result in a clear interfaith voice speaking in times of celebration and crisis. Through creative leadership these threads continue to weave a rich and diverse societal tapestry from which the protection of spiritual and intellectual freedom and security may be formed. It was because of this work that Kerry and I were invited to the Doha Interfaith Conference in 2016 and were privileged to be one of the recipients of the International Award for Interfaith Dialogue.

This all eventually proved too much for a group of Islamophobic right-wing extremists who in August 2016 invaded our church on a Sunday morning dressed in fake Muslim attire, interrupting the service. While this was distressing, it was proof that we were an effective threat to their divisive agendas.

RACISTS, GET OFF THE BUS

The Mufti was the first one on the phone after this invasion, offering his emotional and practical support. The only result to this intrusion was that two weeks later hundreds of people from all faith traditions and none packed the church for an interfaith service where the Mufti and I once again shared the microphone promoting unity in diversity through word and deed. During the service those present built a 'tree of hearts', the dedication of which read: 'Created by all who came together to honour and celebrate diversity . . . in the knowing that we are all connected.'

This cooperation between Christians and Muslims is not new by any means; in fact, it reaches right back to the days of the Prophet Muhammad (peace be upon him). In 628 CE, The Prophet confirmed the rights of the Christian monks of St Catherine Monastery in Mount Sinai to freedom of worship and movement. He also confirmed their right to appoint their own judges and to own and maintain property, as well as exemption from military service. He praised them for their humility and offered them protection in time of war.

This tradition continues to this day, in that the holiest places for Christians are in Jerusalem; the most revered being the Church of the Holy Sepulchre where the heart of Christianity beats. Yet, few know that it is a Muslim who opens and closes the only door to this most sacred of Christian sites.

In fact, it is two Muslims from two different Jerusalem Palestinian clans who have been the custodians of the entrance to the Holy Sepulchre since the 12th century. Every morning, at 4.30, one travels from his apartment outside the walls of the Old City to bring the cast-iron key to the church, just as his forebears did before him.

Once there, he entrusts the key to the other, who knocks at the gate to call the priests and the pilgrims who spend the night praying inside. From inside the church, a wooden ladder is passed through a porthole to help him unlock the upper part of the enormous door. Then, he unlocks the lower one before handing the precious key back to the first. The ritual is reversed every evening at 7.30, after the hundreds of tourists and pilgrims have left the church.

Why the elaborate ritual? As often happens in Jerusalem, a city holy to several religions, there are different versions to this story. After the Muslim conquest in 637, the Caliph Omar guaranteed the Archbishop that the Christian places of worship would be protected and so entrusted the custodianship to a family which originated in Medina and was related to the Prophet Muhammad.

It happened again in 1187, after Saladin ended the Crusader Kingdom of Jerusalem. He chose the family again to look after the peace between the different Eastern and Western Christian confessions, which were at odds over control of the Sepulchre. What does it mean to hold the key to the heart of another's faith, and what does it mean to have that key held for you?

These two Muslim families have for almost 1000 years been conscious of the privilege of serving the Christian community, and the Christians have for that same millennium been conscious that their freedom to worship is held gently in the hands of another. And so it is for us in this nation today, our freedom to pray or not to pray is held in the hands of others – we hope in the gentle hands of honourable friends and caring neighbours. Our particular expression of secular democracy ensures our religious freedom and our religious freedom ensures our secular democracy. We continue to preserve this great privilege only by opening the door to each other.

DO 2 ALL AS U WOULD WISH HAVE DONE 2 U – ISLAM

SHADOW
AND LIGHT

37

Domination Systems – It's a Broken Hallelujah

'FEAR IS THE path to the dark side; fear leads to anger, anger leads to hate, hate leads to suffering.'[1] So said Master Yoda to Anakin Skywalker the first time they met. If I wasn't a Christian, I think I would have liked to have been a Jedi.

MAY THE FORCE BE WITH YOU

In the *Star Wars* mythology, there is a struggle for dominance between the Jedi and the Sith because they have wildly different ideas about the meaning of power and how it should be used. Master Yoda recognises the power of the dark side; the Sith presides with fear, anger and hate. The light side, the side of the Jedi, uses wisdom, knowledge and ultimately love to order the lives of beings. You can see why the Jedi philosophy is appealing to me, and why *Star Wars* continues to provide a stark metaphor for the dark arts used by prevailing domination systems in our societies 41 years after the film's release.

Ever since European invasion, the domination system in Australia has been characterised as white, Western, nominally Christian, male and heterosexual. This could also be said to be true for most Western democracies. The second-half of the 20th century saw a number of sociological shifts, which has placed that traditional domination system under considerable stress. Post-war migration saw an influx of Eastern Europeans, followed by Asian immigrants in the 1970s and, more recently, those from the 'Arab' world.

This has placed some pressure at least on the perception of the white, Western Christian community's feelings of being in control. The rise of feminism and more recently the developing consciousness of the rights of people who identify as LGBTI has caused further questioning of the dominant place of the male heterosexual in the traditional pecking order.

In November 2017 in response to the success of the marriage-equality plebiscite, the Anglican Rector of St Mark's Darling Point in Sydney, Reverend Dr Michael Jensen, said on ABC's *The Drum* that up until now we haven't needed a Bill of Rights. And I did a bit of a Donald Trump: I shot off a tweet, which is probably not particularly wise when you are feeling a little bit explosive.

I said, 'You are a white, male, heterosexual Christian; of course, you didn't need a Bill of Rights. Everybody else needed a Bill of Rights, but you didn't!' So, all of a sudden, one little crack appears in the domination system, where we can marry gay, lesbian, transgender and intersex people, and we white, male, heterosexual, Christian, Western men need a Bill of Rights? How infuriating!

There are Christians in power in our nation today who are calling upon the International Covenant on Civil and Political Rights, something this country has actually signed up to, and asking for a clause to be entered into the Marriage Act: Article 18, which mandates for freedom of religion or belief.[2] As if we don't already have freedom of religion and belief.

IT'S NOT THE THING, IT'S THE SPIN

In that same declaration, these politicians are ignoring Article 9, which says: 'Article 9 recognises the rights to the liberty and security of the person. It prohibits arbitrary arrest and detention and requires any deprivation of liberty to be according to law. It obligates those who are deprived of their liberty to challenge their imprisonment through the courts'[3]; it's called *habeus corpus*, which we have suspended. 'These provisions apply not just to those imprisoned as part of the criminal process, but also to those detained due to mental illness, drug addiction, or for educational or immigration purposes.'[4]

So, I would say to those who identify as Christian who are part of the domination system in our nation today: if you want to call upon Article 18, then you damn well need to call upon Article 9 as well. Because unless all people are free, no-one is free.

'I dream of an Africa which is at peace with itself,' said Nelson Mandela.[5] Perhaps we could share a similar dream for Australia.

In order for us to be at peace with ourselves, we need to understand what it is that causes our internal conflict. While the traditional domination system is under pressure, and there is the perception that it is under attack, it is in practice still firmly in place, if experiencing something of a somewhat painful evolutionary process. The issue of most interest in the current socio-political context is our nation's reaction to the perception of the threat to the domination system.

Politically conservative, populist politicians in Australia, such as Pauline Hanson, George Christensen, Cory Bernardi and their ilk have an appeal to those who perceive themselves to be, by association, part of the domination system. Although, it must be said that those who feel most threatened, who actually do pose a threat to our society, exist at the outermost environs of that structure.

RIGHT WING EXTREMISTS NOW GREATER THREAT

The extremists will use the perception of threat to their political advantage, seeking to turn sensitivities into realities through self-fulfilling prophecies. Their fearmongering is for the most part unworthy of our attention or consideration. However, what does require attentiveness and considered responsiveness are those who live in a perceived state of insecurity.

In order to be transformed from this unhappy condition into a much more agreeable state, there is required a visionary form of leadership expressing a dream that has its foundation in the potential of a future reality. The domination system, however, must be enabled to be a significant and guiding influence in its own evolution, rather than to live in fear of a revolution. In this subtle complexity lies the role of true leadership.

We are yet to hear a response to our aching need for someone to lead us into a happy, healthy future that honours the potential of all citizens to contribute to a diverse, productive nation. We eagerly wait to hear a voice echoing across our land with the words, 'I have a dream.'

As you have probably by now guessed, Dr Martin Luther King Jr is one of my heroes. He understood that to free the oppressed we must first free the oppressor. If I have learned anything as a priest who is an advocate for social justice, it has been to not only hear the cries of the oppressed but also the cries of the oppressor. The oppressors are so insecure and afraid of the other that they are compelled to seek control and domination. The burden of this must be intolerable.

When domination systems are threatened they behave in only one way: they move to eliminate the threat. We need only look at our current dog-eat-dog political landscape to understand this dynamic, with character-assassinating attacks on opposite sides of the chamber now the custom.

In an earlier draft of this book an editor suggested the following two paragraphs were full of sweeping statements, and even although it was impassioned, it did feel like a bit of a rant:

'Our Parliament House is more removed from us than ever, a giant monolithic bunker atop a hill in Canberra, now surrounded by a huge impenetrable fence. Here the elites preside over us from afar sidled up to their cosy compliant press corps. These people, paid by us, the Australian people, to serve us and our democracy, are now so detached from the ordinary everyday lives of the citizenry that it appears they have become delusional and intoxicated with their own sense of entitlement and power.

'Lies abound from the mouths of politicians blasted to us in never-ending 30-second soundbites. Even when proven wrong they still continue to lie, or shout over the top of questioners. Most have lost the capacity to speak in terms of more than three-word slogans. They insult our intelligence and treat us like mugs, and we don't seem to care very much about that. We don't seem too perturbed about their political rorting and abuses of the system either.'

CAN'T MORALLY BLACKMAIL THE MORALLY BANKRUPT

I quite like the odd sweeping statement. I believe they are much underrated because they communicate a general theme of thought, however here the editor is most probably right. Nonetheless I leave the original text here to illuminate the powerlessness I feel most days with regard to our political system. It is very difficult not to become completely cynical and/or disengaged. I believe our democracy is in danger, and while on a good day I can recognise that of course there are decent, honourable, hardworking men and women in our parliament striving to make good policy decisions for a more just and equitable society, they are often drowned out by those who are politically self-serving. Current scientific research reveals that being in a position of power, especially for long periods of time, impairs empathy, makes one less risk aware, more impulsive, and less able to see or understand the position of others.[6] Disturbingly, I think we could all think of politicians in our nation today who meet this criterion.

For those of us who reside in the domination system, the bad dream of oppression has not visited us in our sleep or in our waking, but if you reside with the marginalised, you will know from your own experience that the nightmare is real. I have touched on some of these issues in the 'Fair Go Australia?' section, however please allow me to recap . . . I find it even more disturbing to witness these arguments when placed together in the context of domination systems.

We live in a society where women continue to be slut-shamed, are paid less than men, are less represented in positions of power, continue to die each week at the hands of intimate partners, and are casualties of such distorted expectations around their beauty and body image that they buy into a culture that tells them pumping their faces full of fillers and enhancing their bodies with plastic surgery is the norm. I was astonished to hear recently that women are now concerned about showing their 'arm vaginas' when they wear strapless clothes. If you have an arm and a torso you have an 'arm vagina', because it is the naturally occurring fold of flesh where the arm meets the body. Not so normal now, as women in Hollywood are ensuring their armpits are as fat free as possible. Women remain subordinates in a male domination system that continues to treat them as 'less than' and servants of the male ego.

LGBTI people in Australia continue to suffer immensely because of their sexual orientation, with six in 10 experiencing homophobic abuse, two in 10 physical abuse, and they are three times more likely to suffer from depression than the rest of the population.[7] Young LGBTI people often hide their sexuality or gender identity because 80 per cent of homophobic bullying occurs in schools.[8] The recent plebiscite on same-sex marriage released an avalanche of homophobic bigotry, lies and damaging media campaigns against the LGBTI community, members of which continue to remain collateral damage of the dominant heterosexual culture.

First Nations Australians still do not have a voice in our parliament, still no meaningful acknowledgment in any form as the traditional owners of this land. Their life expectancy, employment, literacy, numeracy and school attendance all failed to meet their targets in the 2018 'Closing the Gap Report' released in February. Twenty-five years after the Royal Commission into Aboriginal Deaths in Custody, Indigenous incarceration rates reflect 27 per cent of the national prison population, while only 3 per cent of the overall population, and they are 13 times more likely than non-Indigenous to go to prison.[9] First Australians continue to be held captive by the myth of white, colonial superiority.

Muslims and immigrants are vilified by the media and our government politicians; if you happen to live in Melbourne I hope you were live-tweeting Mr Dutton from your restaurant table when he recently made the astonishing remarks that Melburnians were too afraid to go out to dinner at night for fear of African gangs. Pensioners, the unemployed, those with a disability are all attacked by those corrupted by power with any number of accusations such as being a drain on our society, leaners, bludgers, welfare cheats and drug addicts. For these marginalised people, lives are lived in ever increasing isolation and poverty, the domination system crushing their spirits and disabling their futures.

How obscene. These are not the signs of a healthy society. Something is very broken.

APPARENTLY EQUALITY 4 ALL IS NOT AN AUSTRALIAN VALUE

The meeting of violence with violence begets nothing but violence, whether it be physical, verbal or psychological, but the meeting of violence with love and compassion turns the whole world upside down. So, this is the choice that lies before us.

We must ask ourselves: can we be part of this revelation? And if so, what does this mean for us? I believe it means we do not participate in the systems that disadvantage the vulnerable, the poor or the marginalised. We say no, we are not going to play that game, and further, we will speak out against these unjust systems.

Now, you may think this is some lefty, liberal, progressive, Christo-Marxist, Rod Bower thing. No, it is the teaching of Christianity. I didn't make this up. There is another way to live, and it's just not about getting more people to join 'the club', because really the problem is we already have far too many Christians, and not enough disciples of Jesus.

Christian or not, we are all called upon to stand apart from the domination systems; not only must we avoid colluding with them, we must challenge their very existence. In doing so we must respond to human need by acts of loving service. When we see people pushed to the margins it is our job to respond, to reach out our hand and draw them back. We must seek to transform unjust social structures and offer a better way; not just in a way that benefits us, but in a way that benefits everyone.

38

Nationalism – The Good Samaritan

THE RISE OF various forms of nationalism across the globe troubles my spirit. This nationalism can often and erroneously be confused with patriotism, but the nationalists who claim the title of patriot do so with no understanding of the tradition they claim, or the dynamic that actually drives them.

NATIONALISM IS NOT PATRIOTISM

A true patriot finds an identity in the actual story of their country with all its triumphs and shame. In that narrative the patriot finds a good story to tell and wants others to share in that reality. The nationalist, on the other hand, concocts a narrative that may hold little or no resemblance to the true story of the people. It is a fantasy construct, fabricated for the purposes of manipulation and political gain.

The patriot is compelled to tell the story of the objective good 'us'. The mature patriot may even come to tell the story of the objective good 'other'. The nationalist becomes addicted to the tale of the subjective bad 'them'.

Perceived threat often brings about the abandonment of patriotism and the adoption of nationalism, along with the accompanying rejection of objectivity for the more comforting subjectivity. This dynamic leads directly to the situation aptly named by the word of the year for 2017, 'post truth'.

Judea in the first century of the Common Era could be characterised by this dynamic, an anxious people occupied by a foreign power, a melting pot of nationalism of the subjective good 'us' and bad 'them'. Into this context came a wandering prophet. On one occasion he was travelling through Samaria, a risky business at the best of times; for the Jews there was no good Samaritan and likewise for the Samaritans, no good Jew. Unsurprisingly the villagers in Samaria rejected this itinerant rabbi.

When a lawyer asked Jesus, 'Who is my neighbour?' Jesus replied

A man was going down from Jerusalem to Jericho, and fell into the hands of robbers, who stripped him, beat him, and went away, leaving him half dead. Now by chance a priest was going down that road; and when he saw him, he passed by on the other side.

So likewise, a Levite, when he came to the place and saw him, passed by on the other side. But a Samaritan while travelling came near him; and when he saw him, he was moved with pity. He went to him and bandaged his wounds, having poured oil on them. Then he put him on his own animal, brought him to an inn, and took care of him. The next day he took out two denarii, gave them to the innkeeper, and said, 'Take care of him; and when I come back, I will repay you whatever more you spend.' Which of these three, do you think, was a neighbour to the man who fell into the hands of the robbers?' The lawyer replied, 'The one who showed him mercy.' Jesus said to him, 'Go and do likewise.'

Luke 10:30–37

The experience in Samaria seemed to change Jesus in some way, perhaps from a nationalist to a patriot, at least to a patriot of a world that was yet to be. He began to speak incessantly of the good other, the good leper, the good Roman, the good tax collector, the good woman, the Good Samaritan.

This is of course not exclusively a Christian story; the exaltation of the good neighbour is universal and held in all cultures and religions not least of all in Islamic traditions where the act of hospitality is so highly honourable. I once had the privilege of attending a barbecue in Mt Druitt organised to welcome Syrian refugees. The young Muslim man who had organised the event told me this story. He was driving along in his local suburb when he saw a car obviously broken down on the side of the road. He pulled in behind the car only to see a bumper sticker supporting the racist organisation 'United Patriots Front'. Undeterred, and dressed in his thobe – traditional Muslim attire for men – he offered help. Upon learning that the gentleman (tattooed with the Southern Cross) had run out of petrol, he drove him to the nearest petrol station, bought a Jerry can, paid for the petrol, drove him back to his car and gave him an extra $50 to fill his car with petrol.

C'MON OZ SAY SALAM ALAYKUM. IT MEANS G'DAY FOR MUSLIMS

I would love to be a fly on the wall of the next UPF meeting. Would the stranded driver begin the journey from nationalist to true patriot? Could his internal conversation begin with, 'All Muslims should be deported . . . except this one guy?' Is it possible that even unwittingly he could begin to tell the story of the good other? Because of one story, the name of the hated Samaritans has become synonymous with compassion, love and true neighbourliness. That is the power of story.

We who love our country must understand the difference between nationalism and patriotism, and come to tell the story not only of the good 'us' but also of the good 'other'. It is in so doing that we come to realise the other is the 'us' and go on to celebrate the unity in diversity that is truly the Australian way of life.

I am not speaking here of the mythical 'Australian way of life' that white Australians love to talk about, where they not only perceive themselves as the 'norm', they also have a sense of themselves as tolerant. However, 'tolerance' implies a position of power; usually over a non-white person, or people. In defining themselves as tolerant, white Australians are mostly unaware that this represents a position of dominance. It would be an absurd proposition to suggest a new immigrant is going to be 'tolerant' of white Australia. Those in the subordinate position of 'the tolerated' can only endure.

An event in 2005 in the beachside suburb of Cronulla, Sydney, illustrates perfectly an example of 'tolerant white Australians' taking this privilege to a violent extreme. On Saturday 11 December, 5000 white locals and their cohorts congregated on Cronulla beach in a response to the alleged attack on three lifesavers by a group of men of Lebanese background. In their mission to 'claim back their beach',[1] they sang the national anthem and carried Australian flags, their bodies painted with racist slogans. A violent, alcohol-fuelled riot ensued as they pursued and assaulted anyone of Middle Eastern appearance.

Commentary on the riots overwhelmingly denied them as a racist act, an argument supported by the then Prime Minister John

Howard. On a day infused with nationalistic myth, white males stood together defending their country against an alien enemy, validated by media reporting that their actions were a justifiable response to the assault of the three lifesavers.

IN TIME OF CRISIS WE NEED RESPONSIBLE JOURNALISM

In a study on Australian nationalism, Farida Fozdar and Mitchell Low reveal an expectation held by white Australians that migrants coming to this country should 'follow the law' and uphold 'Australian values'[2]; implying following the law is, 'proxy for expectations of normative behaviour in Australia, which in turn is proxy for culture'.[3] In this context the riots were seen by white Australians as the failure of the Lebanese community to successfully conform to Australian culture, or take on 'Australian values'.

Ironically, in the Cronulla riots, we witnessed white Australians imitating the behaviours of those they reject as 'un-Australian' by breaking their own code, revealing itself in the widespread denial of racism as the cause of the riots, 'ownership' of the beach as exclusive white territory, minimising and/or excusing the destructive behaviour of the white rioters, justifying the assault of innocent people of Middle Eastern appearance by reducing them to lesser others, and transferring blame for the destructive riot to the Lebanese community. As academic Peter Gale notes, 'whiteness continues to inform the symbolic boundaries of inclusion and exclusion in contemporary Australia'.[4]

CITIZENS OF GOODWILL AVOID CRONULLA

In 2015 there was an attempt by nationalist groups to regroup at Cronulla to mark the 10-year anniversary of the Cronulla riots. The 'reunion' was a fizzer, the nationalists defeated by those Australians of goodwill who value the truth of the 'good other' over ignorant narratives fabricated for the purposes of manipulation and political gain.[5]

In 2017 in the Melbourne suburb of Eltham, plans were underway to house 120 Syrian and Iraqi refugees in a renovated former aged-care facility. However, those from far-right groups such as United Patriots Front, True Blue Crew and Party for Freedom instigated a campaign of hate and lies against the initiative, calling it a 'Muslim-first' resettlement plan that displaced elderly Eltham residents.[6] You may not be surprised to know none of this is true. On a designated Saturday these groups, none of them local, planned to travel to Eltham and protest in what they promoted as 'The Battle for Eltham'.[7]

The residents of Eltham had other ideas. Asking questions of themselves about how they could meet the hate that was about to rain down on their suburb they came up with a plan; they came up with butterflies. They decided to meet the protestors with symbols of joy, love, colour and creativity, and in so doing created 'the butterfly effect'. Residents joined together to create 8000 colourful handmade butterflies, and in the early-morning hours teams inundated the park where the protest was to be held, placing these treasures on fences, roads and footpaths. The protest was a fizzer . . . but the butterfly effect was an astounding success. Following the 'protest', Eltham was still decorated in beautiful artwork, and clever, funny and poignant social media campaigns with hundreds of thousands of views were continuing to spread positive cultural capital. The butterfly effect was so successful in fact that many people brought their children to visit Eltham to see the butterflies . . . and added their own. We too travelled to Eltham to see this living metaphor of love and generosity . . . and got to place our butterflies there as well.

LOVE WINS

39

Lest We Forget – The Other

I HAVE A deep emotional connection to Anzac Day. As a young boy I remember watching the march on television and then going out into the shed where my grandfather's tin hat from WWII hung on a nail. I would take the helmet down, put it on and strap on his canvas army belt, then head off to spend the rest of the afternoon fighting the enemy.

For the past 19 years I have presided at the Anzac Day Dawn Service and marched and presided at the 11 am service in Gosford.

I am always conscious of my grandfathers, one who fought in New Guinea and the other who was torpedoed just off Norah Head on the Central Coast. I think of my great-uncles who rode in the charge of the Aussie Light Horse at Beersheba in the First World War. I count it an honour and privilege to remember them and the unique role I have in helping others to honour their family members who served the cause of freedom.

I am also deeply conscious of the first people to fight for, and to die, in defending their nations. The unknown thousands of First

Australians who took up arms and fought in the Frontier Wars to defend their lands from an invader of overwhelming power. This conflict continues to go unacknowledged by the Australian War Memorial.

While I deeply appreciate the privilege that Anzac Day affords us in honouring those who gave their lives opposing tyranny, I am also conscious that the most meaningful way to honour their sacrifice is to continue to oppose tyranny in all its forms and expressions.

I believe that this particular approach to the commemoration of this very special day in our nation's history helps to guard against the slide into destructive nationalism that seems to be being attached to this most sacred of secular commemorations.

On Anzac Day 2017 Yassmin Abdel-Magied, a well-known media personality, tweeted:

Lest we forget: Manus Nauru Syria Palestine.

The intensity and ferocity of the response, which included threats of murder and rape, drove her from our shores.

A year later on Anzac Day 2018, I echoed Yassmin Abdel-Magied's words from the previous year with a sign:

LEST WE FORGET MANUS AND NAURU

The response was instructive. There was a great deal of support, but the character of the abuse was interesting. The vast majority of opposition was not so much about what I said, but that I had echoed Yassmin.

In other words, it's bad enough when a white, male Christian questions our destructive slide into nationalism, but it is totally unacceptable when it is done by a brown, Muslim woman.

Anzac Day has been spoken of as our secular nation's sacred day, and it has served as an expression of state religion. For the most part it has served that purpose pretty well. But like all religions over time it has become corrupted, the outward form becoming more important than the inner essence. When we see over $100 million being spent on a memorial in France while veterans are left at home unsupported, we know we are reaching the point of a corrupted religion. This is almost always the case following the death of the founders of a faith, whose influence up until that point has been able to keep the ship on its original course.

The next generation ministers of that religion, detached from the anchor of their founders, will then see their own corruption as 'orthodoxy', and those who disagree with them as heretics to be burnt at the stake.

Therefore, when nationalism becomes the orthodox political dogma of a nation's culture, and otherisation a tool to retain power, it is entirely understandable that a member purporting to belong to our country's defence force would feel the need to defend his nation against the threat of inclusion and compassion; even to the point of threatening to burn churches for the crime of the most abominable heresy of kindness.

The threat came via a Facebook post, from someone who, dressed in Australian combat fatigues, claimed to be a member of the Australian Defence Force. The ADF later confirmed this particular individual was not a current serving member, although his LinkedIn profile indicated that his military engagement was still current.

However, this was not the first time we had been warned the church would be burnt down. These other occasional threats of arson, always from the extreme right of our nation's political spectrum, often come from individuals attached to groups such as True Blue Crew and the United Patriots Front. Ironical. Such groups who claim to love their fellow citizens and country but are filled with violent hate and rage for those with whom they disagree. These threats against us from the very same people who warn that Muslims will 'burn your churches down'. No Muslim has, in reality, ever threatened me in any way.

The kind of nationalism that causes someone who has allegedly served in our own defence force to turn on Australian citizens simply for questioning the direction in which our culture is heading is truly frightening, but it shows the coercive power of culture and manipulative influence of otherisation on the communal psyche.

I had the privilege of attending the opening of the Anne Frank exhibition when I was in Auckland, New Zealand in February 2018. It was there that I had the honour of meeting Inge Woolf, a Holocaust survivor. Apart from the overwhelming privilege of being in her presence, I will never forget what she said to me.

Having told her that I spend a lot of time advocating for refugees and my concern about the way the Australian Government was behaving towards vulnerable people, she patted me on the arm, looking at the photos surrounding us of the Holocaust and said, 'Keep up your work, it is so important. Because this can happen so easily.'

Till the day I die I will remember her words, and the incongruity of the foreboding tone coming from such a gentle soul.

LEST WE FORGET

40

Ship of Fools – Jumping Overboard

MANY WORKS ENTITLED 'Ship of Fools' are said to have been inspired by Book 6 of Plato's *Republic*, which is recognised as one of the most important philosophical and sociopolitical works of all time. It makes the case that at a state level we should never allow mob rule to make our decisions.

Indeed, it calls for wise discernment in suppressing our least noble instincts. However, Plato reveals his deep understanding of human nature, suggesting that when the darker side of humanity emerges victorious, and democracy descends into chaos, a wise captain is required to guide the dysfunctional ship out of the pandemonium.

In Plato's discourse the ship is filled with foolish people who begin to act in ever-more asinine ways once the repercussions of their ill-considered decisions become apparent. Sadly, however, they are too inept to change the course of the ship. In this country, over the past couple of decades, we have witnessed politicians and others motivated by self-interest refuse to act with the integrity and transparency our modern democracy demands.

Like the people on Plato's ship, those in this tragic allegory have continued to escalate the farce as the diabolical repercussions of their actions have been revealed; defending the indefensible, denying responsibility, hiding or minimising abhorrent truths, all the while complaining they are being victimised.

Here we see people in positions of power across the spectrum of our society who have clearly lost their moral compass, people who – regardless of mounting evidence – continue to operate from their most base instincts. There is no suggestion they understand the ship has sailed. And so, a nation sails onward toward the death of its soul, its citizens finding themselves with nowhere to turn for truth, love, compassion or kindness. We need to turn the ship around and sail away from the insanity of the darkness back into the sanity of the light.

Many of us in our nation today still don't feel we have a ship's captain or crew with a moral compass. What to do? We know what a decent society looks like. We can choose to be our own wise captains. We can choose to stand with our brothers and sisters in solidarity for all that we know is good . . . because we really don't want to sail with a ship of fools.

**THINK
RELATION
SHIP**

41

Compassion – the Foundation of All Else

NOT LONG AFTER we were married Kerry came home from work
deeply upset, telling me she had been called to arrange a funeral
with the parents of a small boy who had died after an accident in
the home. She was troubled; something hadn't seemed right, but
she dared not let her concern run away with itself, so had kept her
suspicions to herself when at work.

Just prior to leaving the family home the mother had handed
Kerry a small bundle of her son's clothes with the request that Kerry
bathe and dress her little boy on her behalf. This is not an unusual
request when a child dies, Kerry had done it countless – too many –
times before. She always accepted, knowing she was performing a
loving service, feeling honoured to be entrusted to carry out such a
sacred act. The clothes were returned to the office and held until the
time the coroner authorised release of the boy's body to the funeral
home. Usually this can take up to a week, but in this case his release
continued to be delayed.

Two weeks following this little boy's death, the coroner's office finally released his body and he was transferred into the funeral-home morgue. When Kerry went to the mortuary to bathe and dress the boy, she found the staff reeling with anger. When she saw his body, she knew her initial suspicions were correct; this little boy had not died in an accident. Her shock quickly moved to grief. She wept. She wept as she went about gently bathing this tiny broken child; she wept through the lullabies she sang to him as she put on his clothes; and she wept as she whispered her sadness to him that he had not known gentleness in his few short years on this earth.

OUR HEARTS ACHE FOR DIMINISHED HUMANITY

Kerry came home that night in turmoil and white-hot anger. To add to her rage, she was rostered to be the funeral conductor of the boy's funeral service the next day. Her role included looking after the parents. Kerry was also privy to the fact detectives would surreptitiously be in attendance to arrest the parents at the conclusion of the service.

She asked me what she should do, how she could encounter these two people with dignity and respect when she felt as if she wanted to spit in their faces. I had never heard Kerry say such things in this way before, but I understood her pain and desire to lash out, and also her wish to rise above these powerful feelings.

The only response I could give her was to ask how she thought Jesus might feel about the parents. 'That's it?' she replied. '*How would Jesus feel?* How would I know? If that's all you've got to give me, thanks for nothing!'

And as she sobbed with exhaustion and despair and frustration, my gently spoken response, 'I'm sorry, darling, it's all I've got . . . I am a priest, after all,' did not help one bit.

And so, she went off to work the next morning sick with anxiety and worry, having had very little sleep. While initially rejecting my suggestion, she tried her best most of the night to think of the parents 'as Jesus would' because, like me, she had nothing else to work with. She wasn't at all convinced she knew what that meant, and even if she did she wasn't sure she could pull it off. She decided 'emotionally neutral' was probably the best she could hope for.

It was a huge service. Kerry set about organising logistical details such as placing flowers, liaising with the priest officiating the service, making sure the hearse had arrived and the funeral team was in place, and so was able to avoid the parents other than a passing greeting when they arrived.

Just prior to the start of the service, as was her duty, she escorted them into the chapel and sat them in their places in the front row. She checked in with her emotions, pleased she had made it to neutral. Yet when she went to walk away, she was overcome with a powerful impulse and moved to do something out of the ordinary.

She knelt before them.

Now at their level, Kerry placed one of her hands on each parent's knee and momentarily bowed her head and closed her eyes to centre herself. She then looked up into their faces. Instantly, she was overcome with a fierce and penetrating compassion for them and their dead son. For the first time, she saw two broken kids. They were so young and vulnerable and scared, and for a moment she wondered how their life's journeys had brought them to this terrible day; a day when neither would leave the chapel free.

This overwhelming moment has stayed with Kerry. The law will hopefully do its job well, but no matter what, we are all broken, we are all human, and we all exist in this mess together.

WE DREAM OF A WORLD WHERE ALL CHILDREN ARE SAFE

On 25 November 2017 the Diocese of Newcastle elected a new bishop, Bishop Peter Stuart, and so it was on the Bishop-elect's first day in the office I texted him late in the afternoon and said, 'Hi, Bishop Peter. I hope your first day in the office has been a good one. And, by the way, I've just been arrested.'

But not in a bad way, and of course he realised what was going on as he saw images of me being escorted into a police wagon in Kirribilli, Sydney. It was 27 November 2017, and following days of covert and cryptic communications, five Christian leaders from the 'Love Makes A Way' movement chained ourselves to the gate of Kirribilli House, the official Sydney residence of the Prime Minister. This was an act of solidarity with the men who were in prison on Manus Island. For me it was an expression of my concern not only for the Manus men, but for the people of Australia, whose very being has been diminished by the deprivation caused to these men for political purposes.

COMPASSION CAN NEVER BE EXPRESSED BY DEPRIVATION

All the press turned up: Channel 7, 9, 10, ABC, Reuters, AAP, Buzzfeed . . . there were people posting live to social media. All of a sudden Australia and the world were listening and watching.

And then in a moment it all changed. Prince Harry got engaged, and it was like, 'Oh dear, isn't that terrible, look at what's happening on Manus Island. Look at those poor men . . . Oh, wait. A royal wedding!' There are so many things in the world today that will distract us from what is important. I hope Prince Harry and Meghan live happily ever after, have a wonderful marriage and bring many blessings to their country and the world, but celebrities and wealthy people do not need our attention, do not need our focus.

It is the poor and the marginalised and the oppressed who need our attention and focus, and we need to start with what is going on inside us. We must ask ourselves: what are the movements of my heart today, am I being driven by fear, confusion, or am I being driven by compassion and love?

After the event at Kirribilli House our phone rang incessantly with all kinds of hateful messages and enraged people; and we got hundreds and hundreds of awful, threatening posts on social media. In light of this experience I resolved never to have a conversation with anybody about anything that I care about until I have laid the foundation of compassion. I will not enter into a conversation until I know that they are coming from a place of compassion and empathy, because otherwise there is no point having that conversation; it cannot go anywhere that is good.

One of the leaders locked on to the Kirribilli gates was Jarrod McKenna, the teaching pastor at Cornerstone Church in Perth, a great leader of compassion and the 'Love Makes A Way' initiative. Jarrod had travelled to Manus Island a few weeks before with Father Dave Smith from Dulwich Hill in Sydney. They were smuggled onto the island and met with the Manus men, but when they were about to leave they got busted trying to get into the boat.

The floodlights came on and Jarrod ran back into the old camp, and in doing so cut his foot on corrugated iron. The men of Manus Island gathered around him. Now, just remember that these men had had no medical attention or medical supplies for weeks and were down to the last couple of Panadol and bandages, and they used those last Panadol to ease his pain, and those bandages to bind Jarrod's foot. They used their precious rationed water to clean his wounds and wash the blood from his skin.

Here was compassion being shown by the very people to whom we are denying compassion, by the very people to whom we are stopping Médicins Sans Frontières giving care. Compassion has to be the foundation of all else, not contained to what is happening in our own hearts, but what is happening all around us. The ability of one human being to see the need in another, to appreciate the suffering of another and be moved to do something about it . . . this is compassion in action.

While the chaining of five people to the gate was a dramatic and powerful act, well covered by the media, the most powerful moment came after we were released from custody. One of the men from Manus, the Kurdish–Iranian journalist Behrouz Boochani, sent a message to one of the locked-on participants – Hwvar, a young emerging Christian leader who is a Kurdish refugee. I was privileged to bear witness to this exchange when Behrouz sang Hwvar a song in their native language – a language that had been banned by Saddam Hussein. It was an incredibly heartbreaking moment, a stunning expression of solidarity from a man in prison on Manus, and overwhelming in its expression of gracious humanity.

With Hwvar's permission we posted her Facebook post about Behrouz's song to our social media the next day . . .

The most poignant moment was after we were released when Kurdish refugee Behrouz Boochani who has been imprisoned on Manus for years sent me a recording of his voice singing a Kurdish song. I was so overwhelmed and overcome with emotion. I wish you could hear him sing, the gentleness of his song, the sweetness of his voice, the strength to sing still and the power in singing in our outlawed language. This is my brother. He knows we see him. They are getting the messages that we care. It was a deeply spiritual and profound moment where our shared culture connected us, and I wish I could reach out to him and hug him – but I couldn't. He is so full of life and love and has so much to give. For so many years these men's lives have been stolen.[1]

Here is a man whom we as a nation have imprisoned for over four years on an island gulag yet who has retained the grace, compassion and open-heartedness to think of others, to rise above his despair and broken spirit and offer us a gift of pure love. It was astonishing.

Behrouz's actions are a reminder that the men imprisoned illegally on Manus Island are our brothers, and an eloquent example of the deep and abiding beauty and connection that we human beings are capable of when we choose to share the road as companions on the way.

HUMAN/KIND. CAN'T BE ONE WITHOUT THE OTHER

42

Forgiveness – Freeing Up Those We Have Wronged

THE WORDS THAT changed my life forever were spoken by Bishop Geoffrey Parker on 21 December 1992 at my ordination to the priesthood. As he placed his hands on my head he said: 'Receive the Holy Spirit for the office and work of a priest in the Church of God. Those sins you forgive, they are forgiven, those sins you retain, they are retained. And be a faithful dispenser of the Word of God and the holy sacraments.'

I often have to remind myself that of all the myriad tasks a priest has to do, there are only three things I am actually ordained to do, and the first and foremost is to forgive. I think it a great pity that in recent times forgiveness has lost its central place in the ordination service, and therefore in the life of priesthood.

Forgiveness is the essence of a just society, so it is no surprise that in Jesus' prayer for such a society, forgiveness ranks just after our need for food, 'Give us today our daily bread and forgive us our sins as we forgive those who sin against us.'

The words of the act of ordination are derived from John's Gospel Chapter 20 where on the night of resurrection Jesus comes among the disciples and, breathing on them, says, 'Receive the Holy Spirit, if you forgive the sins of any, they are forgiven them, if you retain the sins of any, they are retained.' Most scholars would agree that this text is a glimpse into the life of the early Church. If this is so, then it is interesting that forgiveness is seen to be at the centre of a healthy community.

Let me say that there are some things that forgiveness is not. It is not about letting people get away with unjust or damaging acts. It is not about the suspension of justice. I like to think about forgiveness in this way: when we are harmed by another it is as if they shoot an arrow into our psyche, into our soul, and it is deeply wounding. It is as if there is a rope attached to that arrow, and the person who has harmed us continues to move it. And because that arrow is deep within our psyche it causes us continual pain. It keeps the wound open. It keeps it fresh.

Forgiveness is about cutting that rope. It is about taking away the power that the person who has caused the harm has over us. It doesn't necessarily initially remove the arrow or heal the wounds or take away the pain, but it stops that event controlling us. That is what forgiveness is about. And when that event no longer controls us, we can set about the process of removing that arrow, that painful operation of taking that out of our lives and allowing the wound to eventually heal.

Forgiveness is not only letting go of the cause of our own ongoing pain, but also enabling others to let go of the pain we have caused them.

*

As I stood at the lectern conducting a 10 am funeral, the phone in my pocket vibrated incessantly. I knew that there must be something wrong but there was nothing I could do about it. After the funeral concluded, I discovered a chain of messages from a panicked funeral director wondering where I was, and why I wasn't where he thought I should be to conduct another funeral. I consulted my diary and saw that funeral wasn't scheduled until 1.30 pm that day. The time of the funeral had been changed twice, and while I am sure the funeral director had told me, I have no recollection of it being changed a third time and had double-booked myself.

As a priest, you only have one chance to get a funeral right, and when that doesn't happen you can disable the grief process in families for years. I had visited Noel to arrange his wife Annette's funeral a few days before. They were both retired professionals. He was a lovely, gracious man whose beloved had died with Alzheimer's disease. It wasn't as if I had forgotten the funeral time; it was as if its designated time never existed in my consciousness. I was mortified and devastated. The funeral director managed to get a celebrant to conduct the funeral, albeit an hour late.

I sat down that night and wrote an email to Noel begging his forgiveness and asking if he might allow me to visit him the next day so that I could apologise in person. He replied by suggesting 11 am.

I arrived at the appointed time, ashamed and anxious about what reception I might receive. I was greeted with reserved warmth and offered a cup of tea, which I accepted. I made no excuses, but simply acknowledged that this special moment at the end of this couple's long life together had been marred by my incompetence and that I took full responsibility for that and I was deeply sorry.

I expressed to Noel that I hoped that one day he could forgive me for robbing him of this precious memory. And then it happened: this extraordinary man forgave me then and there. In that moment, we were both released – he from the potential of his wife's memory being infected by the pain and confusion of the funeral, and me from the guilt of ruining this special day. My memory of that devastating day is now filled with grace.

UNCONDITIONAL FORGIVENESS

Upon Noel's death five years later, his family opened a file containing his funeral arrangements, recorded after Annette's death, only to discover he had requested that I conduct his service. I didn't sleep the night before the service for fear I would be late.

Forgiveness is as necessary for society as it is for an individual.

If all justice is social, then a just society must be a forgiving society with a focus on restorative justice over punitive justice. Restorative justice means that the offender must be able to admit their guilt and to make recompense. It allows those who have been offended against the personal empowerment of being released from the need to continually oppress the offender to create the illusion that their own suffering is being alleviated. Punitive justice does nothing for the offender, nor does it release the survivors from the pain of the wounding event.

When Jesus forgave his executioners from the cross he was not excusing their behaviour, but freeing his followers and the early Christian community from anger and bitterness following the crucifixion. The Easter narratives confirm that one of the elements of resurrection, that is renewed life, is forgiveness.

As the former Archbishop of Canterbury Rowan Williams says: 'There is no hope of understanding the Resurrection outside the process of renewing humanity in forgiveness. We are all agreed that the empty tomb proves nothing. We need to add that no amount of apparitions, however well authenticated, would mean anything either, apart from the testimony of forgiven lives communicating forgiveness.'[1]

WORK ON FORGIVENESS

43

Vulnerability – No Place for the Weak

CHRISTMAS EVE 2014 marked 100 years since the guns fell silent over Flanders Fields, where through the eerie silence a familiar melody emerged from the German trenches:

> *'Adeste fideles læti triumphantes, Venite, Venite in Bethlehem.'*
> *Those lyrics were answered from the English trenches:*
> *'Come and behold him*
> *Born the King of Angels.'*
> *Then the Germans:*
> *'Venite adoremus, Venite adoremus,*
> *O, come let us adore him Dominum.'*[1]

The strangest thing happened. First of all, candles began to appear above the lips of the trenches. Then, as the carol continued, empty helmets on rifle muzzles. Then the first tentative but brave head appeared.

No shot was heard over the melody, so a few more heads popped up . . . another . . . then another. Cautiously brave souls made their way across no-man's land, where British and German soldiers met in the middle and shook hands. Others emerged; there were embraces, cigarettes shared, souvenirs swapped, cards played, and even a friendly football game held.

This miracle repeated itself up and down the front lines of the First World War during Christmas 1914 . . . until those far removed from the humanity of the war heard about it and forbade fraternisation with the enemy.

The soldiers had abandoned the safety of the trenches and embraced vulnerability so that the human in them could reach out to the human in the other. Mirroring what God had done almost two millennia earlier, embracing vulnerability, reaching out, touching the divine face of humanity, and inviting us to risk vulnerability. Reach out and touch the human face of divinity revealed in the form of a fragile child. This is the path God chooses to walk towards humanity.

A CHILD . . . NOW THAT'S A SIGN

This is, in fact, the only path that can lead us to each other.

We live in a world that wants to lead us down a very different path. We live in a world where media barons benefit from encouraging us to be afraid of the other, the different, and the stranger.

TABLOID TERRORISM

Then once we are afraid enough, there are those waiting to tell us that they, and only they, can keep us safe. They will protect our borders, our way of life, our very 'Australianness'. It's not long before we find ourselves in the paradoxical state where, while the illusion of vulnerability is amplified, we, at the same time feel safe, and grateful.

So safe, so grateful, so alone, so diminished, so *not* fully human.

In 1914, soldiers fighting at the front in the Great War glimpsed for a moment a truth: that what they had been told was a lie, and that the enemy was indeed human.

So, where are our trenches, who is the other for us?

In December 2014, as the terrible Lindt Café siege unfolded and we saw innocent people held captive by a man who had chosen the path of violence, Rachael Jacobs journeyed on a train. She noticed a Muslim woman removing her headscarf. At the next station, Ms Jacobs felt compelled to reach out to the woman and let her know she had a friend in her. She then posted about her experience on her private Facebook page, which was shared by her friends, and a hashtag was born, #illridewithyou.

It was such a simple thing, one human reaching out to another, then another, and another, and then a whole community reaching out to another whole community. Some would call this a social media phenomenon, and they would be correct. Some would call it an act of corporate consciousness, and they, too, would be correct. For me, it is not only the movement of one human towards another – although it is certainly that – it is the movement of the *more* in that human towards the *more* in the other. For me, it is also the movement of the *universal more* towards the *more* in us. Now, many will not feel the need to take that last step, but I remain unsatisfied without it.

Each year I have the privilege of being invited to deliver a series of talks to groups of Year 9 students at risk of falling through the cracks of the education system. Understandably, some of the students have behavioural issues, and the classes vary considerably in terms of manageability and engagement.

I remember particularly one class who had chosen teenage mental-health issues as their area of interest, although I had been invited to focus on the issue of diversity in my talk. About 20 minutes into the one-hour class, I was dying on my feet. I was being met with folded arms and downcast eyes. It was tough going and I was being frozen out.

I changed tack. I asked the question, 'You know, what I'm really interested in is what's going on in this group. Can someone tell me what's happening?'

There was more silence until one of the group ventured, 'We can't tell you, sir.'

I said, 'Why not? I'll be gone in half an hour and you'll probably never see me again. Why not take the risk?'

'We're tired, sir; we're just really tired.'

'So, how's it feel to have to get up at six on a Friday morning to get here for this class at 8.30?' I asked.

'A bit annoying,' one suggested.

'I'll bet it's a bit more than annoying,' I prompted.

'We're pissed off,' came another voice, accompanied by murmurs of agreement.

And then I could feel the energy begin to shift in the room. Arms began to unfold and eyes began to connect. A little bit of vulnerability leading to some honesty allowed community to form and connections to be made. I told them that their anger was normal for people whose circadian rhythm didn't actually wake them up enough for serious engagement until lunchtime.

There were nods of understanding and acknowledgment of affirmation.

Then another anxious voice said, 'Don't tell miss, sir.'

'Why not?'

'She'll be angry, sir.'

'I'm not so sure. I think it would be a great idea to have this conversation with your teacher.'

The last half-hour went quickly, with all sorts of real emotions and energy flying around the class. Then the teacher re-entered the room.

'Miss, we're tired and pissed off.'

'I can understand that,' said the teacher. 'I feel the same way.'

Suddenly there was vulnerability, reality and the potential for a more engaged education experience.

As I was leaving, the student who had originally broken the ice said, 'But, sir, there are some good things about coming here, too.'

Because the negative had been named, acknowledged and dealt with, it allowed the positive to be embraced. None of this would have been possible without one person being willing to be vulnerable and others being courageous enough to join in. Could it possibly be that if one archetypal human can embody both the immanent and the transcendent, then – perhaps – so can we? If one archetypal human was made from both the dust of the earth and the dust of heaven, then could it be that we are, too? If in one archetypal person the yearning of the human and the universal can meet in an eruption of love, then, could the possibility of this exist in us?

What might that look like?

It may look like a young girl in a backwater town, in a backwater province of a great empire, holding a child with the dreadful sense that he will change the world.

It may look like bitter enemies taking the risk of glimpsing the human in each other in the midst of war.

It may look like standing in solidarity with a stranger in a train.

It may look like a stepfather writing of his love to his children.

It may look like a funeral director kneeling at the feet of two parents charged with killing their child.

It may look like an illegally incarcerated human being singing a song in his outlawed language to a protestor fighting for his rights.

It may look like a hijab-wearing bride coming to Martin Place on her wedding day to lay her bouquet at the Lindt Café flower memorial.

It may look like meeting face to face with a man to ask his forgiveness in failing to turn up to take his beloved wife's funeral.

It may look like a group of young students expressing their weariness and annoyance at the education system to their teacher.

If we seek to be fully human, then this is the path we ourselves must journey. It is to risk vulnerability, to take a chance on the humanity of the other. God took that very same risk in the child of Bethlehem, not just to share in humanity . . . but so that we could find our divinity.

NOT A
SELF-HELP
BOOK

44

Igniting Active Self-definition

A VERY CLEVER woman once came to interview me for a Master's thesis she was writing on leadership. She found my particular style of leadership difficult to categorise, so eventually she made up a new definition in the context of how our encounter affected her personally. This academic went away from our meeting having decided to 'do something' about justice in her particular patch of the world. She had what she described as an experience of 'Igniting Active Self-definition' and went on to ascribe this as a model of leadership. This definition resonated with me at the time, and I still use it to describe what I do and how I do it.

Consequently, I do not tell people what or how to do anything. I am much more interested in people defining for themselves who they are, and then acting out of the clarity of that identity.

This is not a self-help book. I am not attempting to give anyone a plan for their life, or a path to enlightenment. For as much as my story is of any use to you, it can only be in so far as it ignites a memory from your own journey that is relevant in your understanding of who you are. Whatever insights I have gained about myself on my journey have often been gleaned from grappling with the words of those much wiser than me and allowing those words to ignite fuel buried deep within my own core.

What follows needs to be understood in that context.

45

Stages of Spirituality

MANY PSYCHOLOGISTS WHO have studied religion, or basic human development for that matter, have acknowledged that we go through various stages of evolution. I have found this concept helpful in understanding my own journey as well as helping others to understand theirs. While there are various interpretations of this process, one of the most notable is that of James Fowler, who was an American theologian and Professor of Theology and Human Development at Emory University. Fowler devised a fairly complicated six-step process of spiritual development, however I tend to think along with American psychiatrist M. Scott Peck of the journey in four steps.

The first stage is rather self-centred; some have called it the 'criminal stage'. Occasionally I visit a juvenile justice centre where 100 young men are incarcerated. While these boys should have grown out of this stage by the time they were seven or eight, they remained in it for varying and complex reasons. Consequently, they have become increasingly narcissistic, seeing the world as an extension of their own personality and therefore theirs for the taking.

The spiritual manifestation of this is often heard in statements like, 'My personal Lord and Saviour', as if Jesus were like a servant whose only purpose is to satisfy our every whim, a Santa Claus who finds us car parks and smooths our way in life. We see this particularly in some forms of Pentecostalism with expressions of prosperity theology; come to church, tithe generously and you will be blessed abundantly – code for financial wealth – by your very own personal God. This juvenile expression of spirituality is chaotic, and ultimately destructive when held by an adult.

Like all stages, stage one is necessary for healthy human development as it begins to form the ego, but by the time of early adolescence we should have moved into stage two. This is the structural stage where the ego can develop within safe boundaries. If these boundaries are not found naturally they can be imposed sometimes with high fences and barbed wire, as my friends at the juvenile justice centre have discovered. This is the time of finding out who we really are. This requires rules and regulations, containment. Churches and other religious organisations are brilliant at providing spaces for people in stage two. It's all about who's in and who's out, we understand and judge ourselves in a dualistic universe, over and against the 'other'.

Churches are full of stage-two people. In fact, it is the best business model for a Church. As I look back to my seminary training I can now see that I was trained to keep people in stage two precisely because it is how an institution is maintained. Eventually, some time in our mid-30s, the work of stage two is usually done: we have had a family or built a career; we have a mortgage and have to some extent worked out who we are and are beginning to become comfortable and secure in that identity. Those who do not evolve out of this stage, and they are legion, tend to become overly judgmental and genuinely perceive those who have moved on to the next stage as heretics and backsliders. The trouble for the Church, of course, is that as people move into stage three, they no longer need the institutional framework and they leave the group for what they now perceive as a less restrictive landscape.

Stage-three people, having become secure in their identity and abandoning institutionalism and authoritarianism, often become interested in others, not for the sake of their own ego or for the benefit of their institution, but simply because they are 'other'. This is the stage of genuine empathy and compassion. Stage-three people get involved in the world for the sake of the world; they are committed to social justice and human rights and are very rarely found in Churches. This is in fact the absolute worst model for a Church, and so the question must be asked: why would I choose to attempt to build a stage-three Church?

The answer to this is complex, but theologically speaking, it is because of what I see in the life and teaching of Jesus. He only ever spoke of one thing and that was what he called the Kingdom, a state of social justice.

The Spirit of the Lord is upon me,
because he has anointed me
to bring good news to the poor.

He has sent me to proclaim release to the captives
and recovery of sight to the blind,
to let the oppressed go free

Luke 4:18

I believe that the ultimate goal of the Church and society as a whole is to be a manifestation of this reality. The trouble is that the very necessary stage-two Churches have never been able to facilitate moving people into stage-three communities, and thereby continually thwart the purpose of the founder of the firm. The same dynamic can also very adequately describe political parties and governments.

Not that Jesus was a stage-three human. He was much more a stage-four personality. This is the modality of the mystic. The founders of the world's great religions have all attained this way of being. Moses, the Buddha, Muhammad and Jesus all had an overwhelming sense of the unity of all things, of being one with all that is. It is called by various names: 'enlightenment', 'salvation' or simply 'being'.

Mystics can be found in all churches, mosques, synagogues, temples and also in secular society. They just blend in, they are rarely oppositional. It's not that they do not care about the pain of the world, they do deeply, but as another great mystic St Ignatius intimated, they don't care that they care.[1] Because of their deep sense of connectedness, their ministry is often to experience in themselves the world's aching, while fully appreciating that there are many good people willing and able to address the issues causing that pain.

Whenever I think of a mystic in our midst I remember Liz Baker. Liz was already an elderly woman when I came to Gosford. She had never married, probably because she had cared for her mother, who lived well into her 90s. Liz had received very little education and had never worked in a paid job. I doubt she had ever been outside Gosford. Yet there was a unique maturity in her soul; she was one of God's special ones, those Jesus called the 'poor in spirit' (Matthew 5:3).

I will never forget a parish camp that Liz attended. During the free time when the 'adults' were doing their thing, Liz could be found sitting on the floor telling stories to the kids. Children have a sixth sense when it comes to mystics because they experience them as having no agenda other than to be in the moment with them. At that particular camp we had invited a group of people living with intellectual disabilities to spend some time with us. The group arrived late and had to walk into what must have been a rather intimidating room of over 100 strangers. These six people made a beeline for Liz because they intuitively knew that she was safe, she was a mystic. I have met mystics in every age and stage of life, from older people assigned by a narcissistic world as irrelevant, to 12-year-old children in cancer wards having had to grow up far too quickly.

Sadly, because of our human brokenness, we always see the person who has evolved to the next stage as having abandoned the 'truth' and it is not until we have reached stage four that we can fully appreciate that the truth is in the journey.

A stage-two spirituality fitted perfectly into sociological modernism following the Enlightenment, but not so well into postmodernism; hence the decline in institutional religion in Western society. If Christianity has a future, it will not be ultimately in its current institutional form but in a stage-three/four movement that reflects much more deeply the original being and intentions of the wandering mystic carpenter and healer, Jesus of Nazareth.

We will always need stage-two institutions, but we are now desperately in need of more stage-three movements. We are discovering that people will also remain on their particular spiritual path if they are provided the necessary stepping stones, if they are not only allowed but encouraged to evolve. This for many begins with an understanding of where they sit with regard to their spiritual development.

Often when I explain the four stages to people, they experience a lightbulb moment; it is very empowering for them to be able to articulate why they experience their own particular spirituality the way they do. It is often a moment of the ignition of active self-definition.

46

Dualistic Thinking

In 2017 a story broke in the media regarding the Queensland Education Department's move to consider banning references to the name of Jesus in primary school playgrounds. This became for a moment an official policy, which took aim at junior evangelists in primary schools.

Now, you can imagine the outrage that came from Christian groups – from the Australian Christian Lobby and from Scripture Union. I must admit I was for a moment taken aback and shocked that the Education Department might want to stop little kids even mentioning Jesus' name in the playground. But then I read further and found that there were some churches that were getting these tiny kids to go into their playground and try to convert other tiny kids to their version of Christianity.

I can tell you that if I were a parent of a primary school child, I would certainly be anxious about that, and so was the Education Department. Then I was overcome with sadness because it is not the Education Department's fault that they considered this option, it is the fault of Christianity. It is the fault of the churches. They have placed the community in a position where they can be understandably afraid of Christianity. Understandably afraid of having people speak the name of Jesus. And then I stepped back even further and looked at the big picture. What I can see is that there are two forms of fundamentalism clashing with each other: a form of very secular humanist fundamentalism, and a form of Christian and religious fundamentalism coming together, and what was really at play in this situation was two forms of dualism.

The Franciscan priest Richard Rohr writes a lot about dualism and suggests the dualistic mind is essentially binary. It is 'either/ or' thinking.[1] It knows by comparison, by opposition and by differentiation. It uses descriptive comparisons such as 'good and evil', 'beautiful or ugly', 'smart or stupid', while not realising that there may be 100 degrees between the two ends of every spectrum. Dualistic thinking works well for the sake of simplification and conversation, but not for the sake of truth or the immense subtlety of actual personal experience. Most of us settle for quick answers instead of any deep perception, which we leave in turn to poets and philosophers and prophets. Yet depth and breadth of perception should be the primary arena for all authentic religion.

How can we possibly search within the mystery of the Divine with a dualistic mind? Rohr goes on to say that we do need the dualistic mind to function in practical life, and we do need to work as teachers, as nurses, as scientists, as engineers or whatever we do. It's helpful and fully necessary as far as it goes – but the problem is, it does not go far enough.

The dualistic mind cannot process things like infinity, mystery, God, grace, suffering, sexuality, death or love. This is exactly why most people stumble over these very issues when they operate in the dualistic mind. Unfortunately, Christians will bring the dualistic mind to the mystery of God. And that is why we get ourselves into the position where the world starts to say, 'No, we do not want you involved in this conversation. We don't want to hear what you have to say.' The dualistic mind pulls everything down to some kind of tit-for-tat system of false choices and simplistic contingencies, which is largely what fast-food religion does. It sets up that 'either/or', that 'in-or-out' dualistic mind.

WE DENOUNCE EXTREME RADICALISED CHRISTIANS

Without the non-dualistic mind, the contemplative mind, the converted mind, the honest and humble mind, much religion is, quite frankly, dangerous. And that is why the Queensland Education Department considered forbidding students from speaking the name of Jesus in the school playground. An extraordinary thing, but it is something that Christianity itself has to take responsibility for. When one dualism meets another, there is no way to take a step forward. We will throw the baby out with the bathwater. We will say, 'Oh, that's old; throw that out. This is new, isn't it great!' Or, 'I don't like this new thing. I like the old thing.'

But if we understand, we are able to bring out what is old *and* what is new, forging them together in a way that provides understanding and is safe and life-giving. What the Queensland Department of Education was saying is, 'We don't trust that you have been able to do that.' That is when we throw out the old; the three . . . four . . . five . . . six . . . seven-thousand-year story, the tradition, the understanding that comes from the great story – the metanarrative, as we call it.

It would be a tremendous tragedy for humanity if we could not live in that continuation of the old and learn from everything that the name of Jesus represents for us – the great tradition, the great wisdom, the great human story of triumph and tragedy, holiness and sinfulness, of human greatness and human brokenness. There is so much we can learn from that story. What a tragedy it would be if we could not mention the name of Jesus.

But we must learn how to do that in a non-dualistic way. How do we engage with the modern world that is so different to so much in that story? How do we engage with the new, embrace the extraordinary things that technology and science bring as we watch the wonders of the universe being unencrypted in front of our eyes? How do we bring out both the old and the new and understand them, bring them together, decipher them?

THE BIG QUESTIONS DO NOT HAVE
BLACK AND WHITE ANSWERS

That is the task not just for Christians, but for everyone who is called to embrace the non-dualistic mind. It is when we have succeeded in doing this that no-one in any playground will be threatened by hearing the name of Jesus. Because it's not about converting people, but offering a gift of wisdom.

47

Divinity and Humanity Are Lovers

WHAT DOES IT mean to be fully human? As far as I can see, people have been asking similar questions for millennia. The way we answer that question has extraordinary global ramifications, because ultimately our view of humanity dramatically affects our attitudes towards the 'other' and therefore our actions. To perceive that there resides a shared spark of divinity in all humanity precludes the possibility of diminishing another person by thought, word or action without intentionally diminishing ourselves. That changes everything.

The Christians of the second and the third centuries pondered little else apart from this question. The presence of Jesus in their lives prompted them to contemplate not only his very nature but also their own, and ultimately what one has to do with the other. They all came to a similar conclusion: that the fullness of humanity in some way touched on Divinity.

So Clement of Alexandria (c. 150–215) can say, 'Yea, I say, the Word of God became a man so that you might learn from a man how to become a god.'[1] In the second century, Irenaeus Bishop of

Lyons (c. 130–202) said that God had, 'Become what we are, that He might bring us to be even what He is Himself.'[2]

These are somewhat confusing – possibly even frightening – concepts for us to grapple with. We have been schooled in dualistic thought for so many generations. We have been taught that divinity and humanity are, in some cosmic way, natural enemies that can only be reconciled by human sacrifice. Ironically, while that is the antithesis of the Jesus message, it has been the dominant theme of Christian teaching for more than 1000 years.

The reality of Jesus tells us something wholly different. Divinity and humanity are not enemies; on the contrary, they are lovers, and as the marriage rite reminds us, when the two become one, there is an explosion of life.

ON ABOUT WHAT JESUS WAS ON ABOUT

To turn away from those concepts is a loss to all humanity. The insights of those early Christians reflect the reality of what it means to consciously and intentionally live within the space that's created exclusively for humanity.

I see something of the 'Igniting Active Self-definition' model of leadership in the life of Jesus. When he said, 'Follow me,' he didn't mean, 'Hang around with me,' he meant, 'Know who you are and get on with creating a better world.' There were many who took up that challenge and just as many who rejected it, but if we look closely at people's responses to him, we will see humans actively self-defining. It may well not have always been the definition Jesus was hoping for, but he was always clear about what particular relationship those he encountered would have with the society he was attempting to create.

The question is: how do we define ourselves in the context of what deep down we know to be the definition of a just society?

48

Known . . .

WHILE OUR SELF-DEFINITION is essential, we must not fool ourselves that it is the ultimate, the end or the fulfilment. That mindset as a destination can only lead us back into the narcissism out of which we have been called.

Being the ultimate romantic, I tried to woo Kerry with roses, expensive dinners, theatre tickets and of course my own unique and undoubtable charisma and charm; how could she resist? However, the thing she remembers most about that early time in our relationship is a short piece of prose I gave her, *Known,* written by Reverend Dr Charles K. Robinson in 1974. It immediately struck a chord, moving her to tears by words 'put into the mouth of God'.

When I asked Kerry where her tears came from she told me she had never held conscious ideas about an exclusive transaction between God and humanity that one must 'attend church to be loved by God'. She had briefly tried church in a number of settings over the course of her adult life, and found it to be at worst incredibly damaging, and at best confusing and irrelevant.

Regardless, in her heart she always felt forgotten, always felt she wasn't good enough, always felt she had somehow failed God. She was acutely aware she certainly did not deserve to be loved by God, because she had surely done nothing to deserve God's favour. These were astonishing beliefs from someone who had rarely attended church. Obviously, Kerry had received them from a nominally Christian society; numerous, subtle, covert and pervasive judgments, and she had anchored them deeply into her being.

However, when Kerry read the words of *Known* she was able through them to experience a reality that God knew her and loved her absolutely, categorically, entirely, without conditions . . . no questions asked. She felt liberated. Hence the tears. I might add here that Kerry once gave this poem to one of her friends who reacted in the negative, suggesting it made God sound like a stalker. Interpretation is subjective.

This experience did not 'convert' Kerry to a church-going Anglican, but it gave her a doorway through which to enter into relationship with the mystery of God, and consequently of her own volition, in her own time, she chose to become a church-going Anglican . . . occasionally. Kerry's spirituality was sometimes confronting for me, and it took me some time to process the learnings she offered, but ultimately her influence has enabled me as a priest, and us as a parish, to better connect with a secular community seeking spiritual expression in what still remains a Christian context. Our journey together has allowed us to influence and evolve each other in ways we could never have imagined.

We share with you the words that brought so much healing and grace to Kerry all those years ago:

I know you. I created you. I have loved you from your mother's womb.

You have fled . . . as you now know . . . from my love, but I love you never-the-less and not-the-less however far you flee.

It is I who sustain your very power of fleeing and I will never finally let you go. I accept you as you are . . . you are forgiven.

I know all your sufferings. I have always known them. Far beyond your understanding, when you suffer, I suffer.

I also know all the little tricks by which you try to hide the ugliness you have made of your life from yourself and others.

But, you are beautiful. You are beautiful more deeply within than you can see. You are beautiful because you, yourself, in the unique person that only you are, reflect already something of the beauty of my holiness in a way which shall never end.

You are beautiful also because I, and I alone, see the beauty you shall become. Through the transforming power of my love, which is made perfect in weakness, you shall become perfectly beautiful.

You shall become perfectly beautiful in a uniquely irreplaceable way, which neither you nor I will work out alone, for we shall work it out together.[1]

LOVE IS EVERYTHING

This life, our relationships, all that we have been, all that we are, and all that we will become is an intimate partnership between us and Divinity. Marriage, for us, is modelled on the same mutually self-sacrificing and mutually self-enhancing dynamic.

Here I can't help revisiting what I said to Kerry on the night I proposed: 'If I am who I am because I am who I am, and if you are who you are because you are who you are, then I am who I am and you are who you are.'

I did go on that night to say, 'We can only be us if we are us.' This book is a manifestation of the many facets of the 'us'.

49

Alchemy of Mourning

WHEN MY SISTER Anne died my grief was compounded by the pain of all the other times I felt alone, isolated and not understood. These feelings overwhelmed me, pouring in on me as if someone had opened a floodgate of sorrow above me and I felt like I was drowning.

LIFE IS PRECIOUS

This is what grief does to us and that is why it causes us so much difficulty. It is why most people live their lives on the precipice of grief, but never really have the courage to dive in, to feel it, to process it. We mostly live our lives with only a toe in the waters of grief, but this avoidance is enough to rob us of joy.

We live in a pain-denying culture. The word 'dead' has been replaced in contemporary language by euphemisms such as 'passed' or 'departed'. Passed to what, or departed for where? Funeral services now often begin with 'We are not here to mourn, but to celebrate'. Well, if we are not here to mourn, why is everyone crying?

Of course, we can celebrate a life, however that should never be at the expense of mourning it first.

The grieving are often chastised by friends and family if seen to be unable to move quickly enough through their mourning period. It makes no sense, apart from being incredibly damaging, insensitive and unkind, to say to a widow or parent that three months after burying their cherished husband or beloved child they should have 'moved on' by now.

While we have much to be grateful for with regard to medical advancements, the medicalisation of dying has meant people have lost much of the ability to feel and stay connected to death. In times past, most people died in their homes surrounded by family and remained in the home until burial. Here people came to pay their respects and spend time with the deceased. They touched, laughed, wept, told stories, and were corporately joined by this sharing of their loss. Clothing worn by those closest to the deceased for prescribed periods of time alerted others that they were in mourning.

Now, I am not suggesting some kind of return to Victorian era mourning rituals; however, I am making the point that we in Western societies have become detached from many of the individual and communal aspects of mourning. It is heartening to see some practices being introduced that allow people a much closer proximity to those who have died, as for parents of deceased babies who are able to spend time with their child over a number of days to facilitate their grieving process.

Mourning does not just apply to death. To live with joy, we must mourn the many continuing losses in our lives, from the monumental such as moving into retirement, kids leaving home, changing jobs, getting divorced, to the more trivial such as grieving the inability to replicate the best New Year's Eve we ever had. Otherwise we are left in the perpetual cycle of trying to endlessly recreate what we had. If we grieve for what is gone or what we have lost, we are then truly free to celebrate its being, and then move into and appreciate the new. This is the alchemy of death and resurrection.

And so it was for me. Like many others who delay processing the death of a loved one, three decades after my father's death, the nudges to address this issue could not be ignored any longer. I was fortunate that with the support of my loving family and having journeyed enough through life to know what I needed to do, I was able to finally farewell my dad.

I had just finished officiating at a graveside funeral service in a beautiful local cemetery overlooking the water. I knew I was in the right place and this was the right day. As I sat surrounded by gravestones, I closed my eyes and, in my imaginings, returned to that last day with him.

Back in the kitchen at Warakeela I went to him and hugged him, and we held one another for a moment. I heard him whisper to my soul, 'Be the best man you can be,' and I simply turned and walked away. On reflection I was astonished that there had been no need to turn around, run back or delay my departure. I didn't even wave goodbye, it was simply okay to turn and leave.

Anyone present in the cemetery would have seen me wracked with grief as I sobbed in fits of tears, however I had never felt more at peace. I was mysteriously comforted in a way that I could not have imagined. For 30 years this burden of grief had sculpted my inner and outer landscape; it was now gone. This then allowed me the freedom to mourn my own mortality. Ironically the more I embrace this, the more I am free to live, and the more comforted by life I become.

Our children, although they had been missing for great swathes of time as they travelled and lived overseas, both moved out of home in their early 20s within three months of each other. This was devastating for us both, however while I continued to immerse myself in work, Kerry was left floundering. At around the three-month mark she felt lost and lower than ever, and took herself off to a local silent retreat for five days. As she was unloading her bags in the carpark she encountered a woman who was just leaving her retreat. Kerry, not in the mood for chats with random strangers at this point, tried her best to disengage, but the woman seemed oblivious and continued her conversation.

She asked Kerry why she was on retreat, and by now resigned to the fact she was actually in conversation with her new-found friend, Kerry told the woman she had come to process her grief at the kids leaving home. At this point the woman confided that she had gone through this same process a number of years ago, and at the time a friend had given her *The Autumn Sonnets [2]* by May Sarton. Madly searching in her bag for pen and paper, she hurriedly wrote the sonnet down, and folding the paper into four handed it to Kerry with her blessings and hope that it might accompany her on her journey through grief, as it had done for her years before. As they embraced and parted, Kerry was acutely aware that in her initial resistance to this kind woman, she could so easily have thwarted this wondrous gift. Once in her room Kerry opened the paper and read the sonnet. And she couldn't stop crying.

She didn't go to dinner, she just stayed in her room and cried, and reread the sonnet, and cried again.

It was the beauty and simplicity of the sonnet that Kerry found so touching. It speaks about trees in autumn 'so casually, one by one' letting go of their leaves and of our yearning to share their wisdom about the naturalness of the changing of seasons. As May Sarton wrote, autumn isn't 'harsh or strange', because love sometimes merely needs 'a time of sleep'. The strong root is 'still alive under the snow', and 'love will endure – if I can let you go'.

The next morning Kerry woke with a plan. She went to breakfast and then snuck back to the carpark and took herself off to the nursery, where she made her initial purchases of plants and potting mix. Then home to begin her Autumn Sonnet garden. Each day she would leave the retreat centre after breakfast and be back before dinner, falling into bed each night exhausted. If anyone noticed her absence, no-one said anything. She carted heavy bags of soil and a terracotta bird bath, she dug and wheelbarrowed and planted, and said goodbye as she did. She was angry and sad and lost and confused.

But a couple of miraculous things began to happen; not only did a neglected corner of the garden become transformed over those five days, so was Kerry. It was like she physically worked her grief out of herself, and through that process created beauty, like the phoenix rising from the ashes. I had no idea this was going on. As Kerry was away I worked long days and didn't notice the works going in a corner of the back garden. This small sacred space, with visiting birds and its carefully chosen plants so that at least some lost their leaves in winter, represented Kerry's love for Kate and John. It was her way of acknowledging that they had grown up and left home, and it was right that she should let them go. As she further acquainted herself with her grief she told me there were times when she found sweetness and comfort as respite, and when the garden was complete was consoled by the knowledge that those strong roots, her love for them, would always endure.

Kerry has paid this favour forward many times, passing the sonnet to many a woman in need of some comfort.

50

Finding Better Angels

'Do small things with great love' – Mother Teresa.[1]

In the last few days of the final edit of this book, an exacting and intense process, friends from Canberra called in for an overnight stay on their way north. On arrival they found us, as they knew they would, stressed and poring over pages of manuscript. With their bags they also carried in a large esky and proceeded to unload beautiful fresh produce onto the kitchen bench . . . organic spinach, fresh farm eggs, olives, fetta cheese. At first, we were a little confused as we had previously arranged to go out to dinner due to our workload. And then they revealed all. They had shopped in Canberra and carted this wholesome food all the way to Gosford, so that on arrival they could cook and prepare enough food to last us through these last couple of intense days.

It was such a precious and thoughtful gift, and it meant more to us than anything else they could have done or given us at that time. Sometimes we get all caught up worrying that our acts of kindness aren't expensive enough or grand enough, but our friends exemplified how simple it is. This is better angels stuff. While it may be easier to ponder this from an individual level, it's harder to consider how we might go about engaging our corporate better angels.

A couple of years ago I happened to appear in a music video produced by Greg Gould, the runner-up on *Australia's Got Talent*. 'Don't Let Go' made the iTunes top 20, even in Grammy week, and has now had 70 million views on social media. Not bad, given that it was produced in two days on the Central Coast with a primarily amateur cast. The success of this video is attributable to its powerful storytelling ability to engage our better angels. And this is the crux of the matter: our better angels are not being courted by many of our political representatives and much of our media.

We seem to be increasingly heading in the other direction, with some media and politicians appealing not to our better angels at all. Add to this the lack of the general population's motivation to investigate or challenge the status quo, so their personal experience is not able to contradict what they are being told. We find ourselves in the fragile situation where we have a crisis of the corporate soul from which to date we have been unable to extricate ourselves. Are we losing our connectedness to one another and morphing into an 'every person for themselves' kind of nation? Or even more concerning, are we becoming a nation of rivals? It would seem so.

THE OPPOSITE OF LOVE IS NOT HATE BUT INDIFFERENCE

In July 2017 Queensland MP Andrew Laming made a comment about inequality:

> *Inequality is staring over the fence and noticing another guy has got a jet ski and you don't have one. Inequality doesn't cause suffering or falling out of the education system or poor health.*[2]

I will leave you to think about the ramifications of what that statement really means but I want to focus on the idea that inequality, at least for Mr Laming, is staring over the fence and noticing that another guy has got a jet ski and you don't have one.

This idea of desiring something that someone else has was explored deeply by René Girard. He was, in my opinion, one of the greatest theologians of the 20th century. He was by profession an anthropological philosopher but a brilliant theologian as well. Girard said that our desire is mimetic.[3] In other words, our desires are the product of observing what other people seem to be attracted to. We see someone else with something, and therefore we want it.

I remember observing two little boys, sitting in the front row of a funeral service with their parents and grandparents; they would have been barely two years old. One little boy had two Thomas the Tank Engine trains – Edward and James – and the other little boy had Thomas. The little boy with the two trains just couldn't help wanting Thomas. And so, a small kerfuffle ensued in the front row of this funeral. This is what Girard meant when he was talking about mimetic desire: we see what somebody else has and we want it. So, what Andrew Laming was really identifying was mimetic desire – not an equation for inequality. We look over the fence; we see the other guy has got a jet ski, and we feel as though we are lacking something. We want the jet ski.

We have all been in a restaurant and, as we have pondered the menu, seen the waiter deliver a delicious meal to the table next to us. Immediately we think, *I think I'll have that*. That is mimetic desire. We see what someone else has, and something within us just has to have it.

The trouble occurs when the waiter comes to us, and we say, 'I'll have what she's having over there at that table,' and the waiter says,

'Sorry, that was the last one.' What Girard says happens then is that, immediately, the person at the other table becomes our rival, setting up what Girard calls 'mimetic rivalry'. He goes on to say that the only way then to settle that rivalry is to find a scapegoat.

I want to give you just one example of how mimetic rivalry is set up in our nation today, and then think about how we might respond to it: 'These [immigrant] people would be taking Australian jobs, there's no question about that.'

THE NATION THAT STOPS MANY RACES

Those words were spoken by Peter Dutton during an interview with Paul Murray on Sky on 17 May 2016. 'These people would be taking Australian jobs.' That's a classic set-up of mimetic rivalry. What Dutton is telling us unambiguously is that, 'You need to see these people as rivals.' But the reality is, immigrants and refugees stimulate the economy and create jobs. Therefore, the experience of rivalry is an illusion, not a reality.

If we look at this situation in another way, we can see it as abundance rather than scarcity. Girard helps us to understand the dynamic and see it for what it is; mimetic rivalry. This rivalry is often expressed in a form of rampant materialism and capitalism. I'm not saying there's anything wrong with capitalism – it has brought great things to modern society – but when it dominates and excludes and robs the poor and oppresses the marginalised, then there is something wrong.

There is the well-known story of the loaves and fish, when Jesus feeds a crowd on a hillside with only five loaves and two fish. This is not a story about miracles or magic; it is a story about consciousness. There is a hungry mob and one defenceless boy with his lunch in a bag. This is the perfect set-up for mimetic desire that can quickly turn into mimetic rivalry and then move on to scapegoating. Jesus challenges the crowd to shift their consciousness from one of scarcity to one of abundance; that shift in consciousness is a far deeper and more abiding miracle than simply feeding a crowd.

Can we be evolved enough to form a consciousness aware enough to know when we are acting out of mimetic rivalry and beginning to scapegoat other humans? Can we shift our consciousness from one of scarcity to one of abundance? A consciousness of abundance is necessary for a society that is just.

GET INTENTIONAL ABOUT GENEROSITY

As Charles Dickens says in his 1841 novel *Barnaby Rudge*, 'The shadows of our own desires stand between us and our better angels, and thus their brightness is eclipsed.' Across time and culture, stories have been instrumental in personal transformation, in part because they change our brains. Research is giving credence to what storytellers throughout time have always known: real-life stories affect us, as shown by the response to Greg's powerful video. For many thousands of years, we have intuitively known that hearing the stories of others can change our thinking and the way we relate to our world.

Using modern technology and MRI scans, we have come to understand that we are impacted physically, emotionally, mentally and spiritually when we tell and hear stories. These scans show activation in the area of the brain that helps us imagine other people's feelings and emotions; this is incredible stuff because this is compassion in action, on view for us to see. It can be said, therefore, that stories help us map the brain of the storyteller.

Neuroscientist Mary Immordino-Yang articulates this well when she says, 'We argue with stories, internally or out loud. We talk back. We praise. We denounce. Every story is the beginning of a conversation, with ourselves as well as with others.'[4]

This goes further, because these kinds of reactions can also produce strong feelings of moral conviction, and it is these gut-level empathic responses that can inspire people to strive to behave in harmony with their better angels in the real world. These internal and external conversations can be utilised to unleash the power of stories and bring about change-creating potential. That is the power of story.

We recognise that politicians have to listen to the people, but let it be a well-informed, rational voice that they respond to rather than fear-induced cries to be saved from the monster under the bed. Our elected leaders have the responsibility to lead the people through the provision of the standard of information typified by a proper balance of facts and truth. Imagine, if they were to act from their better angels, we would have a society blessed with a 'trickle-down-better-angels-movement'.

They could begin to heal the divisions and inequality we are now facing by taking a leaf out of Abraham Lincoln's book, who in his inaugural address in 1861 to a divided nation, said:

> We are not enemies, but friends. We must not be enemies.
> Though passion may have strained, it must not break our bonds
> of affection. The mystic chords of memory . . . will swell when
> again touched, as surely they will be, by the better angels of
> our nature.[5]

We need a national better angels movement to reach deep down within the Australian psyche and to draw out the decency and generosity that we know dwells there, even if in an increasingly dormant state. This is not a chicken-or-egg process but rather a multi-faceted, multi-disciplinary parallel functioning movement aimed at changing the heart of the Australian people. An integral and indispensable part of that movement is political leadership. While we encourage our Canberra leaders, those who dwell in our nation's political heart, to offer that leadership, I also encourage each and every one of us to search our own hearts for decency and generosity, and upon finding it, apply it lovingly, kindly and gently to ourselves and our fellow brothers and sisters. Sometimes it is our children who remind us how this is done best.

Every autumn we do a blanket drive to assist the local homeless shelter. Last year a mum and her seven-year-old son were driving past the church and saw the sign: 'BLANKETS PLEASE'.

Carmello asked his mum why a church would need blankets, to which she explained they were for local homeless people to keep them warm over the impending winter. Carmello enthusiastically suggested they should buy a couple, however his mum had a better idea. She suggested he earn some money by doing chores around the house during the upcoming school holidays, and then he could buy a blanket himself. Carmello enthusiastically shared his plans with his classmates and they joined in the campaign. All in all 26 blankets, all bought with hard-earned pocket money over the school holidays, were donated to the drive. The children received a life lesson in accessing their better angels, the joyful gratification that acts of service bring to the one who serves.

CAN I BE A MORE LOVING NEIGHBOUR?

51

Thin Places

I SUPPOSE MANY children have a special place that they call their own. Mine was down the gully from my house near the orange orchard. It was what could be described as a dell, beside a brook, overgrown by vines that formed a cave-like structure. It was the place where I felt closest to myself, and I headed there most afternoons after school. The ancient Celts would have called this a thin place. In the early Christian era they built their churches on such 'holy' streams and wells.

One of my greatest joys these days is to watch my grandchildren play. They inhale life in its purest and most beautiful form, fully immersing themselves in every experience; climbing trees, playing in cardboard boxes, walking with dinosaurs, discovering fairies in the garden, singing, skipping, laughing and dancing. Every day they have the ability to totally immerse themselves in thin places.

CHILDREN FIND MAGIC BECAUSE THEY LOOK FOR IT

Thin places manifest themselves in all spiritual traditions, from Aboriginal sacred places, to the Wailing Wall in Jerusalem, the Kaaba in Mecca, the Bodhi Tree and countless other streams, rocks, chapels and mountains.

I remember once saying mass in the church on the Celtic island of Lindisfarne at an altar where bread had been broken and wine blessed for over 1500 years. I was overwhelmed by the presence of all those saints who had performed these very same actions countless times in that very same place.

That's what thin places are. They are places where the veil between Heaven and Earth is thin, where the illusion of the separation between the physical and the spiritual is harder to maintain. It's just easier to say your prayers in these places, and we humans are universally gifted in recognising them.

An Indigenous Aunty once told me that there was a stream that flowed under St Mary's chapel in Gosford. She said that it had been a special place for the people, a healing place. After she told me this I began to notice that children were particularly drawn to sit in the corner of the chapel where the stream was said to intersect with the building. So, I started to sit there too, and found it easier to say my prayers.

Thin places are not only geographical, they are also personal and emotional. They can be found in great works of art and literature, in human relationships and in music, in unexpected moments and in ritual. Wherever the illusion of separation is revealed as just that, an illusion, we have found ourselves in a thin place.

These days I tend to find them everywhere every day. Maybe that's one of the things Jesus meant when he said, 'Unless you become like a little child, you cannot enter the kingdom of heaven' (Matthew 18:3). The gateway to the Kingdom is a thin place.

For little children the whole world is a thin place, but as we grow up we lose that level of perception. Spiritual maturity is about finding that perception again as an adult. Becoming like a little child.

There are humans who have reached the stage of the mystic and they often have a childlike simplicity. I am often struck by the behaviour of the Dalai Lama and Archbishop Desmond Tutu when they get together – they giggle like two school kids, as if in on a joke that nobody else gets. And I suspect that they are.

Those developing spiritually – who expect complex answers to simple questions – will often feel disappointed when they actually meet such individuals. People who have themselves become a thin place will perceive the beautiful and elegant simplicity of what, to the rest of us, can be quite overwhelming.

We need to discover and connect to our own 'thin places', those sacred spaces where we can find wholeness and healing. If we wish to change the world we must first change ourselves, for it is when we have peaceful hearts that we best serve humanity.

PRACTISE PEACE

52

Non-Violent Direct Action

MY SEMINARY TRAINING in the late 1980s did not provide any preparation for the kind of ministry I was eventually to undertake, that of Socially Engaged Christianity. While we certainly touched on and appreciated the writings of the liberation theologians of South America, with their radical commitment to social justice, it was never considered that any of us might be called to a similar ministry. We were only ever prepared to be parish priests and pastors, preaching sermons on Sunday, visiting the sick and having cups of tea with parishioners during the week.

In 2015 I was invited to become involved in non-violent direct action by the organisation 'Love Makes a Way', which provides training and organises non-violent actions, sit-ins in politicians' offices advocating for asylum-seeker rights and demanding an end to detention-centre incarceration. This process was based on the work and ministry of Martin Luther King Jr and the American civil rights movement.

Kerry and I decided to participate in a direct action at Parliament House, Canberra, in order to highlight not only the inhumane, unjust and illegal treatment of refugees and asylum seekers, but also to attempt to alert our fellow citizens to the damage we were doing to our own corporate soul.

On the morning of the protest, after an early meeting for a final strategy briefing, over 40 people – both clergy and laity – inconspicuously wandered into the main foyer of Australia's Parliament House. At the appointed time we began to sing and then move together into the centre. One of the things I remember from that day is the extraordinary acoustics in the main foyer of that building and how our voices reverberated in melodies and harmonies as we sang our own lyrics to the tune of the old African-American spiritual 'Were you there when they crucified my Lord?' What we sang was, 'Were you there when they turned the boats away?' I like to think that somewhere deep, deep down in the unconscious soul on our nation that those words continue to echo.

We were of course very quickly bundled up and removed forcibly from Parliament House. I still find myself wishing that we would get asylum seekers out of detention as quickly as the guards got us out of Parliament House.

NON-VIOLENCE IS THE GREATEST FORCE AT OUR DISPOSAL

Not long after that, some of our parishioners were inspired to cover the front lawn of the church with over 3000 cardboard hearts to symbolise those whose hearts were being broken by the regime of indefinite detention. This coincided with a visit to the Central Coast of the Minister for Immigration and Border Protection, Peter Dutton. I invited the Minister to come and view the installation, and while he declined that opportunity he did agree to meet with me. At this meeting I was able to plead for one particular asylum seeker whose life was being considerably diminished by detention.

He heard me out as politicians do, and went on to speak to an invitation-only gathering at the local leagues club.

Interestingly, the media exhibited some fascination with our private conversation and were more interested in that than what the Minister had to say. The only news footage of that day is of the Minister running away from a group of mums and children holding up their cardboard hearts, then him speeding off in his secure motorcade. I began to discover that there was power in powerlessness and that effective messaging does not require words.

In 2015 in the run-up to a visit of the then Prime Minister Tony Abbott to the Central Coast, there were plans to hold a number of protests. I have always been deeply uncomfortable with protests that involve offensive signs and loud chanting. Even if these gatherings do not turn violent as such, there is, I believe, an element of violence in raised voices and the hurling of insults. I decided on this occasion to hold a silent protest.

About 150 local residents deeply committed to social justice stood outside the venue at which the Prime Minister was to speak. When his motorcade arrived, we simply stood in silence and turned our backs. Once again this was the only action that made the evening news. It completely robbed Mr Abbott of his media oxygen for the day.

I made it plain in media statements on the day that by turning our backs as the Prime Minister arrived, there was no disrespect meant to the office of the Prime Minister or to Mr Abbott as a person, but that we were turning our backs on the policies being executed in our name. Even though this statement was made clearly and repeatedly, the local branch of the National Servicemen's Association decided to withdraw their endorsement of me as their honorary chaplain, such was the extent of their disapproval.

While inconsequential in itself, this is symbolic of what can happen when clergy move from the role of tacit supporter of the regime to openly challenging it. One wonders whether this particular branch of the National Servicemen's Association are fully aware of the freedoms fought for by the servicemen and women whose memory they try to honour.

Individuals and organisations invested in the status quo, with its hierarchy of power and system of domination, are often the first to cry foul when church and state get too close. What they are usually seeking is for the church to be silent. But when the church is actively silent and the separation between church and state is clear, then those people will seek to define what kind of silence the church is allowed to have. In the Socially Engaged Christianity I subscribe to, there is no such silence.

On 23 November 2017 I sat outside the office of my local LNP member, Lucy Wicks, for another 'Love Makes A Way' initiative to stage a non-violent direct action to protest the government's treatment of the men incarcerated on Manus Island.

Among the group outside the office were young William and his mum. I had baptised William just the previous weekend and was powerfully moved by the presence of this six-month-old whose first act as a Christian was to plead with his cries for the lives of others. What kind of world had he been born into? What realities would emerge for him out of the symbols of death and resurrection contained in his baptism?

A former nun in her 80s stood with us also. She had greeted me with a request to conduct her funeral. It seemed she was conscious of the impending death around her. The previous day at a similar event in Perth, a nun had been strip-searched by police. I imagined her bravely bearing such an indignity as a badge of honour.

A man who had just lost his job stood there, more concerned for the Manus men than his own wellbeing. What had he lost compared to these men who had nothing left to lose? Another woman stood unsteadily with us. In her 80s – I had visited her in hospital barely weeks earlier – she occasionally gasped for breath but was determined not to remain voiceless. The presence of a young couple and their pastor from a Baptist church communicated that this was an issue of universal consequence for Christians. The biblical narrative makes no allowance for the oppression of the stranger.

Others, too, were present, both young and old. All of us – each with our own brokenness – stood outside the office of the Honourable Lucy Wicks. Only she and her parliamentary colleagues had the power to save these men and – along with them – the soul of our nation. But she, and they, remained silent.

We stood there, the broken and the powerless in Gosford, holding in our hearts the broken and the powerless on Manus. In practical terms we could do nothing; the majority of the Australian people had spoken. We do, however, continue to stand firm.

HUMAN RIGHTS CANNOT BE DECIDED BY MOB RULE

How do we maintain our sense of honour and dignity when we feel overpowered and metaphorically 'slapped around' by current domination systems, or even another person or persons? It is helpful at times like these to take a lesson from the biblical imperative to 'turn the other cheek'. Like all often-quoted biblical texts, however, turning the other cheek is often misunderstood and misrepresented.

You have heard that it was said, 'An eye for an eye and a tooth for a tooth.' But I say to you, do not resist an evildoer. But if anyone strikes you on the right cheek, turn the other also; and if anyone wants to sue you and take your coat, give your cloak as well; and if anyone forces you to go one mile, go also the second mile. Give to everyone who begs from you, and do not refuse anyone who wants to borrow from you.

Matthew 5:38–42

Biblical culture assumes right-handedness, so to strike someone on the right cheek requires the use of the back of the hand. This is more than physical violence, it is a form of insult that is intended to diminish the victim. It is as if the assailant is not prepared to infect themselves through touching their victim with the palm of their hand. Yet it is possible to shift the power imbalance when you force the assailant to strike you on the left cheek, because the only way they can physically do this is to use their open palm. This thereby raises the status of their focus from victim to equal. This biblical warrant is the foundation of all non-violent direct action, and requires courage, strength and resolve that those who resort to violence simply cannot have.

Non-violence is a powerful and just weapon. It is a weapon unique in history, which cuts without wounding and ennobles the man who wields it. It is a sword that heals.[1]

Martin Luther King Jr

53

Hospitality

AFTER BEING IN detention for a total of five years, Shirin's family were released into community detention, even though the family were still awaiting their immigration interview to determine their refugee status. Initially they were living in a shell of a house devoid of even the barest essentials, so Kerry and I helped set them up with basics such as sheets and towels and cooking utensils. When they finally got their meagre entitlement of Centrelink money, 80 per cent of the Newstart allowance, they went out and bought food. When Kerry and I went to visit them, other friends and asylum-seeker helpers descended on their house, some unexpectedly, to welcome them too. Together we made a group of about ten people.

This incredible woman, Shirin, had a tiny quantity of food, which she had bought for herself and her children. In that powerful Middle Eastern hospitable way, this woman went about cooking what little food she had, preparing a small plate of lamb cooked with beautiful Middle Eastern spices, salad, dates and nuts, adding as much rice as she could to pad out the meal. I'm sure the next day they had nothing left to eat, but Shirin saw this as an opportunity to be gracious. She saw this as an opportunity to be hospitable. She saw this as an opportunity to return, I guess, some of the favours that had been done for her by these people. Shirin didn't see this tiny bit of food as lacking, but she blessed it. In effect she said, to the food, 'You are enough. You are good. And I'm going to break you, and I'm going to share you with this crowd.'

Shirin is a shining example of the Sodom and Gomorrah narrative with regard to hospitality. I wish Mr Dutton would share a meal at this wonderful woman's table; would it be enough to touch his humanity? Change his mind? Could this encounter reveal to him that she is really his sister?

HOSPITALITY WELCOMES THE STRANGER

We have much to learn from these gracious, generous, resilient refugees and asylum seekers that we seem to need to harm so dreadfully, because when it comes to hospitality, they do it so much better than we do. However, we Australians obviously don't want people in this country who see the world like that. And I say that without a hint of irony. Because what Shirin did challenges our very framework of existence. I glimpsed the Kingdom in that small house with that tiny offering of food, and a gracious, generous woman who had suffered so much, and lost so much, and been deprived of so much at the hands of our nation. That's hospitality, that's big-heartedness, that's forgiveness, that's grace right there. That is the joy of generously living out in our shared humanity.

AUSTRALIA NEEDS MORE WELCOME DINNERS

From the extraordinary example given to us by Shirin, we can look to another who came before her 1400 years ago; The Negus of Abyssinia, known today as Ethiopia. The Negus, a Christian king, welcomed and gave refuge to Muslims fleeing persecution, not only offering refuge to those in need, but also confronting the fears and prejudices of his own people. We find ourselves in a situation where we are in desperate need of leaders with the compassion and political sensitivity of The Negus. Whatever subsequent legend and mythology has done with The Negus's story, the basic truth remains that he is honoured for his willingness to open his doors to those seeking sanctuary.

I, along with many others, remain committed to the same principles that guided the decisions of The Negus of Abyssinia. Human need always comes before ideology; the spirit of hospitality always overcomes the fear of the stranger, and at the end of the day bridges will always make us feel safer than walls.

The offering of sanctuary to someone fleeing persecution has a long and venerable tradition in the Judeo/Christian world. The ancient principle goes back to the Hebrew scriptures and was enshrined in English common law. In the Middle Ages Benedictine monks set a watchman at night to make sure anyone who sought protection would be received into their midst. The ancient 'sanctuary knocker' on the door of Durham Cathedral is testament to the long-held practice.

Where an authority is causing grievous harm, churches can provide sanctuary and immunity from arrest by that authority. The legality of this refuge has never been tested under Australian law, nevertheless from February 2016 churches throughout Australia have stood ready to offer sanctuary to asylum seekers and refugees who are in danger of being detained or deported back to countries where they have a well-founded fear of persecution. This is the imperative of hospitality that lies at the core of the seeking of the fullness of humanity.

SANCTUARY HERE FROM DUTTON'S BLACK SHIRTS

54

Engaging Buddhism
and Christianity

EARLIER I DISCUSSED Thich Nhat Hanh's Engaged Buddhism movement, and I have been inspired by the precepts he formulated in his book *Interbeing: Fourteen Guidelines for Engaged Buddhism*. I have used the Beatitudes, which form part of Jesus' Sermon on the Mount found in Matthew 5, to formulate a similar framework. While I may have covered some of this in earlier chapters, I believe this makes an excellent summation, providing for me an architecture for living life in an intentional and authentic way.

DEAR HUMANS. I BELIEVE IN EVOLUTION.
GIVE IT A GO. LOVE GOD

Blessed are the poor in spirit, for theirs is the kingdom of heaven
True humility is not only knowing yourself, but also knowing yourself as truly worthy of love and respect. When we know ourselves in this way we do not need outside influences to bolster our fragile egos. When we know ourselves in this way we understand

that what we call truths can only be provisional. We understand doctrines and ideologies as signposts to deeper realities that we can neither capture in words nor impose on others. This humility recognises that we are on a lifelong journey of learning.

Blessed are those who mourn, for they will be comforted
Accept loss; life is a peeling away of the non-essential. Generosity is the joyful and willing embracing of loss. Recognise that possessing any more than you need for a reasonable life is stealing from the poor. Live as simply as you can and never profit from the deprivation of others. Learn to embrace emptiness. Sorrow is the raw material from which joy is created.

Blessed are the meek, for they will inherit the earth
Do all things quietly and reflectively. Meditate, contemplate, pray, think, embrace silence. Share your thoughts but never impose them on others. Don't be a control freak. Be a tour guide not a travel agent.

Blessed are those who hunger and thirst for righteousness, for they will be filled
All justice is social. Get involved in your community, do the right thing and encourage others to do the same. Lovingly but firmly stand against injustice. If something isn't loving and decent and compassionate and humane, it's okay to say so. Choose a vocation that blesses the world. Embrace non-violence.

Blessed are the merciful, for they will receive mercy
Empathise. Feel your own pain and the pain of others – that's how we process it. Pain that is not processed is passed on, and there is already enough suffering in the world, so try not to make any more.

Blessed are the pure in heart, for they will see God
Love and allow yourself to be loved. Fear is the opposite to love; have courage. Embrace your inner child. Your God is the you that others see; see your own beauty, be awed, be surprised, be moved to tears and laughter.

Blessed are the peacemakers, for they will be called children of God
When you speak only truth, you will say less. Truth needs no explanation. Absorb as much anger as you can, turn it into understanding and forgiveness. Be reconciled within yourself and you will be contagious.

Blessed are those who are persecuted for righteousness sake, for theirs is the kingdom of heaven
This will hurt. The powers of the world will not like your inner freedom, your lack of need to consume their products, your lack of fears to be manipulated. You will, for a while, feel the excruciating pain of the outsider, the excluded, until you realise that you are at the centre of something so much more beautiful and abiding.

Laugh, dance, sing.

PRACTISE KINDNESS, SEE IT MANIFEST

EPILOGUE

We Are The Answer

I STARTED MY priestly life, like my predecessors, as part of the establishment, and I was fine with that. I had always seen our governments – federal, state and local – as relatively benign institutions and, apart from the occasional hiccup, not requiring prophetic consideration from the church. Rather, the relationship between church and state, while constitutionally separated, had usually been one of close cooperation, with a common goal – to help foster a social order in which citizens could flourish.

For the first 20 years of my ministry I was a willing participant in that cosy relationship. A sizeable part of my role as a community chaplain as I saw it in those decades was about supporting the system, sanctifying the order, saying 'a nice little prayer' on Anzac Day. At significant community events I believed in my place on the podium alongside the politicians – the local member of parliament and the mayor. I was very much a part of the club, as an Archdeacon, very much a part of the establishment.

But there came a time when I began to feel a tension within myself as I went about fulfilling that role, and I was eventually unable to fulfil it without question. Something had definitely changed from the time of my predecessors, and it had impacted my priestly ministry profoundly. That tipping point was the government's asylum-seeker policy.

My grief was twofold. There were the human beings fleeing the persecution of corrupt and brutal regimes overseas. And there were my fellow Australians. What had we become? Through what sickness in our hearts had we accepted a morally corrupt leadership, one that punished and hurt? Australians were standing by and allowing this to happen, many of them buying into the spin and misinformation put out by the government with the aid of the tabloid press. In the process, we were allowing our own collective soul to be sold to the devil, to be diminished in a way that would lead to the self-destruction of our own society.

No, I could no longer actively collude with such a process. Nor could I stand by silently and allow it to happen. It is why I do not act the way my predecessors acted. Something has changed. I could not – will not – sit in silence.

Why am I different? My answer to the question posed by the man on the waterfront in the autumn of 2017 is now clear to me. You, sir, are the reason I am different to my predecessors. You, sir, are a good man and yet your goodness, as our society perceives it, continues to enable the oppression of the poor and the marginalisation of the powerless; to perpetrate injustice on those who have no voice. You, sir, and the society you represent have for far too long kept Jesus out of Christianity. I refuse to do that, and that is why you perceive me as different.

I was born into an unjust society, and the natural response to injustice is anger. You, sir, helped me to access and name my feelings about injustice and I thank you, profoundly, from the bottom of my heart.

We have the power to create a better world for generations to come by living a better society into existence. It doesn't matter what the question is because *we* are always the answer. It is in our power to create a more just society; we just need to keep finding our voice for justice.

SALAAM SHALOM PEACE

ENDNOTES

11 On Being Adopted

1 Adoption Fact Sheet, Children By Choice Association Inc., www.children
   bychoice.org.au

25 Facebook and 'That' Post

1 Cited in CB Davis, *The Simplicity Connection: Creating a More Organised,
   Simplified and Sustainable Life*, Trafford Publishing, Bloomington, 2009,
   p 350.

29 Rising Secularism

1 'Ipsos global study shows half think that religion does more harm than
   good', 12 October 2017, https://www.ipsos.com/en-au/ipsos-global-study-
   shows-half-think-religion-does-more-harm-good

2 Cardinal Joseph Ratzinger (Pope Benedict XVI), *Faith and the Future*,
   Ignatius Press, San Francisco, 2006.

3 'Benedict XVI: Cardinal Meisner died a "cheerful" man', *Catholic Canada*,
   17 July 2017, http://www.catholicanada.com/2017/07/17/benedict-xvi-
   cardinal-meisner-died-a-cheerful-man/

32 Captain Cook: 'May We Come Ashore?'

1 Clements, Nicholas, 'Tasmania's Black War: a tragic case of lest we remember', *The Conversation*, 24 April 2014, http://theconversation.com/tasmanias-black-war-a-tragic-case-of-lest-we-remember-25663

2 Liddle, Ryan, 'Pemulwuy and other Indigenous heroes now in HSC mix', NITV, 21 July 2016, https://www.sbs.com.au/nitv/article/2016/07/21/pemulwuy-and-other-indigenous-heroes-now-hsc-mix

3 Cited in Manning Clark, *History of Australia*, Melbourne University Press, 1997, p 204.

4 Ibid.

5 Australian Human Rights Commission, 'Bringing Them Home Report', Chapter 13, April 1997, https://www.humanrights.gov.au/publications/bringing-them-home-chapter-13

6 Medhora, Shalailah, 'Remote communities are "lifestyle choices", says Tony Abbott', *The Guardian*, 10 March 2015, https://www.theguardian.com/australia-news/2015/mar/10/remote-communities-are-lifestyle-choices-says-tony-abbott

7 Booth, Andrea, & Ahmat, Natalie, 'That Adam Goodes war cry used a boomerang not a spear: choreographer', NITV, 3 August 2015, https://www.sbs.com.au/nitv/article/2015/08/03/adam-goodes-war-cry-used-boomerang-not-spear-choreographer

8 Holmes, Tracey, 'Australia laid bare in Adam Goodes booing saga', ABC News, 30 July 2015, http://www.abc.net.au/news/2015-07-30/holmes-australia-laid-bare-in-adam-goodes-booing-saga/6660634

9 Commonwealth of Australia, 'Uluru Statement from the Heart', *Final Report of the Referendum Council*, 30 June 2017, https://www.referendumcouncil.org.au/final-report#toc-anchor-ulurustatement-from-the-heart

10 Ibid.

11 Pearson, Noel, 'The Turnbull government has burned the bridge of bipartisanship', *The Monthly*, December 2017, https://www.themonthly.com.au/issue/2017/december/1512046800/noel-pearson/betrayal

33 XX and XY

1 Australian Human Rights Commission, 'Face the Facts: Gender Equality 2018', https://www.humanrights.gov.au/education/face-facts/face-facts-gender-equality-2018

2   Ibid.

3   Ibid.

4   Ibid.

5   Domestic Violence Prevention Centre, 'Domestic Violence Statistics', http://www.domesticviolence.com.au/pages/domestic-violence-statistics.php

34 I Do . . . I Don't

1   Ford, Mazoe, 'SSM: Sydney Anglican Archbishop defends $1m donation to same-sex marriage No campaign', 11 October 2017, http://www.abc.net.au/news/2017-10-11/archbishop-defends-1m-donation-to-same-sex-marriage-no-campaign/9040322

2   United Nations, Universal Declaration of Human Rights, http://www.un.org/en/universal-declaration-human-rights/

3   Ibid.

4   Ibid.

5   Commonwealth of Australia, Constitution Act, http://classic.austlii.edu.au/au/legis/cth/consol_act/coaca430/s116.html

6   Church of England, 'Five Marks of Mission', https://www.churchofengland.org/sites/default/files/201711/MTAG%20The%205%20Marks%20Of%20Mission.pdf

35 Asylum Seekers

1   Museum of Democracy Old Parliament House, Election Speeches, John Howard, 28 October 2001, https://electionspeeches.moadoph.gov.au/speeches/2001-john-howard

2   National Museum of Australia, 'The *Tampa* Affair', Defining Moments in Australian History, http://www.nma.gov.au/online_features/defining_moments/featured/tampa_affair

3   Trioli, Virginia, 'Reith rewrites history to hide the shame of children overboard lie', *Sydney Morning Herald*, 1 September 2012, http://www.smh.com.au/federal-politics/political-opinion/reith-rewrites-history-to-hide-the-shame-of-children-overboard-lie-20120831-255u3.html

4   Crowe, David & Callick, Rowan, 'Kevin Rudd unveils "hard-line" PNG solution for asylum-seekers', *The Australian,* 19 July 2013, https://www.theaustralian.com.au/national-affairs/immigration/kevin-rudd-to-unveil-manus-island-expansion-plan-in-bid-to-stop-boats/news-story/c8abc607070875a4788c16ed246c153d

5   Leslie, Tim & Corcoran, Mark, 'Operation Sovereign Borders: The
     First Six Months', http://www.abc.net.au/news/2014-03-26/operation-
     sovereign-borders-the-first-6-months/5734458

6   Human Rights Law Centre, 'New migration Bill would allow Government
     to breach international law and sideline the courts say leading human
     rights organisations', 14 November 2014, www.hrlc.org.au

7   Anderson, Stephanie, '"Forgotten Children" report calls for Royal
     Commission', *SBS News*, 23 April 2015, https://www.sbs.com.au/news/
     forgotten-children-report-calls-for-royal-commission

8   Moss, Philip, 'Review into recent allegations relating to conditions
     and circumstances at the Regional processing Centre in Nauru', Home
     Affairs Department, 6 February 2015, https://www.homeaffairs.gov.
     au/ReportsandPublications/Documents/reviews-and-inquiries/review-
     conditions-circumstances-nauru.pdf

9   Hurst, Daniel, '"Things happen": Tony Abbott on sexual assault allegations
     in offshore detention', *The Guardian*, 20 March 2015, https://www.
     theguardian.com/australia-news/2015/mar/20/things-happen-tony-abbott-
     on-sexual-assault-allegations-in-offshore-detention

10   Doran, Matthew, & Norman, Jane, 'Amnesty says Australian officials
     who paid people smugglers to turn boats back committed transnational
     crimes', *ABC News*, 29 October 2015, http://www.abc.net.au/
     news/2015-10-29/paying-people-smugglers-to-turn-around-is-
     transnational-crime/6894610

11   Anderson, Stephanie, 'Manus Island shooting may be related to alleged
     incident involving local 5yo, Dutton says', ABC News, 20 April 2017,
     http://www.abc.net.au/news/2017-04-20/concern-for-5yo-may-have-led-
     to-manus-shooting-dutton-says/8457962

12   Human Rights Law Centre, 'UN finds Australia's treatment of asylum
     seekers violates the Convention Against Torture', 9 March 2015,
     https://www.hrlc.org.au/news/un-finds-australias-treatment-of-asylum-
     seekers-violates-the-convention-against-torture

13   Butler, Josh, 'All the times the UN has slammed Australia's asylum seeker
     policy', 25 July 2017, https://www.huffingtonpost.com.au/2017/07/25/
     all-the-times-the-un-has-slammed-australias-asylum-seeker-polic_a_
     23046469/

14 Asylum Insight Facts & Analysis, 'Air Arrivals', 8 April 2016, www.asyluminsight.com/air-arrivals/

15 McIlroy, Tim, 'More than 64,000 people overstaying visas in Australia', *The Canberra Times*, 18 July 2017, https://www.canberratimes.com.au/public-service/more-than-64000-people-overstaying-visas-in-australia-20170718-gxddpj.html

16 Phillips, Melissa, & Boese, Martina, 'From White Australia to stopping the boats: attitudes to asylum seekers', *The Conversation*, 21 June 2013, https://theconversation.com/from-white-australia-to-stopping-the-boats-attitudes-to-asylum-seekers-15244

17 Kirshon, John, *An American Century*, Strategic Book Publishing, Houston, 2012, p 167.

18 Button, Lisa et al., '"At What Cost?" The Human, Economic and Strategic Cost of Australia's Asylum Seeker Policies and the Alternatives', *Save the Children*, September 2016, p 41, http://www.savethechildren.org.au/__data/assets/pdf_file/0009/159345/At-What-Cost-Report-Final.pdf

19 UNHCR, Figures at a Glance, Statistical Yearbook, 30 June 2017, http://www.unhcr.org/en-au/figures-at-a-glance.html

20 Button, Lisa, et al., op. cit.

21 Whyte, Sarah, 'Tony Abbott spends $4.3m on spin doctors', *Sydney Morning Herald*, 5 July 2014, https://www.smh.com.au/politics/federal/tony-abbott-spends-43m-on-spin-doctors-20140705-zsxlh.html

22 Parnell, Sally, 'Submission to the Inquiry into serious allegations of abuse, self-harm and neglect of asylum seekers in relation to the Nauru Regional Processing Centre, and any like allegations in relation to the Manus Regional Processing Centre', Submission 15 to Parliament of Australia, *Jesuit Social Services*, November 2016, https://www.aph.gov.au/Parliamentary_Business/Committees/Senate/Legal_and_Constitutional_Affairs/NauruandManusRPCs/Submissions

23 Parker, Justine, 'Detention centre operator Broadspectrum, formerly Transfield Services, rejects Ferrovial takeover', ABC News, 21 January 2016, http://www.abc.net.au/news/2016-01-21/broadspectrum-transfield-services-rejects-ferrovial/7105192

37 Domination Systems – It's a Broken Hallelujah

1 Lucas, George, *Star Wars Episode I: The Phantom Menace*, Lucasfilm Ltd, 1999.

2 Australian Human Rights Commission, 'International Covenant on Civil and Political Rights – Human rights at your fingertips', https://www.humanrights.gov.au/international-covenant-civil-and-political-rights-human-rights-your-fingertips-human-rights-your

3 Ibid.

4 Ibid.

5 Mandela, Nelson, *Nelson Mandela By Himself: The Authorised Book of Quotations*, Penguin, Auckland, 2011.

6 Australian Human Rights Commission, 'Face the facts: Lesbian, Gay, Bisexual, Trans and Intersex People', 2014, https://www.humanrights.gov.au/sites/default/files/7_FTF_2014_LGBTI.pdf

7 Ibid.

8 SBS News, '"A national crisis": Indigenous incarceration rates worse 25 years on', 15 April 2016, https://www.sbs.com.au/news/a-national-crisis-indigenous-incarceration-rates-worse-25-years-on

9 Useem, Jerry, 'Power Causes Brain Damage', *The Atlantic*, July/August 2017, https://www.theatlantic.com/magazine/archive/2017/07/power-causes-brain-damage/528711/

38 Nationalism – the Good Samaritan

1 Olding, Rachel, 'Cronulla rioters 10 years later speak of pride, regret, death: "I'm not ashamed"', *Sydney Morning Herald*, 6 December 2015, https://www.smh.com.au/national/nsw/cronulla-rioters-10-years-later-speak-of-pride-regret-death-im-not-ashamed-20151127-gl9mrh.html

2 Fozdar, Farida, & Low, Mitchell, '"They have to abide by our laws . . . and stuff": ethnonationalism masquerading as civic nationalism', Wiley Online Library, 22 June 2015, https://onlinelibrary.wiley.com/doi/pdf/10.1111/nana.12128

3 Ibid.

4 Gale, Peter, *The Politics of Fear, Lighting the Wik,* 2005, Frenchs Forest, NSW, p 152.

5 Gainsford, Jim, 'Cronulla riot anniversary response draws mayor's praise', *St George and Sutherland Shire Leader*, 15 December 2015,

http://www.theleader.com.au/story/3567857/cronulla-riot-anniversary-response-draws-mayors-praise/cronulla-riot-anniversary/

6 Vedelago, Chris, et al., 'Battle for Eltham: Welcoming butterflies a background to anti-refugee protests', *The Age,* 5 November 2016, https://www.theage.com.au/national/victoria/battle-for-eltham-welcoming-butterflies-a-background-to-antirefugee-protests-20161105-gsis8d.html

7 Ibid.

41 Compassion – the Foundation of All Else

1 Khoshnow, Hwvar, Facebook post, 28 November 2017, https://business.facebook.com/anggos/photos/a.120959381268037.12242.115067218523920/1695389407158352/?type=3&theater

42 Forgiveness – Freeing Up Those We Have Wronged

1 Williams, Rowan, *Resurrection: Interpreting the Easter Gospel,* London, 1982, p 118.

43 Vulnerability – No Place for the Weak

1 There are many versions of this true story (see, for example, http://time.com/3643889/christmas-truce-1914). I like to imagine it went as I have described . . .

45 The Stages of Spirituality

1 St Ignatius of Loyola, *Spiritual Exercises* (c 1524), various editions.

46 Dualistic Thinking

1 See, for example, http://www.theworkofthepeople.com/dualism-and-identity

47 Divinity and Humanity Are Lovers

1 Cited in Kirby, Peter, 'Clement of Alexandria', *Early Christian Writings,* 2018, http://www.earlychristianwritings.com/clement.html

2 Cited in 'Portraits of Witnesses to Christ: Saint Irenaeus of Lyons', Ateliers et Presses de Taizé, 2008, https://www.taize.fr/en_article6431.html

48 Known . . .

1   Reverend Dr Charles K Robinson, 'Known', Duke Divinity School Review, 1979, volume 44, p 44.

50 Finding Better Angels

1   Mother Teresa: 'Do small things with great love,' Catholic News Service, 9 April 2016, http://www.catholicnews.com/services/englishnews/2016/mother-teresa-do-small-things-with-great-love.cfm

2   Farr, Malcolm, 'Labor talks about inequality as Liberals talk about Liberals', 25 July 2017, http://www.news.com.au

3   See, for example, http://violenceandreligion.com/mimetic-theory/

4   Immordino-Yang, MH (2010), 'Toward a microdevelopmental, interdisciplinary approach to social emotion', *Emotion Review*, 2, 217–220.

5   http://avalon.law.yale.edu/19th_century/lincoln1.asp

52 Non-Violent Direct Action

1   Martin Luther King Jr., Nobel Lecture: The Quest for Peace and Justice, 11 December 1964, www.nobelprize.org

Addendum 1: Australia's Commitment to Asylum Seekers

1   Refugee Council of Australia, 'The Refugee Convention', 14 May 2016, https://www.refugeecouncil.org.au/getfacts/international/internationalsystem/the-refugee-convention/

Addendum 2: Major Policy Shifts

1   Australian Human Rights Commission, 'Asylum seekers, refugees and human rights: Snapshot report – 2nd edition, Appendix 2, 2017', https://www.humanrights.gov.au/sites/default/files/document/publication/AHRC_Snapshot%20report_2nd%20edition_2017_WEB.pdf

2   Bickers, Claire & Nguyen, Kevin, 'Police storm Manus Island forcing refugees to leave', http://www.news.com.au/national/politics/australians-of-the-year-pen-open-letter-to-turnbull-shorten-pleading-to-end-manus-island-crisis/news-story/2f504fd191142f4649ae0fcdf1ecaa4c

3   Aston, Heath, 'Department's new name to cost $200,000', *Sydney Morning Herald*, 20 November 2013, http://www.smh.com.au/federal-politics/political-news/departments-new-name-to-cost-200000-20131119-2xtnw.html

ADDENDUM – INFORMATION ON ASYLUM SEEKERS

IN ORDER TO explore the topic of asylum seekers and come to a place of understanding, it is useful to have a sense of where we have been as a country and how we have arrived at this day.

1 Australia's Commitment to Asylum Seekers

It was during the 1951 United Nations Conference, and in response to the racist atrocities of World War II and all the displacement generated, that the United Nations Convention Relating to the Status of Refugees (commonly known as The Refugee Convention) came into being. Essentially, its aim was to ensure that refugees had legal protections and status, in keeping with the Universal Declaration of Human Rights. Australia, along with 142 other countries, is a signatory to The Refugee Convention, which became legally binding in April 1954. Australia is also a signatory to the 1967 Refugee Protocol, removing geographical and time limitations for refugees from the 1954 convention.

In other words, Australia has committed to legal protections that apply to people seeking asylum. Under Australian law, it is not illegal for individuals to arrive in this country without passports or other documentation if they are seeking asylum. Somehow, this message has got lost.

The Refugee Council of Australia sets out clearly a number of the rights refugees are afforded under the UN Refugee Convention, directly challenging decades of Australian government propaganda around this issue. Here are some excerpts:

- Under article 33 of the Refugee Convention, refugees cannot be sent to a place where they may be persecuted, including their country of origin.

- The Refugee Convention recognises that refugees often need to enter a country without permission, or with false documents, to obtain protection. Under Article 31 of the Convention, countries who have signed the Convention cannot punish refugees for entering or living without permission, or unnecessarily restrict their freedom of movement.

- Under the Refugee Convention, refugees have a number of rights. For example, freedom of religion, the right to work and the right to education. Refugees are entitled to the same treatment as other foreign nationals for most of these rights. Refugees are also entitled to the same rights as citizens in relation to freedom of religion, intellectual property, access to courts and legal assistance, accessing elementary education, labour rights and social security.[1]

2 Major Policy Shifts

- **1992** Keating Labor government introduces mandatory immigration detention for up to 273 days for those arriving by boat without a visa.

- **2001** Howard LNP government refuses to give permission to Norwegian cargo ship MV *Tampa* to enter Australian waters to disembark 433 asylum seekers rescued from their sinking vessel near Christmas Island. 'Children Overboard' incident. Howard wins government for another term on the back of these two issues, and implements the 'Pacific Solution' whereby refugees arriving by boat are transferred to Manus Island and Nauru.

- **2007** Rudd Labor government elected.

- **2008** Rudd Labor government closes Nauru and PNG's Manus Island processing centres, ending the 'Pacific Solution'.

- **2012** Gillard Labor government re-establishes processing centres in Nauru and on PNG's Manus Island.

- **2013** Gillard Labor government passes legislation to include Australia's mainland in migration excision zone, resulting in asylum seekers arriving by boat being sent to a third country for processing and banned from ever settling in Australia. Rudd signs PNG agreement, no asylum seekers arriving by boat after 19 July will ever settle in Australia. Rudd/Gillard/Rudd government loses election to Abbott LNP.

- **2013** Abbott LNP government commences 'Operation Sovereign Borders', which employs the tactic of turning boats around at sea and forcing them to return to Indonesia.

- **2014** Abbott LNP government signs arrangement with Cambodia permitting refugees from the Nauru processing centre to settle there; reintroduction of Temporary Protection Visas; removal of most references to Refugee Convention from

Australia's Migration Act; strict amendments to the criteria for refugee status; and a so-called 'fast track' review processes. Whistleblower legislation, to jail whistleblowers for up to two years for reporting on detention centres. This includes doctors, nurses and other health professionals.

- **2016** High Court rules in favour of Australian government, finding it has the necessary legal authority to send asylum seekers to Nauru. The PNG Supreme Court rules that detention on Manus Island is illegal. Australian government announces resettlement arrangement with United States for those on Nauru and Manus Island.[1]

- **2017** Manus Island Regional Processing Centre closes on 31 October. Approximately 600 men resist moving to the new Manus Island facilities on the grounds of documented, inadequate accommodation and services, and fears for their safety. In addition, it is a protest at still being incarcerated in indefinite detention for more than four-and-a-half years. All men are forcefully moved to new centres on 23–24 November.[2]

- **30 November 2017** Government statistics for asylum seekers who arrived by boat: 324 remain in detention in mainland Australia and 339 are on Nauru, including 38 children. There are now no men detained in the Manus Island Detention Centre (it had been 690 in October); they are all in one of three transition centres. However, none of those men are free to leave Manus Island unless they return to their homeland (ie, the place from which they have fled).[3]

There have been 38 asylum seeker deaths since 2010 in both onshore and offshore detention centres run by Australia, eight of these on Manus Island and Nauru. These include murder, self-immolation and numerous cases of medical negligence.

3   Myth Busting

Boat people are queue jumpers.

There are 65 million displaced people around the world, far too many for the UN to process, and there is definitely not some sort of global register or queue. There are a few things to add. In war-torn countries or nations where oppressive governments abuse and torture their citizens, there are no queues to jump, and/or Australia doesn't have diplomatic representation. Also, there are few countries between the Middle East and Australia who are signatories to the 1951 Refugee Convention, so asylum seekers must continue to travel across unsafe borders before arriving in a country that will offer protection.

Asylum seekers are 'illegals'.

Article 14 of the Universal Declaration of Human Rights states: 'Everyone has the right to seek and to enjoy in other countries asylum from persecution.' People who arrive without authorisation into Australia, without documents, or carrying false documents, are not illegal. They are classed under international law as 'asylum seekers'. 'Illegals' are people who overstay their work or holiday visas in Australia; the majority are from Malaysia, China, Britain and the United States.

Australia takes too many refugees.

Amnesty International reports that one out of every 115 people around the globe is a refugee. In 2015–16 Australia accepted 17,555 refugees. With 65 million displaced people in the world, in this context Australia takes in relatively few refugees by world standards.

They aren't real refugees.
In fact, between 84 and 94 per cent of those arriving by boat seeking asylum in Australia are found to be genuine refugees.

They are rich: they have money to pay people smugglers.
Financial status is not a determining factor for refugees and does not negate a legitimate claim for seeking asylum.

Mandatory detention is the only alternative.
Currently Australia is the only Western country that places asylum seekers in mandatory detention while their claims are being processed. However, asylum seekers are not criminals and should not be treated as such. Successful community-based alternatives can be found internationally and would offer huge reductions in costs.

Boat people are terrorists.
There is no evidence that any asylum seekers who have arrived by boat have links to terrorism.

They destroy their identification, so they can't be genuine.
There are many reasons people travel without documents, but this does not negate their claims for asylum, nor does it preclude them from entering Australia legally. Many people fleeing war or persecution are unable to obtain conventional travel documents. If individuals are fleeing persecution, they would be placed in more danger if apprehended while trying to escape their country of origin.

Detention centres are better than the countries they have left.

Australia's detention centres have been compared to concentration camps, robbing asylum seekers of their basic freedoms and human rights.

Offshore processing solves Australia's asylum-seeker problem.

Australia's offshore detention system is failing – economically, politically and ethically. It has cost tens of billions of dollars, failed to establish a regional solution, and trapped thousands of asylum seekers in Indonesia.

ACKNOWLEDGMENTS

To Nikla Martin from Penguin Random House, who first suggested a book might be possible, we say thank you for starting us on an incredible journey. Thanks to Alison Urquhart for her constant encouragement, and to Anne Reilly for her technical guidance and support, especially to Kerry. With deep appreciation to Professor Marcia Langton for her reading of First Australians' chapters.

I am much obliged to our dear friends Ken and Jennifer and Stephen for their encouragement and insight, and Merilyn Vale for the professional eye of a journalist, which has guided us on our way.

To my beloved daughters Kate, for getting us past the last big impasse, and Cassandra for insight in illuminating the holes in the story, I express my gratitude. This is in part the story of my family as well, a story of two incredible women, both called Mum, and of fathers whose presence is only in thought; of brothers and sisters and grandparents, all who have their own story to tell. I understand that their recollection and interpretation of events may differ to mine. I continue to be enriched by hearing those voices.

The Church, its priests and people, for better and for worse, are also a part of this story. This entails both blessings and curses, and these I acknowledge, too. I also acknowledge the context in which this book has been written. The people of the Anglican Parish of Gosford have accompanied me on a journey for the past 19 years and I thank them.

To our children and grandchildren, whom I love deeply, and for whom I strive to model the living out of an authentic life in the knowledge this work is for them. With all my desiring, my intention has been, and will continue to be for all my days, that I may make some contribution to a better world for them to inhabit.

Thank you.